Predictive Marketing

Predictive Marketing

Easy Ways Every Marketer Can Use Customer Analytics and Big Data

Ömer Artun, PhD
Dominique Levin

WILEY

This book is printed on acid-free paper. ♾

Published by John Wiley & Sons, Inc., Hoboken, New Jersey
Published simultaneously in Canada

For general information about our other products and services, please contact our Customer Care Department within the United States at (800) 762-2974, outside the United States at (317) 572-3993 or fax (317) 572-4002.

Wiley publishes in a variety of print and electronic formats and by print-on-demand. Some material included with standard print versions of this book may not be included in e-books or in print-on-demand. If this book refers to media such as a CD or DVD that is not included in the version you purchased, you may download this material at http://booksupport.wiley.com. For more information about Wiley products, visit www.wiley.com.

Library of Congress Cataloging-in-Publication Data:

Artun, Omer, 1969–
Predictive marketing : easy ways every marketer can use customer analytics and big data / Omer Artun, Dominique Levin.
pages cm
Includes index.
ISBN 978-1-119-03736-1 (hardback)
ISBN 978-1-119-03732-3 (ePDF)
ISBN 978-1-119-03733-0 (ePub)
1. Marketing. I. Levin, Dominique, 1971– II. Title.
HF5415.A7458 2015
658.8—dc23

2015013473

Cover image: Wiley
Cover design: Abstract Shoppers © Maciej Noskwoski/GettyImages

Printed in the United States of America

10 9 8 7 6 5 4 3 2 1

Dedicated to

My darling wife Dr. Burcak Artun for always believing in me

Ömer Artun

My husband Eilam Levin without whom it would not be worthwhile

Dominique Levin

CONTENTS

INTRODUCTION: WHO SHOULD READ THIS BOOK

This book is for everyday marketers who want to learn what predictive marketing is all about, as well as for those marketers who are ready to use predictive marketing in their organizations. Whether you are just getting started with your research, or have already begun to implement predictive marketing, you will find many practical tips in this book.

We share what marketers at companies large and small should know about predictive marketing. We show you how to achieve the same large returns as early adopters such as Harrah's Entertainment, Amazon, and Netflix. We also give you a practical guidebook to help you get started with this new way of marketing. And above all, we share stories from companies small and large, from retail to publishing, to software to manufacturing. All of these marketers have achieved revolutionary returns, and so can you.

About This Book

We are passionate about improving the quality of marketing and about arming marketers with the knowledge and tools they need to make marketing relevant again. We hope that the chapters that follow give marketers the vocabulary and the inspiration to start to understand and use big data and machine learning–powered marketing. We believe this will lead to a win-win for customers, businesses, and marketers. Customers will have more relevant and meaningful experiences, businesses will be able to build more profitable customer relationships, and marketers will gain visibility and respect within their organizations. We look forward to continuing the dialogue on our website www.predictivemarketingbook.com, the "Predictive Marketing Book" LinkedIn group (https://www.linkedin.com/groups?gid=8292127), or via twitter.com/agilone.

This book is divided in three main parts. The first part, "A Complete Predictive Marketing Primer," introduces many of the foundational elements in predictive marketing, including what is happening under the hood of predictive marketing software, how data science and predictive analytics work, and what are fundamentals behind the customer lifetime value concept. The second part of the book, "Nine Easy Plays to Get Started with Predictive Marketing," is a playbook with concrete strategies to get you started with predictive marketing. The last part of the book, "How to Become a True Predictive Marketing Ninja," gives an overview of predictive marketing technologies, some career advice for marketers, and looks at privacy and the future of predictive marketing. Many of the chapters can be read as stand-alone essays, so use the executive summary below to jump to the chapters that are most relevant to you.

What Is in This Book

Chapter 1: Big Data and Predictive Analytics Are Now Easily Accessible to All Marketers

Predictive marketing is a new way of thinking about customer relationships, powered by new technologies in big data and machine learning, which we collectively call predictive analytics. Marketers better pay attention to predictive analytics. Applying predictive analytics is the biggest game-changing opportunity since the Internet went mainstream almost 20 years ago. Although some large brands have been using pieces of predictive marketing for many years now, we are still in the early stages of adoption, and this is the right time to get started. The adoption of predictive marketing is accelerating among companies large and small because: (a) customers are demanding more meaningful relationships with brands, (b) early adopters show that predictive marketing delivers enormous value, and (c) new technologies are available to make predictive marketing easy.

Chapter 2: An Easy Primer to Predictive Analytics for Marketers

Many marketers want to at least understand what is happening in the predictive analytics black box, to more confidently apply these models or to be able to communicate with data scientists. After reading this chapter marketers will have a good understanding of the entire predictive analytics process. There are three types of predictive analytics models that marketers should know about: unsupervised learning, supervised learning, and reinforcement learning. Many marketers don't realize that 80 percent of the work associated with predicting future customer behavior is going towards collecting and cleaning customer data. This data janitor work is not glamorous but essential: without accurate and complete customer data, there can be no meaningful customer analytics.

Chapter 3: Get to Know Your Customers First: Build Complete Customer Profiles

Building complete and accurate customer profiles is no easy task, but it has a lot of value. If yours is like most companies, customer data is all over the place, full of errors and duplicates and not accessible to everyday marketers. Fortunately, predictive technology, including fuzzy matching, can help—at least some—to clean up your data mess and to connect online and offline data to resolve customer identities across the digital and physical divide. Just getting all customer data in one place has enormous value, and making customer profiles accessible to customer-facing personnel throughout the organization is a great first step to start to deliver better experiences to each and every customer.

Chapter 4: Managing Your Customers as a Portfolio to Improve Your Valuation

It is our strong belief that the best way for any business to optimize enterprise value is to optimize the customer lifetime value of *each and every* customer. Customers are the unit of value for any company and therefore customer lifetime value is the most important metric in marketing. If you maximize the lifetime value, or profitability, of each and every customer, you also maximize the profitability and valuation of your company as a whole. The best way to optimize lifetime value for *all* customers is to manage your customers as if they were a stock portfolio. You take different actions and send different messages for customers who are brand-new than for those who have been doing business with you for a while. You will need to adjust your thinking and budget for unprofitable, medium-value, and high-value customers.

Chapter 5: Play One: Optimize Your Marketing Spending Using Customer Data

When asked to allocate marketing budgets, most marketers immediately think about acquisition spending and about allocating budget to the best performing channels and products. However, the predictive marketing way to allocate spending is based on allocating dollars to the right people, rather than to the right products or channels. Most companies are focused on acquisition, whereas they could achieve growth more cost-effectively by focusing more of their time and budget on retention and reactivation of customers. Marketers should learn to allocate budgets based on their goals to acquire, retain, and reactivate customers and to find products and channels that deliver the highest value customers.

Chapter 6: Play Two: Predict Customer Personas and Make Marketing Relevant Again

We will look at the predictive technique of clustering and how it is different from classical customer segmentation. Clustering is a powerful tool in order to *discover* personas or communities in your customer base. Specifically, in this chapter we look at product-based, brand-based, and behavior-based clusters as examples. Clustering can be used to gain insight into differences in customers' needs, behaviors, demographics, attitudes, and preferences regarding marketing interactions, products, and service usage. Using these clusters, you can also start to differentiate and optimize both marketing actions and product strategy for different groups of customers.

Chapter 7: Play Three: Predict the Customer Journey for Life Cycle Marketing

In this chapter we look at the customer life cycle in more detail, from acquisition, to growth, and to retention and see how your engagement strategy should evolve with each and every customer during the life cycle. The basic principle of optimizing customer lifetime value is the same for all stages of the life cycle and can be summarized in three words: give to get. Customers are much more likely to buy from you if they trust you. The best way to gain trust is to *deliver* an experience of value. So to *get* customer value, *give* customer value.

Chapter 8: Play Four: Predict Customer Value and Value-Based Marketing

Not all customers have equal lifetime value. Any business will have high-value customers, medium-value customers, and low lifetime value customers. There is an opportunity to create enterprise value by crafting marketing strategies that are differentiated based on the value of the customer. This practice to segment and target by customer lifetime value is called *value-based marketing*. Spend more money to appreciate and retain high-value customers. Upsell to medium-value customers in order to migrate these customers to higher value segments. Finally, reduce your costs to service low-value or unprofitable customers.

Chapter 9: Play Five: Predict Likelihood to Buy or Engage to Rank Customers

Likelihood to buy models is what most people think about when you use the word predictive analytics. With these models you can predict the likelihood of a certain type of future behavior of a customer. In this chapter we look at programs based on likelihood to buy predictions spanning both consumer and business marketing. We see how in business marketing predictive lead scoring or customer scoring can optimize the time of your sales and customer success teams. We also show you how consumer marketers can optimize their discount strategy and the frequency of their emails based on propensity models.

Chapter 10: Play Six: Predict Individual Recommendations for Each Customer

Another popular predictive technique is personalized recommendations. In this chapter we provide marketers a primer on recommendations and we teach you about different types of recommendations. We explore recommendations made at the time of purchase versus those made as a follow-up to a purchase, and recommendations that are tied to specific products versus those that are tied to specific customer profiles. We also discuss what can go wrong when making personalized recommendations, and we highlight the need for merchandising rules, omni-channel orchestration, and giving customers control when making personal recommendations.

Chapter 11: Play Seven: Launch Predictive Programs to Convert More Customers

In this chapter we cover three specific predictive marketing strategies that can help you acquire more, and better, customers: using personas to design better acquisition campaigns, using remarketing to increase conversion and using look alike targeting. When it comes to remarketing, you should be able to differentiate between customers who are likely to come back, and send them a simple reminder, versus those who are unlikely to come back and may need an additional incentive. This is true for abandoned cart, browse, and search campaigns. Using lookalike targeting features of Facebook and other advertising platforms, you can find more customers who look just like your existing customers, for example, new customers just like your *best* customers.

Chapter 12: Play Eight: Launch Predictive Programs to Grow Customer Value

The secret to retaining a customer is to start trying to keep the customer the day you acquire her. The initial transaction is just the beginning of a long relationship that needs to be nurtured and developed. Engagement with customers should not stop when you convert a prospect into a buyer. In this chapter we cover a number of specific predictive marketing strategies to help grow customer value: postpurchase campaigns, replenishment campaigns, repeat purchase programs, new product introductions, and customer appreciation campaigns. We will also discuss loyalty programs and omni-channel marketing in the age of predictive analytics.

Chapter 13: Play Nine: Launch Predictive Programs to Retain More Customers

We recommend you focus on dollar value retention. If you don't, you could be retaining customers, but losing money anyway. Also, when measuring customer retention it is important to realize that not all churn is created equal. Losing an unprofitable customer is not nearly as bad as losing one of your best customers. Also, it is a lot easier, cheaper, and more effective to try and prevent a customer from leaving than it is to reactivate that customer after she has already stopped shopping with you. In this chapter we look at different churn management programs, from untargeted, applying equally to all your customers, to targeted, and we will cover proactive retention management and customer reactivation campaigns.

Chapter 14: An Easy-to-Use Checklist of Predictive Marketing Capabilities

In order to use the predictive marketing techniques discussed in this book you need to acquire both a predictive marketing mind-set as well as certain predictive marketing technical capabilities. You need to evolve your thinking from being focused on campaigns, channels, and one-size-fits-all marketing to being focused on individual customers and their context. From a technology point of view you need to acquire basic capabilities in the areas of customer data integration, predictive intelligence, and campaign automation.

Chapter 15: An Overview of Predictive (and Related) Marketing Technology

We live in an exciting and somewhat confusing time. A large number of new marketing technologies are becoming available every year. In this chapter, we will give you a high-level overview of the various types of commercially available technologies and describe what it would take to build a predictive marketing solution in-house from the ground up.

Chapter 16: Career Advice for Aspiring Predictive Marketers

There is a huge career opportunity that comes from being an early adopter of new methodologies and technologies, predictive marketing and predictive analytics included. If you are uncomfortable with numbers and math, and fearful of getting started with predictive marketing, there are a couple of things you should know: business understanding trumps math, asking the right questions goes a long way, the best marketers blend the art and science of marketing, and there is a lot you can learn from others.

Chapter 17: Privacy and the Difference Between Delightful and Invasive

In general, consumers are willing to share preference information in exchange for apparent benefits, such as convenience, from using personalized products and services. When it comes to personalization, there are different types of customer information that can be used and consumers may feel different about one type of information over the other. Use common sense when considering whether a marketing campaign is delightful or creepy and consider the context of the situation. This chapter will provide some guidelines for dealing with customer data that will engender trust.

Chapter 18: The Future of Predictive Marketing

Predictive analytics will continue to find new applications inside and beyond marketing. Not only will more algorithms become available, but real-time customer insights will start to shape our physical world, including the store of the future. There are huge benefits for customers, companies, and marketers alike to get started with predictive marketing sooner rather than later. Sooner or later your customers and competitors will force you to adopt a predictive marketing mind-set, so you might as well be an early adopter and derive a huge competitive advantage.

About the Authors

Omer Artun

I am a scientist by training; I am an entrepreneur at heart, driven by curiosity of knowledge and challenging status quo. In elementary school, I saw the opportunity to make a profit collecting fruit from mulberry trees from our school backyard and selling it on the street, enlisting my schoolmates to help me run this small business. With some prodding from my engineer parents, I followed in my older brother's footsteps to enter a PhD program in physics at Brown University, studying under Leon Cooper at The Institute for Brain and Neural Systems. Dr. Cooper has received the Nobel Prize in Physics for his work on superconductivity and later decided that the next big problem to solve was in neuroscience, decoding how we learn and adapt. He is a pioneer in learning theory since the early 70s, using both experimental neuroscience as a base as well as statistical techniques for understanding and creating learning systems, now popularly called *machine learning*. I worked on both biological mechanisms that underlie learning and memory storage as well as construction of artificial neural networks, networks that can learn, associate, and reproduce such higher level cognitive acts as abstraction, computation, and language acquisition. Although these tasks are carried out easily by humans, they have not been easy to embody as conventional computer program.

As I was getting close to graduating from the PhD program at Brown University around 1998, I noticed that the business world was mostly running on simple spreadsheets, and I wanted to apply a data science and machine-learning approach to business. This goal led me to work for McKinsey & Co., the premier strategy consulting firm that helps large companies formulate strategies based on a fact-based problem solving approach.

When I joined McKinsey & Co. in 1999, I was able to test drive some of this data scientific approach in a few studies. My first project was to help a large technology company improve sales coverage, scientifically matching the sales team with the customers based on customer needs, sales team's skill, and experience. The CEO was impressed with the results on paper, but was unable to operationalize the results in real life, in a repeatable way. This is what I call the last mile problem of analytics. I realized that this is a big problem to solve. Analytics is an important enabler in improving commercial efficiency, but can only create value if it becomes part of the day-to-day execution workflow. I saw this theme repeat over and over again in many areas of business, pricing, supply chain, marketing, and sales. Most McKinsey projects I have been part of ended up on a slide deck which had all the right answers but very rarely created any real value. Equipped with McKinsey training, I joined one of my clients, Micro Warehouse as VP of Marketing, in 2002, with the goal to bring data science to everyday operations. I was lucky to be empowered by the CEO Jerry York and President Kirby Myers. Jerry was the most analytically driven person I ever knew in business, still to this day. He was previously CFO of IBM during Gerstner years, and CFO of Chrysler before that. He encouraged me to use data science to help him run the business better.

I knew I had to architect my approach in a way that married data science with execution to solve the last mile problem. I had two important recruits, Dr. Michel Nahon, a brilliant Yale-trained applied mathematician who helped me with machine-learning algorithms, and the hacker extraordinaire Glen Demeraski, who helped me with everything database and application related. I created approaches and systems that used data to more efficiently allocate resources, reduce marketing costs, and uncover new revenue sources. We had significant impact on marketing efficiency, pricing, and discounting patterns as well as salesforce effectiveness. In early 2003 we had real-time systems alerting purchase, pricing, and customer acquisition patterns of the sales team compared to moving averages to take immediate action by the sales leadership. After Micro Warehouse, from 2004 to 2006, I joined Best Buy as Senior Director of Business-to-Business marketing of its newly founded Best Buy for Business division. Best Buy at the time also struggled with the same exact last mile problem, lots of internal resources, tools, many high-flying consultants talking about customer segmentation, and analytics, but when you walked into a store, none of that had any impact at the customer level. This is the true test of analytics; does it impact the customers in a positive way that they can experience it? If not, then you have the wrong setup. Making progress at Best Buy was much more difficult, which I will touch on in Chapter 1.

While working at Micro Warehouse and Best Buy, I was also a regular guest lecturer at Columbia University and NYU Stern MBA programs Relationship Marketing and Pricing courses that Dr. Hitendra Wadhwa taught. I also became an Adjunct Professor at NYU Stern for Spring 2006, teaching the MBA level Relationship Marketing program. During this period, talking to students, doing market research, talking to colleagues at different companies, I postulated that data-driven predictive marketing would become the new paradigm for the next 10 years. The value of predictive marketing was already clear to me, but its importance has accelerated due to digital transformation of commerce, increase in customer touch-points, and exponential increase in the size, variety, and velocity of data (which is now popularly called "big data").

If you ask me what is the one important thing I learned from Dr. Cooper, I would say that it is breaking the problem down to its core and solving it at a fundamental level. He always said the idea behind the solution to any problem has to be clean and very simple. This is how I thought about the marketer's problem. Marketing was easy in the days of the old corner store. People knew our name, our likes and dislikes, and treated us on a one-to-one basis. Marketers lost touch with their customers in the era of one-size-fits-all mass optimization. Customers became survey responders and focus group participants; it was all about products and channels. However, the need for customer-centric marketing has always been there, it just wasn't practical and cost effective to practice. Digital transformation including web, email, mobile, social, location technologies combined with technologies to store, process, and extract information has significantly changed what is practical and cost effective.

Predictive marketing is the approach that restores that personal touch by bringing that human sensibility into our digital and offline lives, by focusing on the consumers individually to understand what they did and what they will do next. Predictive analytics, based on machine-learning algorithms, offers enormous leverage to marketers trying to make sense of these actions. Rather than replacing human decision making, machine learning and complex algorithms could help people amplify their intelligence and deal with problems on a much larger scale, something like giving a bulldozer to people used to digging with a shovel.

I saw the opportunity to solve a problem that a growing number of companies were struggling with, and I decided to disrupt the status quo and solve this problem. In 2006, I founded AgilOne, to bring the power of big data and predictive analytics to everyday marketers with an easy-to-use, yet powerful, cloud-based software platform.

AgilOne was initially bootstrapped for the first 5 years, then backed by top tier VC firms including Sequoia Capital, Mayfield Fund, Tenaya Capital, and Next World Capital. We are helping more than 150 brands in retail, B2B, Internet, media, publishing, and education deliver relevant experiences across channels. Through complete and accurate customer profiles, predictive insights, and built-in life cycle marketing campaigns, marketers boost customer loyalty and increase customer lifetime value.

In my spare time, I claim to be an accomplished potter of 28 years, having studied at Rhode Island School of Design under Lawrence Bush during my years at Brown. A native of Turkey, I now live in Los Gatos with my wife Burcak and two daughters, Ayse and Leyla. As I write this introduction, my daughter Ayse, who is a freshman at Castilleja School in Palo Alto, is reading an article about predictive marketing for her math class, which shows how predictive marketing will become mainstream for the next generation.

Dominique Levin

I credit my education, a combination of engineering school, design school, and business school for my left-brain–right-brain approach to marketing: I have a master's of science (Cum Laude) in industrial design engineering from Delft University in The Netherlands and a master's of business administration (with Distinction) from Harvard University. I recommend all marketers to marry human creativity with technology learning in order to deliver value to customers. Over the past 20 years I have run marketing at companies large and small, on four different continents, targeting businesses and consumers. Above all, I was an early convert to the importance of customer data.

In 1994 I took my first marketing job: a summer internship in Cusco, Peru. I drove around in a pickup truck to visit local farmers and tally how many would join a local cooperative to process fruits into marmalades and liquors. For my next job, at Philips Consumer Electronics, I was asked to find a way to sell more electronics to girls and women. I mingled with teenagers at local high schools to collect data. Philips launched a product called KidCom, an electronic organizer for girls, and proto-typed TeenCom, a two-way paging device for teenagers. My boss on this project was Tony Fadell, who later became the father of the iPod and iPhone, and who went on to found NEST. In 1997, I relocated to Tokyo, Japan, to work for Nippon Telegraph and Telephone (NTT). All employees at NTT, whether in product or finance, worked one weekend in the company store to meet and serve customers. I recommend such "meet the customer" program to any company as no numbers can totally replace meeting customers face to face.

In 2000, I moved to Silicon Valley and ran marketing for my first big data company, LogLogic—later acquired by TIBCO Software. For the first time I had access to lots of customer data in digital form. Log files are like the digital video cameras of the Internet. At LogLogic we used this log data to monitor security, but it also opened my eyes to the possibilities of using similar data to better understand and serve customers.

I went on to work for several other technology companies, including Fundly and Totango, focusing on building highly data-driven marketing organizations. Fundly helps non-profits use social media to raise money. We used data to automate the process from self-service sign-up to fundraising success. Totango offered a predictive marketing solution that monitors customer behavior to identify both promising and struggling customers. In both cases data and predictions helped to accelerate customer acquisition and increase customer lifetime value, while lowering the cost of sales.

I met Omer in my role as CMO at Agilone, where I got to work with thousands of marketers just like you to figure out how they can best use customer data to delight customers. Omer and I are united in our data-driven and customer-centric approach to marketing. Data and humanistic experiences go hand-in-hand. Our passion for customers has led us to this book.

In my spare time, I love to travel with my husband and three children and experience people, places, and cultures around the world. I play ice hockey to blow off steam and was once a member of the Dutch national team. I love to work with entrepreneurs and help them make their dreams a reality.

Acknowledgments

This book was significantly enhanced by the efforts of Anne Puyt, Barbara Von Euw, Rinat Shimshi, Dhruv Bhargava, Carrie Koy, Joe Mancini, Angela Sanfilippo, Hac Phan, and Francis Brero, who not only work tirelessly every day to help companies be successful with predictive marketing, but who also went above and beyond the call of duty to add their experiences, examples, and wisdom to the manuscript.

We also want to thank visionary CEOs and CMOs who were early adopters of the predictive marketing approach, specifically John Seabreeze, VP Marketing at Billy Casper Golf; Joe McDonald, SVP Sales and Marketing of Stargas, Eoin Comerford, CEO of Moosejaw; Levent Cakiroglu, CEO of Arcelik; Ersin Akarlilar, CEO of Mavi; Adam Shaffer, EVP Marketing of TigerDirect.

Additionally, Omer's personal success, the success of AgilOne, and the concepts in this book would not have become a reality without the help from Bonnie Bartoli, Peter Godfrey, and his "adopted sons and daughter" Ozer Unat, Dhruv Bhargava, Oyku Akca, Anselme LeVan, Louis Lecat, Ryan Willette, and Francis Brero.

We would also like to thank our families:

Omer would also very much like to thank his wife Dr. Burcak Artun, always believing and encouraging him for challenging the status quo and being patient with his busy schedule.

Dominique thanks her husband, Eilam, and children Liv, Yanai, and Milo, for their encouragement during the writing process. Similarly, she would like to thank her AgilOne marketing superstars, Chris Field, Johnson Kang, Kessawan Lelanaphaparn, and Angela Sanfilippo for being so independent and professional so she could focus on the book at times.

PART 1

A Complete Predictive Marketing Primer

CHAPTER 1

Big Data and Predictive Analytics Are Now Easily Accessible to All Marketers

Predictive marketing is the evolution of relationship marketing defined and practiced by many direct marketers in the last few decades. Predictive marketing is not a technology, but an approach or a philosophy. Predictive marketing uses predictive analytics as a way to deliver more relevant and meaningful customer experiences, at all customer touch points, throughout the customer life cycle, boosting customer loyalty and revenues.

The rise of predictive marketing is fueled by three factors: (1) customers are demanding a more personal, integrated approach as they interact with marketing and sales through many channels, (2) early adopters show that predictive marketing delivers enormous value, and (3) new technologies are available to capture new and existing sources of customer data, to recognize patterns, and to make it easier than ever to use customer data at the intersection of the physical and digital worlds.

Predictive analytics is a set of tools and algorithms used to make predictive marketing possible. It is an umbrella term that covers a variety of mathematical and statistical techniques to recognize patterns in data or make predictions about the future. When applied to marketing, predictive analytics can predict future customer behavior, classify customers into clusters among other use cases. Other terms you might hear in the media to describe this process include *machine learning*, *pattern recognition*, *artificial intelligence*, and *data mining*. Predictive analytics and machine learning are used interchangeably in this book.

Predictive marketing is fundamentally changing both business and consumer marketing across the customer life cycle. It is transforming the focus from products and channels to a focus on the customer. Predictive analytics is used to improve strategies to acquire new customers, to grow customer lifetime value, and to retain more customers over time.

Innovative, technology driven companies like Netflix and Amazon have been using predictive analytics for years, and so have others like many in the telecommunications, financial services, and gaming industries, such as Harrah's Entertainment. The row of movies and TV shows "you might like" that appear when you curl up on the couch and turn on Netflix is a driving force of the company's success. It's all made possible by the translation of customer data with smart analytics. In fact, "75% of what people watch [on Netflix] is from some sort of recommendation," Netflix's Research Director Xavier Amatriain wrote on the company's tech blog in 2012.

Amazon has been using predictive analytics to drive success since the very beginning of the company. Recommendations that appear under a product you are thinking of adding into your cart is part of what makes Amazon such an e-commerce powerhouse today. The company has stated publicly that 35 percent of its sales comes from recommendations made by their predictive engines. That would equate to $26 billion of revenue in 2013. The company is using predictive analytics in many other ways too, such as predicting which email newsletter to send you, or to nudge you at the right times to reorder an item.

In the gaming industry predictive models can set budgets and calendars for the casino's gamblers, calculating their predicted lifetime value in the process. If a gambler wagers less than usual because they may have skipped a monthly visit, the casino can intervene with a letter or phone call offering a free meal, a show ticket, or gaming comps. Without this type of customer analytics, casino operators might not notice what could be a slight, almost imperceptible change in customer behavior that might portend future problems with that patron. For example, if a long-time customer decides to cash in all their player card points, perhaps it's because they are dissatisfied with their last experience at the casino property. Predictive analytics can quickly spot these trends and alert casino management to the issue so that they can approach the individual to find out if there is a problem. This kind of personalization can go a long way in appeasing a disgruntled customer, which might be the difference between retaining or losing them as a customer.

Harrah's Entertainment's Total Rewards, which was rolled out as Total Gold in 1997 and renamed Total Rewards a year later, is heralded by many as the gold standard of customer-relationship programs and is powered heavily by predictive analytics algorithms. The company's belief in its loyalty program grew so strong that it cut its traditional ad spending from 2008 and 2009 more than 50%. The company spent $106 million on measured media in 2008; for the first half of last year it spent $52 million and in this year's first half $20 million. (*Source:* http://adage.com/article/news/harrah-s-loyalty-program-industry-s-gold-standard/139424/.)

Although some large brands have been using predictive analytics for many years now, it is not too late for other brands, large and small. In fact, predictive marketing is only now finding widespread adoption in medium and small organizations. A good example of a company that has achieved significant success with predictive marketing is Mavi, a high-fashion clothing manufacturer and retailer based in Istanbul, Turkey. Mavi is known for its organic denim favored by celebrities and supermodels. Mavi operates over 350 multinational stores and sales channels in the United States, Canada, Australia, Turkey, and 10 European countries.

Mavi started with a single predictive marketing campaign six years ago. When Mavi first got started, each department, including marketing and IT, used its own set of marketing reports and customer data, including key performance indicators. This led to cumbersome cross-referencing and impeded important decision making. Like many companies, the Mavi marketing team initially did not have access to customer data without relying on IT resources. This was the first problem that the team tackled. Mavi deployed a modern, cloud-based predictive marketing solution in 2009. This allowed the company to consolidate, cleanse, and de-dupe their customer data on a daily basis. They were then ready to start using data in hyperpersonalized campaigns.

One of the first predictive marketing programs that Mavi tested was a program around specific buying personas. Mavi used predictive analytics to find groups of people with distinct product preferences. In predictive lingo these are called *product-based clusters*. Mavi found at least three very different groups of shoppers: customers who favored mostly woven shirts, others who favored beachwear, whereas a third persona mostly shopped for new season high fashion and accessories. Mavi started to use these personas to implement more targeted marketing campaigns via email and short message service (SMS). Specifically, it implemented a reengagement campaign for lapsed customers that featured the right types of products with the right customers. Using these clusters, Mavi was able to reactivate 20 percent of lapsed customers. This was a big breakthrough because every customer saved or reactivated reduces Mavi's need to acquire new customers.

Mavi today is running more than 80 different predictive marketing programs in a year. Collectively, these campaigns helped add 7 percentage points to Mavi's overall revenues in the first few years, which is a huge sum on a dollars and cents basis. Wikipedia reports that Mavi revenues in 2014 were $747 million, so that would be an incremental $52 million. Mavi is still finding new ways to increase customer lifetime value, and with every campaign launched this number is pushed up higher.

Elif Oner, Mavi's head of customer relationship management, recommends all marketers get started with predictive marketing. She says: "Start small and pick just one program and build on that success." Elif is also the CFO's favorite marketer. Every dollar she spends in marketing, every discount she gives, is accounted for, tested, and optimized. The CIO Bulent Dursun also played an important role in realizing the potential of analytics and was a key supporter, which made the approach successful.

The Predictive Marketing Revolution

Anticipating customer needs is not a new concept. What is new is the ability to anticipate and respond to customer needs automatically, near real time and at large scale, for hundreds, thousands, or even millions of customers at a time.

Not too long ago, you could walk into a corner store and the salesperson would know your name, know what kind of things you bought, how long you've been a customer, and other important information about your personality and behavior. This relationship not only makes the buying process pleasant, it also increases the likelihood of the customer to return, spend more, and develop a sense of brand loyalty and trust.

These days we shop in supermarkets where nobody knows our name. The promise of predictive marketing is to bring the personal relationships of the corner store to the modern world of online and offline marketing. Using predictive analytics, it is possible to move from an era of mass marketing centered on the products you sell and the promotions you send to an era of highly personalized marketing centered on the customer you serve.

Today, even small- and midsize businesses interact with customers on an enormous scale through a wide variety of channels, including websites, social media, mobile apps, and store visits. Because of the substantial increase in speed, number, and type of customer interactions, companies have a greater opportunity to maintain the kind of personal relationships that used to be an important aspect of doing business. Of course this is not easy, and many companies fail due to lack of technical, organizational capabilities and strategic focus.

Customer interactions and the digitization of so much of our daily activities have allowed businesses to gather an extraordinary amount of data about their customers that can be put to use to better service customers. For example, when you buy a pair of shoes at Zappos, the company knows many things about you: what type of shoes you like,

your name, gender, where you live, whether your zip code is mainly made up of apartment buildings or single-family homes, whether you typically buy items at full price or at a discount, whether you bought just one product or multiple products, how often you clicked on a Zappos email or visited its website before placing that first order and what you looked at, how often you called the call center, whether you are a first-time or repeat customer, whether you are a VIP customer or an unprofitable customer who returns more products than she keeps, and much more.

Most companies still find it very difficult to put any of this information to good use. The sheer size and breadth of the records make them incomprehensible for anyone without the training and experience to mine insights from large datasets. This is where predictive analytics and machine learning come in. Machines are very good at mining insights

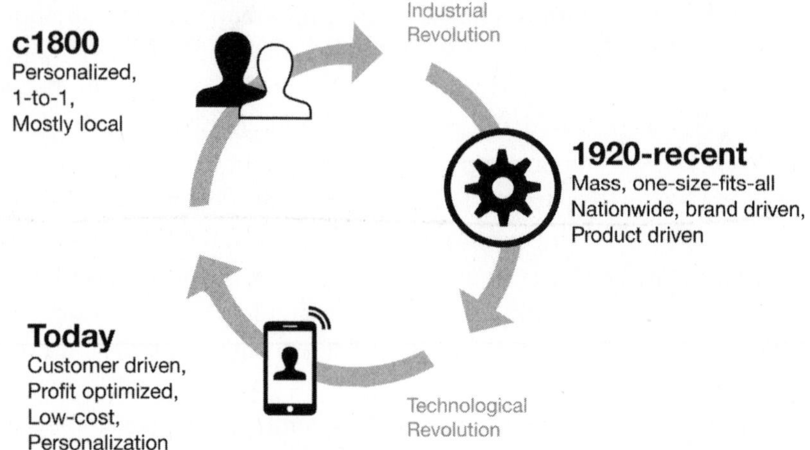

Figure 1.1 The Predictive Marketing Revolution

from large datasets automatically. Machines can remember the names of millions of customers with no effort and greet them accordingly, just as the shopkeeper from yesteryear would have done. In other words, using machines, humans can now bring back the personalized marketing interactions from yesteryear, even if their company has millions of customers. Figure 1.1 illustrates how the marketing revolution has come full circle. In the 1800s, shopkeepers had personal relationships with each and every customer. In the 1900s, during the industrial revolution, these personal relationships fell victim to mass marketing and a desire to scale businesses. Now, thanks to the technological revolution, marketers can bring back the personal relationships from yesteryear, while still operating companies at a large scale.

Predictive marketing is the perfect marriage between machine learning and human intelligence. The point of predictive marketing is not to replace marketers with machines but rather to empower and augment human intelligence with machine learning.

The Power of Customer Equity

Predictive marketing gives rise to a new, data-driven way to approach marketing, with the customer at its center. The ability to collect and analyze data on every single customer, as well as his or her interactions

Figure 1.2 From a Product to a Customer Orientation

with your brand, allows you to serve your customers better and generate more sales. At its core, as Figure 1.2 illustrates, predictive marketing is helping companies to evolve from a product- or channel-centric orientation to a customer-centric orientation. Companies using predictive marketing focus on developing and managing customer relationships rather than just developing and selling products or channels:

- Instead of finding customers who will want your products, it is now possible to discover which products your customers will want in the future.
- Instead of maximizing sales, companies in the customer era focus on optimizing customer lifetime value and share of wallet to drive profitability of the enterprise.

- Instead of organizing around channels and product lines, companies which practice predictive marketing organize around the customer.
- With the customer at the center, companies are using big data and predictive analytics to configure processes and organizations to find ways to customize interactions.
- Communications become much more targeted and the key metric is relevance, not reach.

Predictive marketing allows you to identify and realize the long-term value of customer relations to keep your best customers coming back and buying more. Figure 1.3 illustrates the core principle: if your company acquires more profitable customers, grows the value of each and every customer systematically, and retains these customer relationships for a long time, the firm will grow, too.

Companies should think about managing customer equity in much the same way they manage their stock portfolios: just like stocks, some customers are more valuable than others and their value will rise and fall throughout time. Predictive marketing gives companies an easy and automated way to manage individual customer lifetime value and customer equity.

The key to unlocking this value lies in the information you are able to collect about your customers. The more you can personalize the experiences you offer, the more likely the customer remains loyal to your brand. Think about your hairdresser. She has a lot of information about you. She knows how you like your hair cut and probably knows a lot about your family, friends, and job. This information makes the interaction with your hairdresser very seamless. You sit down, she gets to work, and you have a pleasant conversation. She may call you when it's time for your next appointment and suggest a new hairstyle from time to time. It would take you a long time to start over with a new hairdresser. Your hairdresser has very few clients. Most marketers serve millions of customers. It is not possible for a brand to collect and process the data of millions of customers without computers and software.

Predictive marketing puts customer data and insights directly in the hands of marketers, customer-facing personnel, and applications that deliver personalized experiences to individual customers.

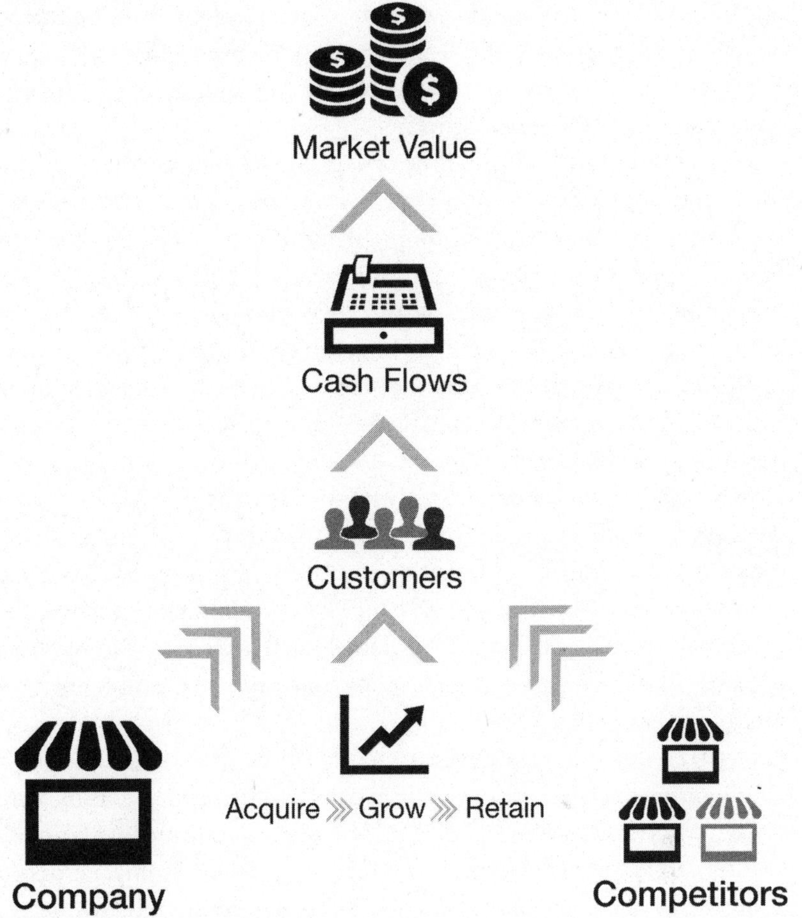

Figure 1.3 Customers Are Key to Market Value

Predictive Marketing Use Cases

Predictive marketing is much more than just providing recommendations. The most commonly use cases of predictive marketing are the following:

- **Improve precision of targeting and acquisition efforts.** With predictive marketing it is possible to know which channels produce the most profitable customers and optimize marketing spending based on this knowledge. Armed with better information about behavioral buying personas, marketers can also design more effective acquisition campaigns that hypertarget a specific microsegment and increase conversions by four times or more.

- **Use personalized experiences to increase lifetime value.** Predictive marketing can predict future customer preferences and interactions (such as a customer's likelihood to buy). Armed with this information, marketers can improve personalization, relevancy, and timing of customer interactions. It is these experiences that will keep customers coming back and maximize customer lifetime value. If you can maximize the lifetime value of each of your customers, you will automatically maximize the value of your entire customer portfolio and thereby the value of your company as a whole.
- **Understand customer retention and loyalty.** Predicting when, why, and which customers will return or leave is a big challenge for many organizations. Predictive marketing can help flag customers who are at risk of leaving so that marketers can take proactive steps to retain these customers. Predictive analytics can also generate insights about loyalty-inducing behaviors that maximize customer lifetime value.
- **Optimize customer engagement.** Predicting who will respond to an email promotion, what would it take to convert a browser into a buyer, what discount is needed to incent the customer to complete the transaction are all methods of increasing customer engagement in real time or near real time that maximizes marketing effectiveness.

Figure 1.4 gives examples of questions that predictive analytics can answer for marketers. These examples, as well as other used cases, are discussed in greater detail throughout the book. The list below is not an all-inclusive list, as the marketing questions that can be answered with predictive analytics are really endless.

Armed with information ranging from likelihood to buy, predicted lifetime value, and future product preferences, brands can better serve their prospects and their customers by delivering personalized experiences.

10 Questions to Answer	How Predictive Can Help
1. Who my best customers will be	Predict which prospects or customers have the highest lifetime value, taking into account revenues, but also the cost to acquire and service these accounts. Use this information to spend time and money on high-potential customers early on.
2. Find more new customers like your existing best customers	Predict which prospects are most like your existing high-value customers using look-alike targeting (B2C) or specialized lead generation vendors (B2B).
3. Find personas in your data to use to acquire more customers like this	Predict the customer clusters that most distinguish buying personas with respect to brands, products, content and behaviors in your customer base. Then develop creative, content, products, and services to attract more buyers like this.
4. Which marketing channels are most profitable	Predict which channels attract the customers with the highest lifetime value, including all future purchases. Use this information to influence keyword bidding strategies and channel investments.
5. Which prospects (nonbuyers) are most likely to buy	Determine who is most likely to buy so you can give the right incentive (in B2C) or prioritize your sales personnel's time with the right prospects (in B2B).
6. Which existing (or past) customers are most likely to buy	Product incentive (or discount) is needed to convince a one-time buyer to become a repeat customer. Prioritize the time of account managers to focus on likely upsell candidates.
7. Which existing customers are least likely to buy	Predict which customers are likely to leave and target them proactively with a "please come back" incentive, a personalized recommendation or by having the customer success manager make a call.
8. What customers might be interested in a specific new product	Predict which customers might be interested in overstock items or a new product release so you can focus your sales and marketing efforts on these businesses or consumers.
9. What other products or content might this customer be interested in	Predict what product or content recommendations to make to a particular customer in order to win, upsell, or reengage this customer.
10. What is my share of wallet with a specific customer	Predict in what markets or customer groups you have high value potential to focus future customer acquisition strategies.

Figure 1.4 Ten Examples of Predictive Marketing

Predictive Marketing Adoption Is Accelerating

A recent survey of 132 marketing executives by our company AgilOne found that 76 percent of marketers used some form of predictive analytics in their marketing in 2015, which is up from 69 percent in 2014. The acceleration is fueled by three factors: (1) customers are demanding the benefits of predictive marketing—mainly highly relevant and timely marketing, (2) early adopters show that predictive marketing delivers enormous value, and (3) new technologies are available to make predictive marketing easy.

Customers Are Demanding More Meaningful Relationships with Brands

Consumers are bombarded with marketing and frankly are fed up. Retail research agency Conlumino conducted a consumer survey in late 2014 that showed many consumers have come to expect some form of personalization—in part because the larger and more established brands have been serving up personalized experiences for some years now. By asking more than 3,000 adult online shoppers about what information they expected companies to know about them and what personalized experiences they appreciate, the survey uncovered that more than 70 percent of shoppers want brands to deliver some type of personalized experience, whether it is sending an alert about a new product that matches their interests, a refill reminder, or VIP customer recognition. Certain types of customized experiences, such as loyalty rewards and personalized discounts, were popular across the board, whereas appreciation levels for other areas of personalization differed greatly depending on age, location, gender, and a number of other factors. The findings suggest that it is crucial to have a deep understanding of your customers, and using hypertargeting is crucial to building brand loyalty:

- More than 79 percent of U.S. consumers and 70 percent of U.K. consumers expect some sort of personalization from brands.
- More than half of consumers in the United States and United Kingdom expect e-commerce sites to remember their past purchases.
- Among U.S. shoppers, the most popular personalized experiences were emails offering discounts on products they previously viewed

(66 percent), alerts when products they like are on sale (57 percent), and VIP customer appreciation rewards (51 percent).
- Consumers in the United States were much more likely to expect online retailers to personalize experiences than those in the United Kingdom: about half of Americans want to receive a new customer welcome greeting, versus only 34 percent in the United Kingdom.
- Shoppers age 18 to 34, part of the "millennial" generation, were more likely to appreciate almost all forms personalization: 52 percent of millennials expect brands to remember their birthday as compared to 21 percent of those aged 65-plus.
- Personalization of email is much more popular than personalization of display advertising, with 66 percent of U.S. consumers and 57 percent of U.K. consumers welcoming email-retargeting, but only 24 percent (U.S.) and 17 percent (U.K.) welcoming web-based retargeting.

In one case, the customers of a high-fashion brand from New York actually wrote to tell the company they felt they were not receiving the personalized experience they deserved. Specifically, this company was conducting postpurchase surveys after each shipment. Some customers wrote that they were frequent shoppers of the brand, yet felt they did not receive any special treatment. It is rare for customers to express their dissatisfaction with one-size-fits-all marketing so directly. It is more likely that customers are letting you know through their actions. Are you experiencing an unusually large number of customer complaints, do you have a small number of repeat buyers, or are you seeing a large number of opt outs from your email campaigns? All of these could be signs that customers are not getting the personal attention they expect.

Another example comes from a small kitchenware company. For years, its products were offered in limited quantities and geographic areas. Word spread about the unique products, and to meet customer demand, the products are now offered through its website directly to consumers and in large retail outlets such as Costco. The passionate customer base was demanding more relevant communications. Customers did not write or call to tell the company about this, but rather it started to experience a rising number of opt outs when sending email. Clearly customers were saying that the one-size-fits-all email campaigns were not suiting their needs. Today customers receive much more relevant and timely email, such as replenishment reminders to reorder barbecue pellets for grilling just around the time they were running out of their last order. Predictive marketing has increased the purchase rate from their marketing emails from 1 percent to 4 percent, while reducing the unsubscribe rate by 40 percent within just six weeks.

Many marketers may think they are delivering relevant experiences, but consumer perception is often very different. A 2013 AgilOne survey of 2,000 marketers and consumers, found that 75 percent of marketers believe that they are sending as many as 15 relevant marketing campaigns to consumers each year. However, 34 percent of consumers say they cannot remember a single relevant campaign from the past year. Clearly there is a disconnect between marketers and consumers. The same survey found that 52 percent of marketers send the exact same email to all of their customers and 65 percent send the exact same number of emails to each of their customers regardless of their preferences.

Marketers need to change their thinking dramatically. Today, marketers may cheer when one of their email campaigns receives a 4 percent click-through rate. In reality that means that 96 percent of customers deemed this email irrelevant. That is a terrible result. We believe all customers deserve to be served relevant and respectful communications. Instead of sending 100 messages with a relevancy of 1 percent, marketers should start sending a single message with a relevancy of 100 percent.

Early Adopters Show That Predictive Marketing Delivers Enormous Value

Marketers better pay attention to predictive analytics. Applying predictive analytics is the biggest game-changing opportunity since the Internet went mainstream almost 20 years ago, because of the unprecedented array of insights into customer needs and behaviors it makes possible. When Bill Gates was asked during a 2013 Sequoia Capital event what company he would start if he were starting out today, he answered with two words: machine learning.

In his book, *Data Driven Marketing*, Kellogg School of Management faculty Mark Jeffrey proves that high-performing companies spend significantly more on data infrastructure than lower performers (16 percent versus 10 percent). High performers were defined as the top 25 percent of the dataset, measured by their excellence at marketing a basket of financial metrics, which validated the high performers indeed get better financial performance. High performers also spend more on customer equity or retention marketing (14 percent versus 11 percent) and less on demand generation (48 percent versus 58 percent). He also describes the success of early adopters of predictive analytics in this book. For example, Earthlink used predictive analytics to identify dissatisfied customers about to churn. Taking proactive steps to contact and retain these customers helped Earthlink reduce churn by 30 percent. Similarly, the supermarket chain Sainsbury Stores used predictive analytics to cluster its customer base in relevant segments. The company then used these segments to remodel its stores and customize the product assortment in each store based on these data. As a result, revenues increased by 12 percent.

There is no limit in the number of campaigns that a company can develop. Mavi, the mid-market retailer we discussed earlier, has developed over sixty individual campaigns, using predictive analytics, gradually increasing revenues and profitability.

New Technologies Are Available to Make Predictive Marketing Easy

So why are all marketers' not using predictive marketing techniques already? Until recently the technology needed to collect, analyze, and act on large amounts of customer data for hundreds, thousands, or millions of customers was inaccessible to most marketers. It was too expensive, time-consuming, and cumbersome to invest in the technology and manpower required to collect and analyze customer data and to deliver customer experiences across channels based on these insights. However, recently predictive analytics has matured to the point that out of the box, standard algorithms and technologies are available, which marketers can access without the help of data scientists or software engineers. In Chapter 15 we discuss in detail the different off-the-shelf tools available to marketers today, which make it significantly cheaper, faster, and easier to use predictive marketing.

Predictive Marketing Is Becoming More Affordable The costs involved with predictive marketing can include the money spent on hardware and software technology, as well as the people time spent on data collection, integration, predictive analytics model development and deployment, and the people time needed—from marketers or data scientists—for the ongoing maintenance of these models and the use of these models in daily marketing campaigns.

Until recently, the data-warehousing infrastructure alone to collect and store customer data could cost you hundreds of thousands or even millions of dollars. In his book about data-driven marketing, Mark Jeffrey documents that a small regional retailer with 10 stores, 100,000 customers, and 1 terabyte of customer data may need to spend $50,000 to $250,000 to build in-house data warehousing infrastructure. That number rises to $2.5 million for a medium-size retail chain with 400 stores and to $250 million for a large, national retailer with 5,000 stores. Nowadays, cloud-based predictive marketing solutions are available for as little as several thousand dollars a month.

Predictive Marketing Is Becoming Easier to Deploy Whichever solution you use—an off-the-shelf package or an in-house solution—you will need to collect and integrate customer data into a customer profile for each customer. In a late 2014 survey of 132 marketing executives, AgilOne found that 68 percent of marketers do not have a single view of each customer. You probably have a lot of information about your customers already, but this data may reside in many different silos. Most companies have separate databases for online transactions, store transactions, and phone transactions. Web behavior has its own silo as does email behavior, social behavior, and service center interactions. Until recently, it could take months or years to accomplish the data integration needed to build a single customer profile and to link and deduplicate all customer data. Recently, more automated solutions have emerged that make data integration and data cleansing much easier. These solutions often use standard data models that make it easier and faster to standardize customer data across channels.

Historically you did not just need in-house infrastructure; you also needed in-house or outsourced data integration specialists and data scientists. Data scientists were needed to build custom models to analyze customer data—probably using a predictive analytics workbench tool. These models also needed to be tweaked and tuned periodically to continue to deliver accurate results. Data scientists are in short supply, and more than 50 new graduate programs have sprung up across the United States alone to fill the gap. Fortunately, nowadays many marketing solutions come with out-of-the-box, built-in models that are proven and tested by other companies in your industry. Some of these models even have self-learning capabilities, which means that they adjust to your evolving customer data automatically over time without requiring ongoing maintenance from a data scientist.

Predictive Marketing Is Becoming More Accessible to Marketers

Even if customer data is available within the organization, it may not be available to you, the marketer. This happened to Omer Artun, when he joined Best Buy as the head of marketing for a new division called "Best Buy for Business" in December 2003:

> I joined Best Buy from Micro Warehouse where I had already built a near real-time customer analytics system to track and analyze orders on a daily basis. I was hired to do the same for Best Buy's new B2B group, which sold products such as routers, printers and computers to small businesses. Best Buy, like many companies, was outsourcing its IT to a third party at the time. If you wanted to talk customer data with this group, it was $10,000 dollars just to meet. I went to the IT guys and asked for a raw data dump, nothing else, but got nothing. After a couple of months, I still wasn't able to obtain a list of customers who had purchased from us in the past. The data was available somewhere, but not accessible to me. I fought the battle for another nine months before I finally gave up. I started a company, AgilOne, to make predictive analytics and customer data accessible to marketers shortly thereafter.

Even having access to data will not drive revenue unless data can be used to deliver more relevant experiences to customers. It can be difficult to integrate and share customer information directly with customer-facing personnel or applications that send out or trigger these types of customer communications. It is not unusual for a company to have a lot of customer data, but for marketers to be unable to use this information to segment customers within their email marketing software, for example, without complicated, time-consuming, and costly data integration. A new generation of marketing software is becoming available, where predictive insights are accessible as drag-and-drop filters to help segment and target customers and to include personalized content or recommendations as dynamic content in emails or advertisements.

What Do You Need for Predictive Marketing?

The fundamental building blocks of a successful predictive marketing initiative, as summarized in Figure 1.5, are:

1. Continuously learn more and more about your customers: capture data, build profiles and unify the information on a daily basis. We discuss how to do this in great detail in Chapter 3.
2. Analyze customer information and assess customer preferences and profitability at a micro (individual/segment) and macro level—both past and future. Chapter 2 gives you an overview of the different predictive algorithms you can use as a marketer.
3. Leverage customer information to profitably personalize experiences across all customer touch points, and to optimize the return on investment of your marketing and sales time and money. Part II of this book is entirely devoted to these practical applications.

In order to do predictive marketing, you need to develop these three capabilities of collecting and integrating customer data, analyzing customer data, and delivering relevant customer experiences across channels. You can acquire these capabilities in one of three ways: (1) build predictive models yourself using a predictive analytics workbench,

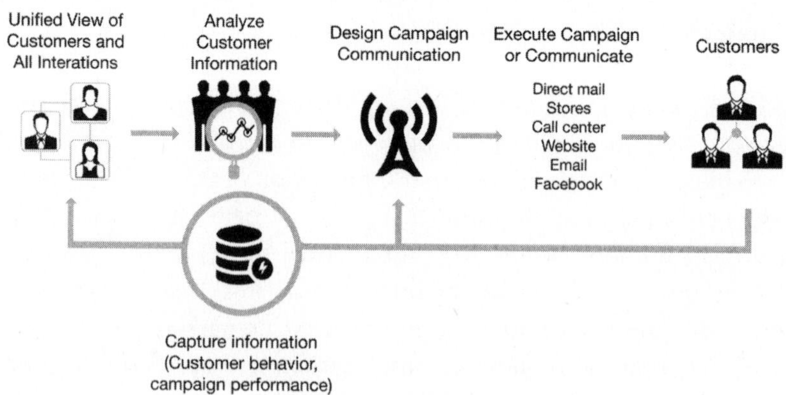

Figure 1.5 The Predictive Marketing Process

(2) outsource customer analytics and predictive marketing campaigns to a marketing service provider, or (3) evaluate and buy a predictive marketing solution, such as a predictive marketing cloud or a multichannel campaign management tool. The first option will cost you millions of dollars and require you to hire an in-house team. Marketing service providers are typically servicing the Fortune 500, and annual contracts for full customer data integration, analysis, and personalized campaign probably start at a quarter million dollars a year. Predictive marketing cloud solutions available at the time that we are writing this book start at about $50,000 a year. Chapter 15 provides more details about each of these options as well as some criteria to decide which route is best for you.

Whatever you do after reading this book, we recommend that you get started with predictive marketing in some way or another. Early adopters of predictive marketing will have significant competitive advantages, including more loyal and valuable customers. Companies that fail to adopt predictive marketing are at risk of falling behind. The key is to start small and grow your efforts over time. Find a quick win that can deliver immediate ROI.

Predictive Marketing = Human Intelligence + (Predictive Analytics) ≡ (Machine Learning)

CHAPTER 2

An Easy Primer to Predictive Analytics for Marketers

A natural nutrition company has been in business for 60 years. While it is an $800 million business, the marketing team is small and the company does not have an in-house data science team nor have the systems to leverage the data it collected over the years about its customers, many of which were very loyal. The company is using cloud-based predictive marketing software to organize, understand, and utilize its customer data with significant results.

The software discovered customers that make their first purchase without any free membership promotions spend 76.5 percent more than customers who join with a free membership offer. It also found that customers who placed auto ship orders were likely to spend three times more over their lifetime. The company was then able to develop smart campaigns around membership programs to encourage customers to sign up and enroll in auto ship when possible.

The software also sorted its customer base into clusters, or groups of customers with similar interests. In doing this, it found a weight-loss cluster that was underserved and sent additional personalized communications, resulting in a 300 percent increase in revenue. It became clear that customers tend to make the majority of purchases within specific nutritional categories and rarely migrate across categories, prompting an initiative to focus communications to each cluster around the most complimentary products for each cluster.

Lastly, the software came with a number of quick-win campaigns, triggered by specific customer behaviors such as abandoned cart and replenishment programs, which resulted in 28 percent incremental web conversions and 22 percent new orders from email reminders, respectively.

The nutrition business story illustrates how everyday marketers can now use predictive marketing methods without ever hiring a single data scientist. The company owns its own customer data, but relies on cloud-based software for predictive algorithms, advanced segmentation, and life cycle campaign templates. Even if they don't have in-house data scientists or develop algorithms in-house, many marketers are curious about what is happening "under the hood" of such predictive marketing software. This chapter is written for those marketers.

This chapter aims to give an easy primer on predictive analytics so you will understand *how* predictive marketing software works. Think about it this way: in order to use a word processor, you don't need to learn to program a computer. However, in the early days of personal computers, people took basic programming classes anyway before using a word processor "just in case." Similarly, this chapter is aiming to teach you the basics of predictive analytics algorithms. It will hopefully give you more confidence using its outputs. You can safely ignore this chapter and jump to Part Two of this book. Knowledge about predictive analytics is not necessary in order to practice predictive marketing.

What Is Predictive Analytics?

Predictive models are used in many areas of business and everyday life including politics, fraud detection, or risk modeling, such as when calculating your credit score. For the purpose of marketing, we are looking to use advanced math in order to predict individual customer behavior and to group customers into the most actionable and meaningful ways. For example, using predictive analytics, you can predict whether and when a customer may be planning to buy next. You might also be able to detect distinct groups of buyers in your customer data, such as customers who only ever buy on discount—so-called discount junkies—or customers who buy a lot but return most items they buy—the returnaholics. Last, using predictive analytics you could predict what specific product a customer may buy next and recommend these products to your customers proactively.

There are three types of predictive analytics that marketers should know about:

1. *Unsupervised learning (such as clustering models)*: Unsupervised learning finds hidden patterns in data, without explicitly trying to estimate or predict an outcome. For example, finding similar customers within a large group of customers, such as those who like long-distance running versus skiing, without explicitly knowing what groups exist or who belongs to them. Unsupervised algorithms such as clustering are thus typically used to unveil the true underlying segmentation of your data.
2. *Supervised learning (such as propensity models or predictions)*: Supervised learning is used to estimate an output given an input, by training it with sample inputs and target. An example is to estimate the lifetime value of a customer, the likelihood a customer will engage with your brand, or a specific product a customer might want to buy next.
3. *Reinforcement learning (more commonly used for recommendations)*: Reinforcement learning allows us to leverage hidden patterns and similarities in the data to accurately predict the best next steps, outcomes, products, or content for the user or a given event. Unlike supervised learning, reinforcement learning algorithms are not provided a training input/output sample but learn from a trial-and-error-based learning scheme.

Unsupervised Learning: Clustering Models

Unsupervised learning is about recognizing patterns in the data without knowing ahead of time what you are looking for or using explicit labels. One of the approaches is called *clustering*. For example, looking at the buying behavior of customers, there could be a cluster of people who usually buy only when they are being given a discount. This group of customers could be detected without imposing any specific pattern or hypothesis or knowledge of the data ahead of time, but rather the pattern of this group would emerge by trying to group customers who are most "behaviorally similar" together.

The difference between clustering and segmentation

If segmentation is the process of manually putting customers into groups based on similarities, then clustering is the automated/statistically rigorous process of finding similarities in customers so that they can be grouped. When you segment you know whom to target ahead of time; when you cluster you discover whom to target. Clustering is a method to automatically discover segments in your customer base by using already known factors about your customers. Clustering algorithms, such as *k*-means and apriori algorithms, can analyze hundreds of customer attributes and previous customer interactions to reveal insights into customer behaviors and the forces driving those behaviors. This is different from customer segmentation in the sense that most segmentation utilizes one or two factors, such as age or income in non-statistical ways to group customers together. Also, as Swedish statistician Hans Rosling put it, "the problem is not ignorance, it is pre-conceived ideas."

For example, if I am selling an expensive cocktail dress, I want to market to people who are most likely to buy the dress. So first I define the limits of the target group: women with annual incomes over $100,000. Identifying and grouping customers who are women and have a high income is the process of segmentation. I make an assumption that people outside this segment most likely would not want a $1,000 dress. I may not have information about household income but can probably estimate income by looking at a customers' zip code.

Clustering will help you discover which women might be most likely to buy your new cocktail dress. Clustering algorithms look at many more dimensions than just zip code. After looking at many variables, such as age, location, time of purchase, similar items purchases, and so forth, a clustering algorithm automatically groups customers with similar behavior. For example, you might discover that it is women of a certain age who buy in the first two months of the year, who are the most likely to buy a high-end dresses (including a cocktail dress) and that household income has very little or nothing to do with it. It is this automatic discovery of customer attributes that matter, and the grouping of customers with similar attributes that we call clustering. Figure 2.1 demonstrates the principle of clustering visually.

In this example we only looked at three dimensions—income, age, and time of purchase. In real life, the power of algorithms is that hundreds

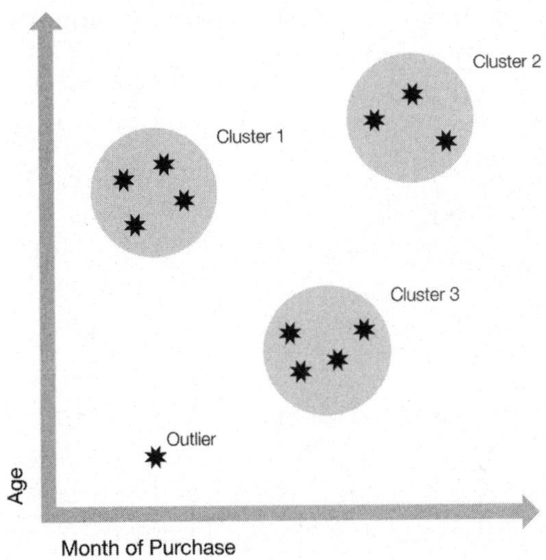

Figure 2.1 The Principle of Clustering

of customer attributes can be analyzed automatically, until the algorithms find the attributes that are significant in teasing apart distinct groups within the customer base. Marketers now have hundreds of characteristics they can look at, such as brand preference, discount preference, time spent onsite, browsing behavior, length of call. It is just not feasible for a person to go through hundreds of types of data to find the relationships between each variable, but for today's powerful computers and software algorithms this is a piece of cake.

Usually about 8 to 15 attributes together describe a customer cluster. You could consider this an automatically discovered persona, who you can now start to market to. You might find that you have a statistically significant group of customers, all young women, who buy every year like clockwork in February, and will only buy designer dresses that are on sale at that time—over the Internet. There might be another group of women who are older, who only buy from you in the store, always at full price, about every two months or so—but don't ever go for the cocktail dresses, only for the casual wear. You get the picture.

Traditional methods often rely on human intuition and guesswork. Clustering, on the other hand, uses what's called *machine-learning algorithms* to create customer segments. This allows computers to quickly study massive amounts of past examples and then learn from the previously collected data to distinguish one customer group from another, find correlations a person might not have looked for, and lead to surprising results that marketers might not have discovered.

For example, let's say you are an online retailer of fast fashion. It is difficult to make specific product recommendations because your inventory changes so quickly. You can, however, cluster your customers around product types in order to discover distinct buying personas. Perhaps you will discover that certain types of products are often bought together, and that some customers are one-category buyers, whereas others tend to shop across categories. Specifically, you might discover that some people who buy active wear also tend to buy sunglasses, whereas another cluster of customers buy sunglasses together with beachwear. Using other customer attributes, such as location, gender, and time of purchase, you can distinguish these two clusters and market to them accordingly. One cluster might constitute women getting ready for vacation, whereas the other consists of avid runners—both men and women. Both segments are best addressed using different creative and content marketing strategies, but if you just look at the purchase of sunglasses you might miss the nuances.

We will learn how to use clusters in marketing campaigns in Chapter 6.

Supervised Learning: Propensity Models

Propensity models, also called *likelihood models*, are what most people think of when they hear the term predictive analytics. In mathematical terms, these models use algorithms such as neural networks, logistic regression, random forest, and regression trees. The names of these algorithms are of little importance to marketers. What is important to know is that propensity models make true predictions about a customer's future behavior by learning from examples from the past. Examples include the likelihood of a customer to buy a product or the likelihood of a prospect to engage with a website.

Propensity models are used heavily in direct mail and are often referred to as *response models*, because these models predict a customer's response, for instance to buy or not to buy, as a result of receiving a piece of direct mail. Propensity models are guided-learning models, which means that it takes some time to train the data and that the models get better over time. As the model observes the actual outcome of the prediction, such as did the customer buy or not, then the model can adjust its algorithm and become more accurate over time. Therefore, most propensity models require a short training period and a testing period before you rely on the predictions entirely. You can accelerate the training period by providing a historical data set as a training data set.

Figure 2.2 demonstrates how you need either a training and testing period or historical data to start making your first prediction using propensity models.

How to Use Propensity Deciles

A key term when it comes to propensity models is *deciles*. Instead of using individual customer scores, most practitioners group customers into deciles, top 10 percent, next 10 percent, and all the way to the bottom 10 percent.

For instance, to predict how much money a customer would spend throughout her lifetime, we would use what's called a *predicted lifetime value model*. The top 10 percent of customers here might have an average predicted lifetime value of $1,000, whereas the average predicted lifetime value for the bottom 10 percent is only $5.

The decile approach is useful in two ways. First of all, it provides the average value for the expected behavior such as lifetime value or spend. Secondly, it essentially provides a rank order of your customers from the most valuable to the least valuable, or from the most likely to buy to the least likely to buy, in 10 equal buckets. You could use this information in many ways, such as to decide to whom to send an expensive catalog

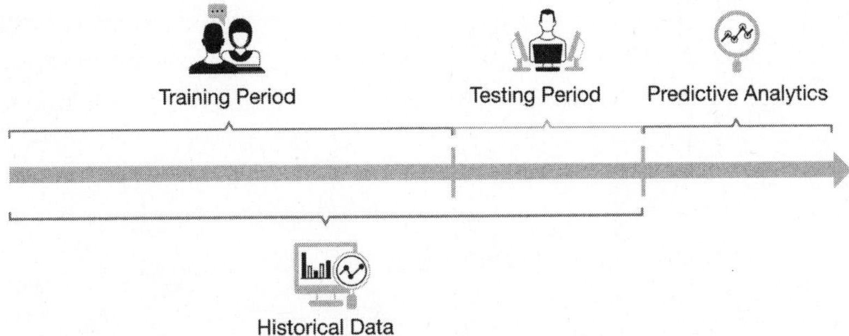

Figure 2.2 Training Propensity Models

or to design a/b lift tests. Catalogs would only go out to the customers in the top one or two deciles or you can test what the lift is in sending catalogs to each decile, and determine the efficacy and effectiveness. Or you could use this model to decide who to invite to the upcoming fashion show of your new sneaker line. It is more advantageous to have customers there who will actually buy something after the show.

Similarly you could decide on different strategies for something as simple as an abandoned browse campaign: prospects who visited your website but didn't convert are an important missed opportunity and many retargeting solutions are available to follow these non-buyers across the web. What if you could differentiate the offer you are making to these customers based on their likelihood to buy? For people with a very high likelihood to buy, a simple reminder might be enough to get them to open their wallets, whereas for people with a very low likelihood to buy you might offer them a discount or free shipping.

Figure 2.3 shows you the predicted customer response to a direct mail campaign. This model is essentially predicting that the top 10 percent of customers, or the first decile, will make up 52 percent of all responses to the direct mailer. Based on this you might decide only to send this catalog to this top decile. If you are aiming for a certain number of responses, say 70 percent, you may need to send this to the top two deciles or you might consider sending to decile two and three because

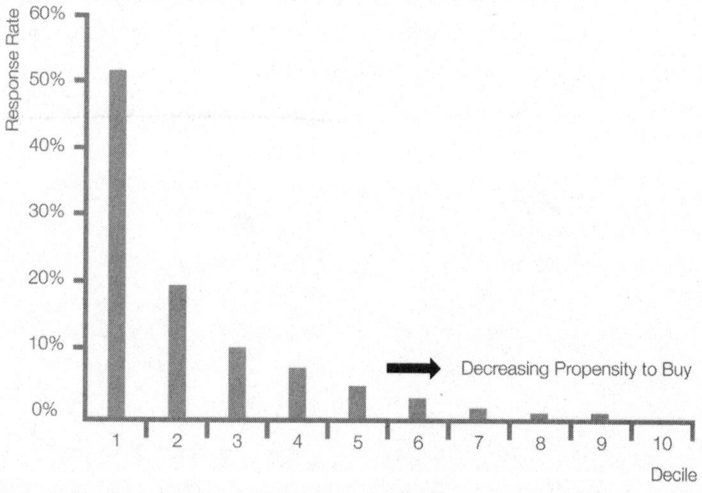

Figure 2.3 An Example of a Direct Mail Response Model

decile one is likely to buy anyway, were as deciles two and three might need the catalogue to incent them to make a purchase. Or if you have a limited number of catalogs, or a limited budget, you can now aim those catalogs at the customers most likely to respond. The other way to use the model is to create a/b tests within each decile to measure the lift to see which decile can justify the cost of incremental catalogs with incremental profits.

This type of model can be used to predict future prospect or customer behavior. For example, from the moment I buy my first Gucci handbag, the luxury manufacturer can predict with a high degree of accuracy how many more handbags I will buy in the future. I may have no intent to ever buy from Gucci again, but the brand knows better. Ironically, by comparing my purchases, website visits, and email clicks, as well as my age, sex, and location, to the behavior and demographics of thousands of other customers who have come before me, Gucci's algorithms can predict my future purchases better than I can myself.

Comparing Propensity Models and RFM Modeling

Before predictive analytics became widely available, the industry standard for identifying who is likely to buy from you was a model called RFM (*R*ecency, *F*requency, *M*onetary Value). However, it has limited utility and can be surprisingly hard to use in real life. Furthermore, even though RFM is often classified as a predictive model, it is nothing but a mere heuristic (using a rule of thumb, an educated guess) approach with no statistical nor predictive foundation.

The idea is that if a customer purchased from you recently, frequently, or has spent a lot of money with you, he or she is likely to buy from you again. There is certainly no argument that "how many days has it been since the customer last bought from us?" (recency), "how many times has a customer bought from us?" (frequency), and "how much revenue has the customer generated for us?" (monetary value) are all excellent variables to try and predict whether the customer will return to make another purchase.

However, this technique has limitations. For one, it severely restricts how companies use their own data. There are so many other variables that can be derived from data that can serve as additional excellent predictors. Also, the old saying, "past results are no guarantee for future performance," holds true for RFM modeling as well. RFM is exclusively looking backward, rather than comparing customers' current behavior to the future behavior of others who came before them. Using RFM you will not be able to recognize high-value customers *before* they have bought from you. You might also ignore past high-value customers who have defected to the competition.

Let's look at an example: there might be a pattern where customers buy a couple of times and then disappear. The only way to find this out is by comparing customer behavior to other customers just like them to make predictions about future behavior. If most customers buy three times and then disappear, then the likelihood of a customer to buy after three times is actually very low, whereas the RFM model would put this customer in a "highly likely to buy" segment. Thus, good, responsive customers might end up in not so valuable segments and thus get ignored for promotional mailings. The opposite might happen as well—not-so-great customers might end up in valuable segments. A response model that ranks customers by their value as opposed to the value of their segment can take care of this problem.

Also, RFM models can only make predictions about the likelihood to buy in an environment where there are frequent purchases, such as retail. RFM models do nothing to predict a customer's lifetime value, a customer's likelihood to unsubscribe from a service, such as a subscription service or your email list, or the likelihood of a web browser (nonbuyer) to convert into a first-time buyer. Supervised learning models can be used to make predictions about all of these customer behaviors and more. In many comparison tests, where the top 50 percent of customers are selected with RFM and propensity models, propensity models are on average 40% more accurate than RFM. This in many cases translates to 20–25% less promotional costs.

Ironically, propensity models are not only more accurate, they are also much easier to use for the everyday marketer. Rather than having to choose which combination of potentially hundreds of possible combinations of recency, frequency, and monetary value to use for a campaign, you can just decide which of the ten propensity deciles to include. With predictive analytics, marketers are presented with a list that automatically ranks customer from the most likely to buy to the customer least likely to buy.

We come back to some specific supervised learning models and how you can use them in Chapters 7 and 8.

Reinforcement Learning and Collaborative Filtering

Reinforcement learning is typically used in combination with collaborative filtering models. The common marketing application for collaborative filtering models is *recommendations*. From a technical point of view, recommendation models make use of the latest machine-learning theories in the field of collaborative filtering, bayesian networks, and frequent item sets. Time-decay functions are used to take into account the fact that recent behavior has more predictive weight than older behavior. Finally, reinforcement learning is applied to "educate" the model to the customer's preferences. Again, we just mention these names in case you want to dig deeper.

Collaborative filtering models can recommend products, content, or just about anything else. These recommendation models were made famous by Amazon with their "customers who liked this product, also liked . . ." suggestions. Recommendation models are a fantastic way to grow the value and retain your customers, by suggesting relevant products or content they will be interested in. Suggesting relevant products will drive revenue directly, whereas suggesting relevant content will increase the engagement with your brand, and indirectly create more happy and loyal customers.

It is important to serve up recommendations that fit the context of where they are presented to customers. Bad or out-of-context recommendations will be viewed as "creepy," "intrusive," or "irrelevant." Recommendations should come at the right time: for example, just as you are about to check out your online shopping cart it makes sense to receive a "customers who bought this, also added . . ." type of recommendation. Perhaps two days after, it is appropriate to receive a thank you email suggesting useful follow-on purchases. Those who bought a wood grill might now be recommended a cookbook or refill wood chips. It is best also to expose this context to the consumer. The more transparent you are, the more consumers will accept and act on your recommendations. Companies that successfully utilize recommendations are now starting to offer explanations of their recommendations to remove the intrusive nature. You will see Amazon use words such as "because you looked at this product, you might also be interested in these products," or "people who bought this product, bought it together with this other product." These brands are also starting to give consumers control over

which products are recommended. You can go to a preference center and exclude certain items from being considered for the recommendation algorithms.

If you have worked with recommendations before you know that there are many details that matter when it comes to recommendation algorithms. First, to stay relevant, the recommendations are ideally refreshed in real time, and the underlying models are refreshed daily for each customer to take into account a customer's recent behavior but also the change in behavior of other similar people.

Also, you want to make sure that the model does not recommend products that are out of stock or products that have a high return rate or bad reviews. Some retailers do not recommend items that are on sale but opt for higher margin items. A good recommendation model also allows for marketers to manually enter merchandising rules that tweak the algorithm.

Different Types of Recommendation Models

There are three good use cases for recommendation models: upsell recommendations, next sell recommendations, and cross-sell recommendations. Each of these has a different place in a marketer's arsenal. Also, recommendations can be made for "products that are generally bought together" or can be made specifically to a person based on past behavior. Let's start by explaining the difference between those two.

Products Generally Bought Together Products that are typically bought together are not customer-specific. At our company, we sometimes call these *product-to-product* recommendations, though this is not a common industry term. These are the type of recommendations that are displayed on a product page, and will recommend other relevant products to all visitors of that product page. Products that are typically bought together are called product-to-product recommendations. They answer the question: "Customers who bought this product, typically also bought what other products?" In this scenario, two people browsing the same product will receive the same recommendations. In Figure 2.4 two people browsing the first bikini set will receive a recommendation for another bikini, a swim cover-up, and a tote bag. These types of general recommendations are especially relevant when you don't know

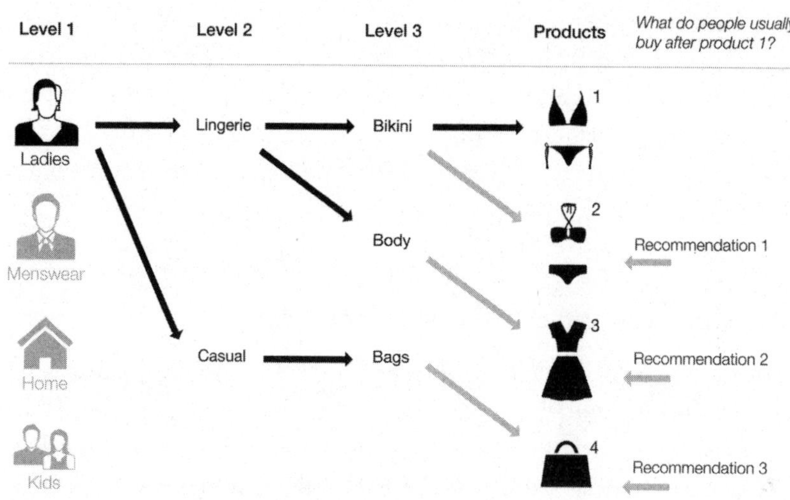

Figure 2.4 Products Typically Bought Together

much about a specific customer, such as an anonymous first-time browser coming to your website.

User Specific Recommendations If you have more information about a specific user, then you can go further than generic recommendations. Let's say you know the person looking at this bikini set is a male and this is the first time that he is looking at swimwear. Normally he browses and purchases electronics from your website. While he is browsing, presumably for a gift or something, it might be appropriate to recommend other bikini tops. However, when sending the customer a thank you email two days after his purchase with recommendations of what to buy next, you would be better off making recommendations specific to this person that take into account the entire history, not just the most recent browsing session.

These are product recommendations specific to a given customer. In our company we sometimes call these types of recommendations *product-to-user* type recommendations. You can replace "product" with "content" or "person" or whatever you are trying to recommend. In this case, two users looking at the same product at your site would receive totally different recommendations.

User-specific recommendations are not limited to physical goods. You can replace the word "product" with "content" or "event."

For example, Shazam is recording the music tastes of consumers when you tag (Shazam) songs you like. Based on your personal tastes Shazam will recommend concerts that are of interest to you, but only if the concerts actually take place in your geographical area. For these recommendations to be successful, Shazam needs to know not only the tastes of its customers but also their physical locations.

The Predictive Analytics Process

Let's walk through the different steps a data scientist, or analytics software, goes through to make accurate predictions or recommendations. Most of what we describe here happens under the hood and marketers don't need to worry about any of this. Figure 2.5 gives an overview about what is happening under the hood, either of out-of-the-box predictive analytics software, or the steps your internal data scientists will have to go through if you are building your own predictive analytics models. We don't mean to scare you by being very specific about some of these steps in this chapter. However, we do want you to realize that the do-it-yourself route to predictive marketing requires highly trained data scientists. There is a lot that comes with developing and deploying predictive algorithms for marketing, and if you are starting new and want our advice, we strongly recommend that you use an off-the-shelf software package suitable for your industry to take care of the steps described in this chapter automatically. When you exhaust off-the-shelf models, and you have the budget and need for a data scientist, you can easily evaluate the cost-benefit equation with the

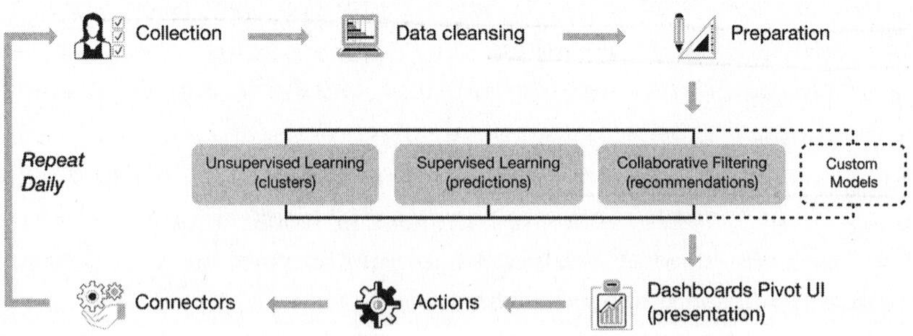

Figure 2.5 Overview of the Predictive Analytics Process

experience you gained (and you'll find it easier to convince the CFO to make the incremental investment).

Data Collection, Cleansing, and Preparation

Data cleansing and preparation is the most important and most ignored stage in predictive analytics. In some cases, the data might be missing or incorrect as collected. Data cleansing is used to correct things like names and addresses to make sure the computer will know that a customer lives in California when her state is listed as CA. We discuss the process of collecting customer data and linking it together to form individual customer profiles in detail in Chapter 3. However, even after building 360 customer profiles, there still is significant work to be done getting your data ready for analysis. Not all data collected is immediately usable and the results could be skewed by missing data or outliers, data measurements that are either too low, too high, or do not fit the underlying data-generating system.

If you are considering building your own predictive analytics capabilities, make sure you address who will do the data collection, integration, cleansing, and preparation. Chances are, your typical data scientist is not going to be satisfied doing this work and is going to expect that you hire a separate software or integration engineer to do this work.

Outlier Detection

Outlier detection often makes a big difference in the accuracy of predictive models. For example, if a customer at an electronics retailer came in and bought 50 televisions for $50,000 when the average customer at the retailer spends $500, this high-spender will skew the average order value metric. In electronics retailing, these types of outliers where there are few users making large purchases are indeed quite common. People making such large purchases could be middlemen who are buying items like televisions to take out of the country and resell. These are not normal consumer customers, but rather gray market resellers. If this situation wasn't recognized and corrected, the retailer would think these are great VIP customers. Not recognizing this creates two problems: distorting the definition of VIP customers so the true VIP customers would be left out and masking an opportunity to market to this group of resellers in a more profitable way.

To correct for the outlier, your data analyst or predictive marketing software will need to detect and either remove the outlier or replace it with a number at the high end of the distribution (e.g., the lowest spend of the top 10 percent customers is $2,400, so replace the $50,000 with $2,400). This replacement is only done for modeling purposes. Alternatively, you can treat these customers as a separate group altogether and create specialty programs for this one segment.

In another example, one retailer was measuring foot traffic at each store but would miss out on data for certain days whenever the measuring device would get knocked off by cleaning crew. To correct for the missing data, the retailer applied an imputation based on the three-week average for the same days in the week as the missing days. Imputation is the art and science of replacing wrong or missing information. Depending on the specific data elements, there are various techniques for this:

- Replace with static or temporal averages.
- Model the data based on other variables available. For example, you can model a vitamin store customer's age based on whether she buys vitamins geared toward women above age 50.
- Random selection from the underlying distribution. For example, if the foot traffic data is missing and this data usually follows a bell curve, then randomly generate a number from the underlying distribution.

Imputation is a great way to make up for missing data until the problem is corrected at the source.

Another example of imputation is asking customers for their birthdays. This is a great piece of information for modeling and action purposes but not all customers want to provide this information. In such cases, the predictive model would either discard the birthday as an input or discard customers with no birthday.

Feature Generation and Extraction

Once your data scientist or predictive marketing software has cleansed the data for missing information and outliers, there are two other factors to consider: (1) the data may be too large to use as is, or (2) data in its current representation may not be suitable for the models. Feature generation and extraction deals with turning data into information that the models can digest and throwing away unnecessary or redundant information. Think of feature generation and extraction as separating the signal from the noise. Feature extraction deals with removing unnecessary information by either throwing it away or transforming it to eliminate the noise. There are quite a few mathematical methods to use, but the short explanation is to utilize algorithms to be able to extract the maximum amount of information from the data, regardless of what you will use it for later on. This optimal extraction leads to less noisy data, hence increasing the accuracy of predictive analytics.

There are tricks you can use to make your data easier to use. For example, when trying to analyze the number of orders from a customer you can look at the numbers in absolute terms or you could take the logarithm of the number, creating a new variable where if a customer has 1 order or 10 orders, it's the same difference between having 10 orders and 100 orders. It is a simple transformation that can have a powerful impact.

Another example could be taking the ratio of certain variables instead of using absolute numbers. For instance, instead of return revenue and shipped revenue per customer, you can calculate the ratio or percentage of revenue that comes through returns.

Classifier and System Design

The next stage in the process used by data scientists or predictive marketing software is choosing, architecting, and fine-tuning the correct algorithm. In machine learning, there are two important concepts that need to be understood. One is the *no free lunch* theorem, which states that there is no inherently better algorithm for all problems out there. This is important to understand so the data scientist chooses the right algorithm for the right problem, and not use the same algorithm for every problem. The other concept is called the *bias-variance dilemma*, which states that if you go deep in developing an approach and algorithm to solve a specific problem, then the system that is biased toward this specific problem gets worse and worse performance in solving "other" problems out there. The lesson learned here is to understand that no algorithm is inherently better than the other. If you develop your own algorithms it means you probably have to develop multiple algorithms for multiple situations. If you buy off-the-shelf predictive marketing software, you want to make sure to choose a vendor that focuses on your specific vertical and business problems, and/or to choose a vendor that has self-learning algorithms that can adjust to your specific situation automatically. Correctly architected software solutions usually have multiple models competing with each other, and the "champion" is selected against "challengers" that is unique to the customer's domain of data. This maximizes performance and eliminates the need for hand-coded custom models.

Just writing an algorithm is not enough when it comes to predictive analytics. Before you can start to use an algorithm, you need to backtest that it actually works. If you use a predictive marketing software package, your vendor will have done this for you already. However, if you are developing your own predictive analytics models in-house you will have to worry about training, testing, and validating your models before you can start to use them. The time needed to develop predictive algorithms can be divided into 80 percent training, 10 percent testing, and 10 percent validation. This means that after writing the algorithm, data scientists need to spend considerable time training and testing the algorithm to make sure it works accurately.

For example, when developing a likelihood to buy model, if 1 percent of 10 million customers buy within the next 30 days, then for training, we use 100,000 customers who bought in the past month and randomly select 100,000 customers who didn't buy anything in the past month, so that the total dataset has 200,000 customers in which 50 percent bought and 50 percent didn't. This oversampling produces better results, because it focuses the model to detect between potential buyers and non-buyers.

The Last Mile Problem of Predictive Analytics

Most data scientists don't worry how marketers will use their predictions. Frankly, most data scientists don't know enough about marketing and marketing systems to embed predictions into the daily routine of marketers. An email marketer at a large national department store once told us: "Brides register with us on our website and leave a lot of personal information. That information is in our customer data warehouse somewhere and we probably even analyze it. However, as an email-marketing manager, I am unable to run a simple campaign that takes into account some of the preferences or dates that the bride has shared with us." We call this the last mile problem of predictive analytics.

Especially in organizations with in-house data scientists, the outcomes from predictive models are often not easily digestible or usable by marketers. It is often very difficult for marketers to put predictive analytics into action—to connect the dots from analytics to the daily campaign management of email, web, social, mobile, direct mail, store marketing, and customer interactions in the call center.

For customer predictions to be profitable, predictions need to be put in the hands of all the customer-facing personnel in your organization. If you can't surface recommendations to the personnel in your call center, the upsell might never happen. If you can't use likelihood to buy segments to decide whether to send an abandoned cart holder a discount or a reminder, you are leaving a lot of profit on the table. In Chapter 14 we look at technologies that bridge this last mile problem.

Now that you have a basic understanding of predictive models and how they can be used for marketing, we get to work. In the rest of this book we give you more examples of each of the three types of machine-learning models discussed in this chapter. We cover how to use each of these models for marketing in much detail. We also propose how to operationalize each of the models, connect the findings to specific marketing campaigns that can drive immediate revenues or profits for your organization. Without marketing actions, there may be analysis paralysis, thus no customer delight nor incremental profits.

CHAPTER 3

Get to Know Your Customers First: Build Complete Customer Profiles

Before you can leverage customer data to find new growth opportunities or hypertarget your customers, you first need to aggregate, clean, and analyze that data. This is no easy task. If yours is like most companies, customer data is all over the place, full of errors and duplicates and inaccessible to everyday marketers. Fortunately, predictive technology can help clean up your data mess. Your information technology (IT) department and potentially outside vendors can also help.

Bosch understood that its customers were no longer only home improvement retailers like Home Depot and Lowe's. Instead, the rise of online shopping allowed their end customers to go directly to its website and engage with the brand, without ever stepping foot into a big box store. That created a challenge for Bosch, which had limited insight into the end-user data of who was buying their products.

Bosch realized it had to do a better job marketing directly to its end customers, but to do so it needed to get a better handle on its customer data. Like many companies, Bosch did not have an internal data team and was relying on an outside service provider. That meant that for every question about customers, it had to ask the external provider to create a new report. So Bosch decided to bring its customer data in-house by using modern cloud-based software, rather than to rely on an outside consulting firm. Now, the company can aggregate customer information from various data sources and link it together into individual customer profiles. It tracks purchases, but also newsletter signups and product registrations. Bosch has learned that even without using customer data for one-to-one personalization, the 360-degree view of customers has made all the difference when making decisions about how to market to its customers. The next step is to understand how this data can be utilized to support marketing activities with partners like Home Depot and Lowes.

A New York boutique fashion brand had the same experience. Once it collected all customer data into a single profile, it was able to give customer service personnel access to these records. Now if a customer writes or calls in to complain, it could look up if this customer was a high-value customer or not, and get more context overall to have a better conversation with this customer, and respond appropriately to the complaint.

The Bosch and fashion brand examples illustrate clearly that even without advanced segmentation or analytics, organizing customer information across all customer touch points, including web, transactions, mobile, email, store, call center, into a 360-degree profile for each customer can be a huge win. The Bosch example also illustrates that customer data is not only for direct-to-consumer marketers. Of course, for those companies that have wholesale distribution, getting consumer data can be a challenge. Industry standard is such that wholesale partners do not pass along customer data. However, brands can develop a program whereby they utilize a registration or warranty program where they put a card in the packaging for consumers to sign up online to register online. The card will often instruct you to go to a specific registration URL with the brand in exchange for registering the product for future issues with the product or simply register their email address to get the latest product information and care instructions directly from the brand. Surprisingly, many consumers are will to do this, and though you may not have all the transactions associated with the purchase, you'll have their email or mailing address. Service records can serve the same purpose. A well-known European retailer of white goods is using repair records as triggers for personalized marketing campaigns. Lastly, brands selling through wholesale may also consider using visits to their corporate website as a proxy for product interest. Clusters can be built based on browsing behavior alone.

This chapter helps you understand what data you need to collect first, if you, too, want to bring customer data in-house as a core competency, and how to prepare your data for analysis. We will also add a few words on how to partner successfully with your IT counterparts to bring customer data projects to completion.

How Much Data to Collect

In this book, we focus on customer data provided to a company directly by its customers, not data derived or purchased from third parties. Marketers have more historical and real-time data on customers than ever before. This type of data is also called first-party data, data that is owned by the marketer that reflects direct interactions of the consumer with the brand and has the richest information compared to third-party data sources. Third-party data sources needs to be anonymized and sometimes come close to breaching privacy boundaries. We talk about this in more detail in later chapters. Each individual consumer generates hundreds of data points each day, which when multiplied by thousands or even millions of customers result in truly *big* customer data. Data is said to be "big" when there is a lot of volume, variety, and velocity. For customer data this is certainly true. In fact, the data most companies collect from their customers has grown so large and varied that no human being can analyze it anymore without the help of computers and software.

Marketers who can find a way to harness the power of all this customer data will have a significant competitive advantage. Figure 3.1 outlines some design principles that may be useful when deciding what data to collect. The most important design principle is to start with the end in mind. Often, marketers make data collection and integration a project on its own without specifically outlining what the data will be used for and how it will be maintained to ensure it is in great shape.

When considering how much customer data to collect, also take into consideration how valuable that data is, as well as how easy it is get. This may vary by company, but remember not to overdo it.

Design Principle for Data Collection	Example
Frequency	How frequently to collect data, and on which event triggers?
Derived data	Derived data are implied data elements. A customer who visited the website and browsed a product five times and each time bought from a store in the following seven days could be labeled as a customer who collects information online, but shops offline.
Granularity	Web data could be collected click by click or in some cases a summary about the web sessions could be enough.
Insights to be derived	If the goal is to predict customer upside potential, the type of products a customer purchases is important, as well as the zip code the customer lives in. The Insights to be derived determine which data we collect.
Actionability	Data collected should be actionable directly or indirectly. Collecting the sports interests of customers is actionable for a sports retailer, but not for a company that does tax consulting.
Accuracy	When asked for age, quite a few customers randomly type answers, more often in cases where marketers use it for gating content or a sign up. Marketers need to deal with these inaccuracies through imputations. Imputations is the process of replacing missing values with substitute values.
Fill rates	Marketers often want to collect data on customers using progressive profiling in order to boost fill rates.
Storage	How much or how long to keep the data depends on the "currency" of data. Web browsing data is often not relevant after a few weeks, whereas purchases stay relevant for years.
Accessibility	Data collected should be accessible to marketers for analysis and action. Too often customer data is stuck in silos, inaccessible to everyday marketers.

Figure 3.1 Design Principles for Data Collection

Many marketers obsess over collecting all customer data at once. That is a big mistake. It is very easy to get caught up in a long and slow data integration project without ever seeing results. Your goal should be to collect just enough data to find new growth opportunities and start marketing programs that deliver results. You will be surprised by how little information you need to get started. Once you can show results from your initial data-driven campaign, it will become easier to get the cooperation from other departments, such as your internal IT team, to collect more customer data.

Big data inherently has a lot of noise in it. So data collection needs to be paired with techniques to find the signal in the noise. The important point here is to know how to extract the information from this large dataset to make it manageable, insightful, and actionable. Figure 3.1 gives an overview of some of the questions marketers need to answer, in collaboration with their technology teams, about the data to be collected, integrated, and analyzed.

What Type of Data to Collect

Traditionally, marketers have mainly used purchase data and customer demographic data. These days, marketers also have access to more behavioral data points, which brings temporal information. This temporal information can be used to derive context and to make marketing more relevant in time. When we interact with a company or a brand, each of our actions leaves a digital footprint, which gets recorded in a database. For example, for every purchase that somebody makes online, we now have about 50 data elements on each customer before that purchase is even made. These include what customers clicked on in an email, whether they clicked on Google Adwords, what reviews they may have left, activity on social networks, complaints, and calls to customer support centers. The amount of behavioral data available has exploded in recent years. It is easy to get overwhelmed, but not to worry. We show you where to start.

While no two businesses are alike, Figure 3.2 gives you an example of what a phased data integration strategy might look like. In this example

Phase 1	Phase 2	Phase 3
Behavioral	**Behavioral**	**Behavioral**
Purchases	Call center interaction	Social interactions
Web behavior	Returns and complaints	Reviews and surveys
Email behavior	Customer meeting notes	Loyalty program interaction
Demographic	**Demographic**	**Demographic**
Household affiliation	Gender	Additional third-party data
Account grouping	U.S. census data	
Location	Vertical and size	

Figure 3.2 Three Steps to Customer Data Collection

the assumption is your end goal is to drive customer engagement and increase customer lifetime value.

High-priority behavioral data for both consumer and business marketers includes purchases, web visits and email clicks. High-priority demographic data for consumer marketers could include the gender, age, and location of a customer, and for business marketers, more likely the industry, size of the organization, title of the buyer, and the location of the buyer's headquarters. Purchases alone will already give you a wealth of information. In fact, every single purchase generates lots of interesting meta-data points, such as time and location of the purchase, product purchased, and the sales person involved in the transaction. Figure 3.3 summarizes more of these points. We will describe each of the different data types and how to collect them in detail in Appendix A.

Data You Can Collect at the Time of Purchase
Time of the purchase
Date of the purchase
Date of shipment
Billing address for the purchase
Shipping address for the purchase
Name of the buyer
Gender of the buyer (derived from the name)
Shipping revenues
How long ago was this purchase
Channel of the purchase (for example, online or offline)
Product that was purchased
Product category that was purchased
Brand that was purchased
Salesperson involved in the purchase (B2B and B2C)
Price of the purchase
Discount applied to the purchase
Revenues generated by the purchase
Cost of goods sold for the purchase
Margin of the purchase
Tax collected on the purchase
Shipping revenues associated with the purchase
Whether this was the first purchase or a repeat order
Number of products in the order
Types of products included in the order
What type of device the customer used to make the purchase

Figure 3.3 The Anatomy of a Purchase

A special challenge exists when it comes to in-store or other in-person purchases. Many store purchases are anonymous. You might try to collect email addresses in the store by offering customers an electronic receipt or an incentive in exchange for an in-store newsletter signup. You might also give store associates a discount or other compensation to collect email addresses.

For a well-run program, expect in-store capture rates above 60% and as high as 95%. Improving data capture rates can dramatically improve the success of in-store clienteling. Clienteling is a technique used by retail sales associates to establish long-term relationships with key customers based on data about their preferences, behaviors, and purchases. Clienteling is intended to guide associates to provide more personal and informed customer service that may influence customer behavior related to shopping frequency, lift in average transaction value, and other retail key performance indicators. From the customer's perspective, clienteling "could add a layer of personal touch" to the shopping experience. Clienteling with big data dramatically improves upsells and consumer satisfaction because the consumer develops a relationship with a sales associate that has a vested interest in securing their loyalty. Retention rates improve dramatically for brands that make 360 customer profiles available to sales associates and that associate consumer transactions with individual sales associates.

Mavi, the international jeans and Apparel Company from Chapter 2, wanted to tie POS transactions to customers to understand customers individually. Mavi introduced a loyalty card program to accomplish this. When it started the program, in its first year, only 20 percent of transactions were tied to individual customer. By year four it had tied close to 90 percent of transactions to individuals. There are a few things Mavi did right when introducing this program: First, it put goals and measurement in place and always focused on improving. Second, it delighted customers with the data it collected, for example by sending them highly personalized offers to come back to the store and get extra points to buy again. By doing so, customers wanted to identify themselves, because they saw the benefits. Third, the store personnel saw the benefits and were always educated about why they did it. It was a cultural focus and shift.

Loyalty program interaction itself is another important data point: the use of loyalty rewards can be very different from customer to customer. In fact, we have found that when grouping customers based on their behavior, the use of loyalty points is often a differentiating factor and some groups of customers— such as men—are more inclined to be swayed by reward offers than others.

In another example, Walmart created a mobile application called *Savings Catcher*, which promised customers who downloaded the app that Walmart would compare the prices of their purchases against prices offered by Walmart's competitors and refund customers the difference when it found a lower price at another retail store. By providing an incentive to customers, Walmart was able to collect millions of email addresses and analyze information, like which products customers bought and what time they typically went shopping.

Business purchases are likely tracked in your enterprise resource management system or customer relationship management system. These systems are also a rich source of demographic information, such as the location of the customer and the relationship between contacts and accounts, as well as between salespeople and accounts.

Preparing Your Data for Analysis

When it comes to your customer database the saying "garbage in, garbage out" holds true. If you base your customer segmentation or predictive models on bad or incomplete customer data profiles, you will get the wrong recommendations for your customers. Therefore, data wrangling is a huge part of the job. Data scientists will tell you that data preparation before analysis can make up 95 percent of all the work.

Without a single view of the customer, it is impossible to truly understand any single customer or to draw any conclusions about customer trends. For example, if you can only see a person's in-store purchases, but that person makes 90 percent of his or her purchases online, you may believe this is an unprofitable customer when in reality this person could be one of your VIPs. Similarly, if somebody frequently browses your website but always ends up buying in the store, you may mistake the website customer as "low value." In a different scenario, a customer spends a large amount and buys often, but returns items just as frequently or makes frequent calls into your call center. This customer looks like a "high value" customer, but is in fact unprofitable.

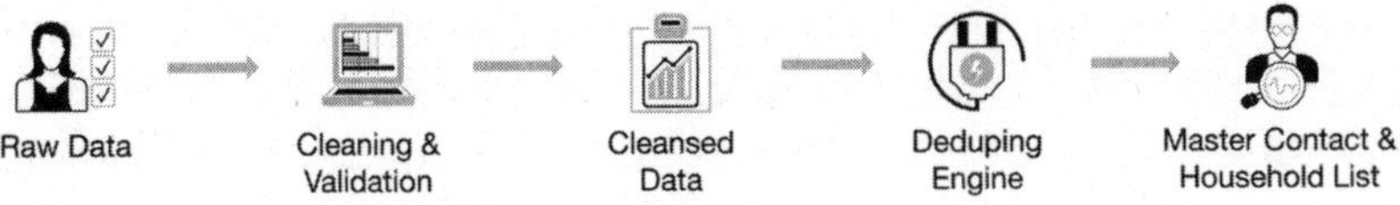

Figure 3.4 The Data Preparation Process

This means that you need to be able to integrate, link, and deduplicate all the information that you have collected. This is not an easy task. Figure 3.4 gives you an overview of the data preparation process at a high level. We will go through each of the steps in the data preparation process briefly.

Cleaning and Validation of Names

After receiving the raw data, the first thing you want to do is to validate the names, postal addresses, email addresses, and phone numbers in the customer files you received. Without this, software algorithms will be unable to link the right activities to the right data records. Examples of common mistakes that need to be corrected before matching records to real people include:

- Middle names or initials might be included or excluded: William L and William Louis might both be variations of the same person—William Morrison.
- Two-person contacts might not be matched unless corrected: "William & Cathy Morrison" should be matched to William Morrison's customer record.
- Replacing abbreviated names: Wm and Bill and William may all be the same person.
- Removing honorifics: Rev. Bill Morrison and Dr. Bill should both be matched to William Morrison's record.
- First and last name swapped: Bill Morrison and Morrison Bill are likely the same person, especially if they live at the same address.
- Slight variations in name spelling, like Katie and Cathy.

There are many common mistakes that software can easily correct. Software can automatically normalize names, such as change Bill to William or vice versa, and recognize and tag men and women.

Metaphonic algorithms are also correct words that have similar pronunciation, such as Katherine, Cathy, and so on. Software can automatically standardize names so that different records from the same customer will now match and be linked to a single customer ID. For example, Michael is the same as Mike and James is the same as Jim, and so forth. As part of name standardization and verification, software can also change the case of the name. So if the name was in all capitals (WILLIAM) or all lowercase (william) we make it have first letter capital, remainder lowercase (William). This may seem trivial, but software algorithms are not people—and tend to take things literally. Without correction and normalization, these records would not be matched to the same person.

Cleaning and Validation of Addresses

For mailing addresses, validation is important to make sure that each piece of expensive direct mail you are sending is actually deliverable. Address validation can reduce mailing costs by as much as 80 percent. These are some ways to validate mailing addresses:

- *Canada and U.S. address coding according to USPS standards.* Make sure that the address is complete and correctly written including a zip code with a four-digit append to have the most accurate address possible.
- *NCOA (National Change of Address).* Each address in your database can be checked against the NCOA database to make sure that the recipient has not moved since you acquired his or her address.
- *CASS certification.* CASS certification is a requirement for all mailers in order to receive certain mailing rates from the USPS based on the quality of their addresses.
- *DPV (Delivery Point Validation).* This is the highest level of address accuracy checking—where each address gets checked against a data file to ensure that it exists as an active delivery point for the USPS.
- *Address type flag.* If relevant, address parsing can also append an address type flag, such as whether the address is a residence or a business.
- *MSA/region append.* Based on each address, software can append the longitude and latitude of the location, but can also match this against administrative regions.

Email address validation is equally important. Email verification services can improve client reach and reduce the danger of damaging your sender reputation. Checks that can be performed automatically include:

- *Syntax correction.* Syntax correction in names and addresses automatically removes illegal characters and fixes host names. For example, software algorithms can automatically fix common domain name misspellings (gmai1.com = gmail.com, for example). Software could also validate and correct illegal characters. For example, if it says gmail,com instead of gmail.com, the correction would be to replace the comma with the period.
- *Mail test.* As part of validating email addresses, software can automatically "ping" the domain in the email address to ensure this domain is available as a mail exchange. Software can also automatically maintain a list of invalid emails.
- *Invalid email filtering.* Certain common default values, such as noemail@email.com, can automatically be detected and filtered out.
- *Casing standardization.* As with names, when it comes to checking emails, software can automatically standardize all addresses to include only lowercase letters.

Linking and Deduplication

To eliminate duplicate copies of repeating data, you can use a technique called *deduplication*. It is important because it can increase the accuracy of key performance indicators and metrics (like the lifetime value of a customer). It also helps you avoid targeting the same person twice, which doesn't look very professional and can be very expensive when it comes to campaigns like direct mail. The attributes of each of your contacts should be merged according to a set of priority rules to obtain a master contact list. At this time, you should also associate the right contacts with the right households or the right corporations.

In order to accurately deduplicate your data, you can use software algorithms to do what's called *fuzzy matching.* Fuzzy algorithms compute a similarity score between attributes such as Names or Addresses. When the similarity is higher than a defined threshold, the entities are considered duplicates. Hence fuzzy logic will "estimate" whether two customer names that are similar, but not exactly the same, might be the same person. Some customer attributes, such as a customer's home address, will have a higher weighting in this estimation. William Morrison and Bill Morrison are likely the same person if they live at the same address, but unlikely the same person if they live in different states.

Now that all the hard work of collecting and cleaning customer data is done, in Figure 3.5 we give an example of the information that may be included in the profile of a single customer. Just with this profile alone there is a lot of value. You could give your sales team, customer success team, call center team, or in-store personnel access to these profiles and they will surely be able to serve customers better with this type of information at their fingertips. In the next chapters we take the next steps to actually using this information for customer analytics and to create unique and meaningful experiences for each and every customer.

It is not unusual to make important discoveries about your customers after integrating all customer data. In the case of a jewelry company, they found that though 70% of the product line featured women's jewelry, 50% of the buyers were men buying jewelry as gifts. This group was virtually untapped until a demographic append was done to uncover this target. Even women purchasing jewelry were often shopping for presents, such as heirlooms for daughters and sons for special occasions like graduations from high school and college. Lastly, after collecting all customer data, this company found that there was very little overlap between metal types. Gold buyers continued to buy gold and silver buyers continued to buy silver. Of course all of these insights changed their marketing strategy entirely.

Working with IT on Data Integration

We highly recommend that you work with your information technology (IT) department when collecting and integrating data into a single, real-time view of the customer, so we want to conclude this chapter with some advice for successfully partnering with your IT team:

Don't go it alone. A study by the CMO Club found that 88% of marketing executives admit that projects run outside of IT control "sometimes" (53%) or "often" (35%) run into problems. According to a 2014 Accenture report, only one in 10 marketing and IT executives say collaboration between the two departments is at the right level. CIOs are in a key position to guide technology initiatives across the organization,

General demographic

- Name
- Email
- Gender
- LinkedIn search
- Address
- Location (latitude and longitude)
- Google Map view of Address

Contact strategy

- Preferred channel
- Preferred store
- Closest store
- Preferred brand
- Marketable by Phone? (Y/N)
- Marketing by Mail? (Y/N)
- Marketable by Email? (Y/N)

Purchase analytics

- Lifetime revenue (for example, $2,007)
- Lifetime margin (for example, $576)
- Lifetime order count
- Last 12 months revenue
- Last 12 months margin
- Last 12 months order count
- Average Order Value
- Last 12 Months Revenue Segment (for example "top percent of customers")
- Prior 12 Months Revenue Segment
- Revenue Trend (Up, Neutral, or Down)

Predictive analytics

- Likelihood to buy ("high")
- Behavior-based cluster ("discount junkie")
- Product-based cluster ("laptop buyer")
- Brand-based cluster ("Dell")
- Life cycle cluster ("new customer")
- Product recommendations

Life cycle cluster values could include

- Prospective customer
- New customer
- Repeat customer
- Lapsed one-time customer
- Lapsed repeat customer
- Inactive one-time customer
- Inactive repeat customer

Behavior

- Last order date
- Last order channel
- Last order revenue
- Last web visit date
- Web visit count
- Last send date
- Last open date
- Last click date
- Email open count last month
- Email open count two months prior
- Email click count last month
- Email click count two months prior
- First order date
- First order channel
- First order revenue
- Distinct channels
- Distinct products
- Distinct categories
- Last five orders (channel/date/product/brand)
- Last five on site search (search term, date)

Figure 3.5 Example of a Customer Profile

ensuring reliability, data privacy, security, and compatibility with the corporate technology stack amongst others. As a marketer you can play the role of "chief experience officer" but accept IT as a strategic partner with marketing, not just as a platform provider.

Be clear in what data you will need. Show the IT team what you will use and what impact it could have. Be prepared to parse out what you need versus what you want just for the heck of it. You'd be amazed at how much the IT folks can achieve once they are "in the know" and you acknowledge how valuable their contribution is!

Ask for self-service access to the data. Too often IT builds a customer data warehouse that can only be accessed through SQL queries. This is bad for IT because now each time you have a question about customers, or need a segment, IT will have to do work. This is also bad for marketing, because with each request you submit you need to "wait in line" behind other projects.

Make sure IT knows your existing technology stack. If you ask IT for help with data integration, make sure you outline what you ultimately want to do with the data. If you ask for data integration only, you may get a customer data warehouse that is hard to access (see #3) but also that doesn't talk to your existing campaign execution tools.

Discuss ongoing requirements. Make sure that IT doesn't only focus on the initial development and deployment, but understands your needs for ongoing updates. Customer data changes so quickly that, at a minimum, you will need daily updated customer profiles and segments. Data integration and cleansing really is an ongoing process, and scheduling IT resources on a one-time basis is not sufficient. Too often, IT will deliver a solution with too many manual steps, making it cost prohibitive to update profiles and segments more than once a quarter. Instead marketing needs near real-time, and therefore automated, updates.

Start small and iterate quickly. Together you can come up with a roadmap that makes sense. Perhaps don't ask for all data to be integrated at once. Start by capturing all digital data from email and your website for example, and get your feet wet with campaigns that use just these data sources. After you have proven success, it will be easier to justify the incremental investment to add other data sources such as your store transaction systems.

Be empathetic to the IT team. Acknowledge the challenges of the IT team. If the IT team is struggling to put the data together, suggest a simpler ask. Have an idea of what your true deadlines are. Don't be afraid to get a drink together. Reach out and ask for their ideas on what they think you are missing, how you could simplify your marketing report or data! Trust helps.

Get outside help. Introduce IT to some of your marketing vendors. They may have expertise in ongoing data integration, cleansing and analysis. Data integration is a specialized skill and it may not be something that your IT group does every day. Also, your IT organization may not be familiar with these vendors so you could champion a solution.

Involve IT early. Early in the project, schedule a data discovery call where you involve the IT organization to define the use cases/business requirements for the data integration.

Assign dedicated resources. Treat data integration as a separate project deserving of its own project manager. The project manager can be in IT or marketing. In either case, make sure there is one specific, named person in IT to work with on scoping your project, selecting a vendor, and seeing the project to completion.

One Hundred Questions to Ask Your Data

Once you have all your data in one place, you can start to understand your business and your customers better using this data. The list that follows is a place for you to start. The questions to ask are endless, but we thought it would be useful to get an idea of some of the things you can learn from centralized customer data.

Sales

1. How many new customers am I acquiring each month?
2. What is our true cost to acquire new customers?
3. What is my revenue per customer? How is it trending?
4. How seasonal are my revenue and margin?
5. Is most of my revenue coming from new or repeat buyers?
6. Is most of my margin coming from new or repeat buyers?

7. What is my annual total number of orders of products I shipped?
8. What is my order value by month: do some months see larger deals?
9. What is my annual average order value and how is it trending over time?
10. How does my revenue break down by access device (mobile, tablet, etc.)?
11. How does my revenue break down by geography?
12. How does my revenue break down by store or by sales representative?
13. How much of my revenue come from non-marketable customers?

Customers

Product clusters

14. How many customers are in each product-based cluster?
15. How much is each product-based cluster member worth?
16. Which product-based cluster produces the most revenue?
17. Which brand-based cluster produces the most margin?
18. What channel does each product-based cluster prefer?

Brand clusters

19. How many customers are in each brand-based cluster?
20. How much is each brand-based cluster member worth?
21. Which brand-based cluster produces the most revenue?
22. Which brand-based cluster produces the most margin?
23. What channel does each brand-based cluster prefer?

Behavioral clusters

24. How many customers are in each behavioral cluster?
25. How much is each behavioral cluster member worth?
26. Which behavioral cluster produces the most revenue?
27. Which behavioral cluster produces the most margin?
28. What channel does each behavioral cluster prefer?
29. What percentage of my customers are discount buyers?
30. What percentage of my customers are frequent buyers?
31. What percentage of my customers are full-price (high-margin) buyers?
32. What percentage of my customers are one-time buyers?

33. Who are my high-return complainers?
34. Who are my seasonal customers?
35. Who are my single channel customers?

Lifetime value

36. Who are my most valuable customers?
37. What is the (predicted) lifetime value of my top 10% of customers?
38. What % of revenues comes from my top 10% (or bottom 10%) of customers?
39. What is the order frequency of my top 10% (or bottom 10%) of customers?
40. What brands do the highest spenders prefer?
41. What product categories do the highest spenders prefer?
42. What channels do the highest spenders prefer?
43. How to define a VIP?
44. How many high-value customers do I have that are at risk of leaving?
45. What is my share of wallet for each customer (by customer segment)?
46. What is my upside in each and every customer?
47. Which accounts have a high potential lifetime value, but a low penetration?
48. What is the predicted lifetime value by gender?
49. Is the predicted lifetime value of bargain hunters lower?
50. Is the lifetime value of mobile shoppers higher or lower?
51. What brand preferences do my most valuable customers have?
52. Is the lifetime value of loyalty program participants higher than average?

Likelihood to buy

53. What is the revenue (and margin) impact of offering free shipping?
54. Did discounts drive incremental sales?
55. Did discounts drive incremental margin—considering the costs of the promotion?
56. What are the best incentives to give to each of our customers?
57. Which are my high potential leads of people coming in?
58. Should I charge a membership fee?
59. Which existing customers are most likely to buy again?

Life cycle stage

60. How many active customers do I have (who bought in the past 12 months)?
61. How many of my customers have lapsed?
62. Is most of my revenue and margin coming from new or repeat customers?
63. How quickly will a buyer typically make their second purchase?
64. How many customers can I re-engage with a replenishment campaign?
65. How many customers can I re-engage with a new customer welcome campaign?
66. How many buyers with known emails have been to my website recently but did not purchase?
67. How many customers have recently opened an email but did not buy in a long time?
68. Should I focus on retention?
69. Are my new customers returning (and is this getting better or worse)?
70. How many multi-time buyers do I have and when did they last purchase?
71. Which customers are at risk of churn?

Demographics

72. How many individual households buy from me?
73. What is the average order value by gender?
74. What is the distance to my closest store for each customer (segment)?

Recommendations

75. What product to recommend to each customer next?
76. What is the primary channel for each of my customers?

Marketing/Channels

77. How many shopping carts are being abandoned each month?
78. How many web searches are being abandoned each month?
79. What is the revenue per email and how is this changing over time?
80. How many engaged subscribers actually read my emails?

81. Is my number of engaged subscribers growing or declining?
82. What is the performance of my direct marketing campaigns?
83. What programs are giving me the best return?
84. Which promotions drive the most sales?
85. Does my catalogue add profits?
86. Which customers have not received any emails from me in the past year?
87. What percentages of my sales come from which channel?
88. What percentage of margin comes from which channel?
89. How are my sales trending by channel (annual revenue by channel)?
90. How are my sales trending by channel (monthly revenue by channel)?
91. How is my margin trending by channel?
92. Which channel gets us the most profitable customers?
93. Which channel gets us the most loyal customers?

Products

94. What is my revenue and margin by product category?
95. How many people can I target with my product introduction campaign?
96. What product categories are performing the best?
97. What is the purchase frequency of certain product categories?
98. Are people in a specific zip code area buying specific products?
99. Which customers will be interested in this new product/content/event, etc.?
100. How many different products types does each customer buy from us?

$$\frac{(\text{\# of opptys})(\text{CR})(\text{Avg Deal})(\text{Frequency})}{(\text{Sales Cycle})}$$

? SAME

(Maximize Lifetime Value) and/or (maximize profitability)

CHAPTER 4

Managing Your Customers as a Portfolio to Improve Your Valuation

The best way for any business to maximize enterprise or shareholder value is to maximize the customer lifetime value, or profitability, for *each and every* customer. Customers are the most important assets for a firm and therefore customer lifetime value is the most important metric in marketing. If you maximize the lifetime value, or profitability, of each and every customer, you also maximize the profitability and valuation of your company as a whole.

The best way to optimize lifetime value for *any* customer is to give that customer the best possible experience throughout the life cycle of their interaction with your brand: from their first exposure to your brand to becoming paying customers, coming back a second time, and eventually turning into loyal brand advocates for your business. Predictive marketing explains *how* you can optimize the lifetime value for every prospect and customer. Now that marketers have more detailed information on past, current, and future needs of customers at their fingertips, delighting each customer one at a time is finally possible.

The best way to optimize lifetime value for *all* customers is to adopt a portfolio approach. Marketers need to recognize that different groups of customers have different value and different behaviors and take different actions based on these distinct customer segments. We cover types of clustering in another chapter, but changing the mentality from single value focus to managing a portfolio of values is important. You need a different strategy for those customers who are at risk of leaving you than for those who already have a high likelihood to buy. You will need to adjust your thinking and budget for customers that are unprofitable compared with more profitable customers.

We sometimes hear marketers get the advice to "fire" unprofitable customers, or just focus on high-value customers, but this is a mistake. Every customer contributes to revenue, and when you acquire customers and manage a portfolio, there is always a mix. The important focus is the mix and how this mix is trending.

What Is Customer Lifetime Value?

In general, customer lifetime value is a term that describes how much revenue or profit you can expect from customers over their lifetime doing business with you. There are a couple of different ways to calculate and use lifetime value, depending on the marketing problem at hand.

Historical Lifetime Value

Historical lifetime value or LTV for short is defined as the *actual* profits—gross margin minus direct costs—from customers over their lifetime so far, adjusted by subtracting the acquisition cost of those customers. Note that historical lifetime value only takes into account past purchases, not future purchases. The only time to use historical lifetime, rather than predicted customer value, is when you are trying to detect if the customer value of a specific customer or customer segment is trending up or down. A customer might have spent \$500 two years ago, but only \$200 in the last year. It is this change in lifetime value that signals underlying trends, risks, and opportunities. If a customer's historical lifetime value is trending down, this is called *value migration,* and this can be an early warning signal of customers unsubscribing from your service or planning to stop buying from your website. Detecting value migration allows you to catch customers before they walk out the door and it is too late to win them back. Identifying a change in historical lifetime value allows you to implement a reactivation or proactive churn campaign to turn the tide.

Beyond value migration, customers may be changing their spending habits in other important ways. A certain customer may have made only one big purchase last year, but this year they are making smaller purchases more often. While the customer lifetime value of this person has not changed, your marketing approach and goals for the person should change.

In order to accurately calculate historical lifetime value, you need to be able to link all purchases made by the same person—even if that person used slightly different emails, names, or addresses. The average American has three email addresses. If you are like most companies, you may have separate order databases for different channels. The orders from the web are often recorded separately from the brick-and-mortar store purchases and those are separate from sales made through the call center. Unless you can link purchases from these separate channels to the same physical person, you will not have an accurate picture of lifetime value. For some products, it might be important to also understand the total value of a household or an account. Perhaps I spend only very little with a brand myself, but by acquiring me, the brand has also acquired the revenues from my spouse and children. When comparing the costs to acquire me to the revenues of my entire household, I could be a very profitable investment. The only way to do this is to make sure you can associate family members of a household to each other. Similarly, in business marketing you need to be able to associate different buyers in the same company with the master account to understand the true value of a customer.

We recommend that you take the cost to service a customer into account whenever you can in order to calculate historical lifetime value. This includes returns and discounts, as well as product cost. On average, 9 percent of all retail sales in the United States are returned by consumers, so ignoring returns would skew the results. Some practitioners calculate LTV without the acquisition cost. If LTV is being utilized to make acquisition decisions, acquisition cost should be taken into account. However, if it is for existing customers, acquisition cost is a sunk cost and should not be used.

Predicted Customer Value

Predicted customer value is the projected value, revenues, and costs, adjusted for the time-value of money, of a customer looking forward several years. Your average retention rate will tell you how many years in the future, on average, you will retain a customer and how many years of future revenues to take into account. We typically look one to three years ahead when calculating predicted customer value.

Predicted customer value is very useful, especially when deciding how much money to invest in acquiring or retaining a specific customer. If you were to only look at historical lifetime value, you would significantly underestimate the potential of a customer and likely underinvest in the acquisition or retention of certain customers. It can also be used to identify high-value customers very early in the life cycle. After her first purchase, a future high-value customer looks just like everybody else. If you could recognize the high-potential customer early in the life cycle, you could start differentiated treatment right then and there and increase the odds this high-value customer will stick with you.

One person might have just bought this expensive jacket but he might have only been a customer for two months, but another customer might have been a customer for five years and bought the same jacket. If you were to look at historical lifetime value, you might draw the conclusion that one customer is more valuable than the other. However, these two might very well become equal value customers and should probably be treated in much the same way. If you look at historical lifetime value you look too much at old customers and will miss the opportunity to acquire or retain more recent, high-potential, customers.

With predictive analytics, you can estimate the future value of a customer by comparing a customer to the thousands or millions of others that have come before them. You can predict future lifetime value by finding customers that look just like them. From the example we used earlier, buying a certain type of jacket may very well be an early indicator of a well-known pattern of behavior for a high-value customer. Even if predicted customer value is not accurate in absolute dollar terms, the rank order it provides gives the marketer focus on the right segment and trends.

Here are some examples of factors that can signal future lifetime value. Predictive marketing software typically looks at hundreds of factors like these but will only use those that actually correlate with future lifetime value in your particular company or situation:

- Recency of engagement: The recency of purchases, web visits, reviews, and email clicks may all be important predictors of future purchases and thus future customer value.
- Size of the first order: Customers who make a large first order are more likely to end up being valuable shoppers.
- Discount on the first order: Customers who buy full price are more likely to become valuable over their lifetime.
- Multiple types of products in the first order: Buying from different categories, such as shoes and electronics, in your first order is a signal of future customer value.
- Time between orders: Most valuable shoppers make frequent purchases and thus a shopper who places a second order quickly is more likely to become a high-value customer.
- Time spent on website: The more time prospects or customers spend on your website, the higher their likelihood to buy and the higher their predicted customer value.
- Social and email engagement: Customer engagement of any kind, including email opens and clicks or social engagement, are great predictors for likelihood to buy and predicted customer value. Often it is not the amount of engagement that matters, but the consistency or frequency of engagement. Spending a little time every day is a more reliable indicator than spending hours sporadically.
- Acquisition source: It turns out that certain channels drive higher value customers than others. The customer who came from a fashion blog may have a higher predictive value than the customer acquired through a banner ad.
- Geography: Customers in certain zip codes have a greater predicted customer value than others. Rural populations tend to be more stable, move less frequently, and therefore have more loyal purchase behavior. Zip codes can sometimes predict what type of products people buy.

For example, zip codes with many apartment buildings have a low predicted customer value for certain products, such as lawn mowers.

- Seasonality: Retail customers who are acquired during the holidays tend to be about 14 percent less valuable than those acquired during other times of the year.
- Personal referrals: People who came to your brand through a personal referral tend to be more loyal than those who buy because of an advertisement.

Predictions about lifetime value are not destiny. Marketers can do much to change the course of history here. Take, for example, the fact that shoppers acquired during the holidays tend to be less valuable and less loyal than shoppers acquired at other times during the year. One skincare company decided to focus its retention efforts on this holiday cohort specifically. It set up an email marketing campaign to increase brand loyalty among new Cyber Monday customers, sending regular reminders for refills and recommending other products of interest. They were able to reverse the trend, and lifetime value of these new holiday customers is now 5 percent higher than the company average. By focusing on specific outreach to underserved customer segments, the company was able to offer personalized promotions that ultimately drove greater brand loyalty. The important lesson is that once customers are acquired, the best strategy is to focus on engaging them to grow and retain them, ignoring the cost of acquisition.

Upside Lifetime Value

Upside lifetime value, which is also called *size of wallet*, calculates how much more money a customer still has to spend with you. This is money that the customer is already spending at your competition to buy the products you offer. Algorithms can figure out size of wallet by comparing a customer to other like-minded customers. It is important for marketers to focus on what size the wallet is, because it is always easier to grow a relationship with an existing customer than to acquire a new one. Unfortunately, most marketers have been taught to focus more on new customer acquisition than on engaging and retaining existing customers. Especially if the customers have high upside potential, marketers should focus on how to deepen their relationship by introducing them to new products or serving them in a differentiated way. Very few companies calculate and utilize the upside or share of wallet potential of a customer, yet it can be a very powerful way to identify customers to focus on.

The critical difference between future lifetime value and share of wallet is often in the types of products that are factored into the analysis. For future lifetime value, you tend to look at just those products that a customer is already buying from you. For example, I may be a hockey player, and I may be buying my hockey tape from a specific outlet every couple of months. Based on this, the company can project that if they retain me, I will buy a lot more hockey tape in the future and perhaps have a predicted lifetime value of $300. However, because I am buying hockey tape, I am likely in the market for skate sharpening, hockey sticks, and occasional gear upgrades. I am clearly buying those things elsewhere right now. If I were to buy all of my gear at the same place I buy my tape, my future lifetime value is probably well over $1,000.

Let's look at another example, this time in business marketing. An electronics company has quite a few customers who only buy inkjet cartridges for printers. They buy these cartridges regularly and spend $20,000 a year on average, leading you to think it's a great customer. But the fact they are buying these high-end cartridges means that they probably also have a big office with servers, laptops, and other products that could use services or add-on products that you are not selling to them. The fact that you are not selling those other products to them is a missed opportunity.

You can use share of wallet analysis to find upsell targets, as one business software company did. It took all of its business customers and broke out those that were similar in size and industry. Out of 100,000 customers, they found 20,000 businesses in the insurance industry with 100 to 150 employees. They then divided these customers into value segments. The top 25 percent of these small insurance companies spent $30,000 a year, the next 25 percent spent $10,000 a year, the third 25 percent spent $5,000 a year, and the bottom 25 percent spent $1,000 a year. All of these businesses are similar, and they all have a similar spending potential. Maybe not all of them will be large customers spending $30,000 a year, but all should at least be able to spend $10,000 a year, or as much as the second group. This means that for all the customers in the $1,000 bucket, you have an upside potential to sell more products and services of $9,000, and for the customers in the $5,000 bucket you have an upside potential of $5,000.

Increase Customer Lifetime Value for One Customer

The customer life cycle is a term used to describe the progression of steps a customer goes through when considering, purchasing, using, and maintaining loyalty to a product or a service. The customer life cycle emphasizes the individual journey of each customer and encourages marketers to think about the right approach to every customer. The life cycle model underscores the importance of customer repeat engagement with a brand. A marketer's job is try to give customers the best possible experience at any point during their life cycle or journey with your brand and—in doing so—increase the loyalty and the value of those customers.

Figure 4.1 gives an overview of some of the strategies a marketer could use in the acquisition, growth and retention phase of a customer's life cycle. Some of these programs have significantly higher return on investment than traditional broadcast marketing techniques. Whereas the average open rate of a broadcast email is about 14% and the average revenue per email sent $0.05, the various campaigns that are triggered by a customer's life cycle can see open rates that are two or three times higher and revenue per email up to $6 per email, a whopping 130 times the average of a broadcast email.

Acquire

It often takes many interactions to acquire a new customer. Once you have acquired this customer, you have engaged in a transaction, but you can't really speak of a customer relationship just yet. In some industries, like retail, 70 percent of customers never come back to buy a second

Acquisition	Growth	Retention
Look-alike targeting	Repeat purchase program	Loyalty appreciation
Remarketing	Cluster-based targeting	Customer reactivation

Figure 4.1 Sample Life Cycle Marketing Strategies

time. Your primary goal when it comes to acquiring new customers it to acquire the right customers. Some people simply have a higher likelihood to become large, loyal customers. When it comes to acquisition you can focus on acquiring these more loyal customers using look-alike targeting. You can also increase conversion of prospects to buyers using remarketing techniques. Both will be discussed in greater detail in Chapter 11.

Grow

Your primary goal for newly acquired customers is to turn them from one-time buyers into repeat customers. Once a customer comes back and buys a second time, you have now started a relationship. It changes the dynamics completely. Whereas retention rates for one-time buyers in retail are around 30 percent, the retention rate for two-time buyers jumps to 70 percent. A repeat purchase program and cluster-based targeting are just two examples of strategies that you might use to grow customer value. Chapter 12 is entirely dedicated to customer growth strategies.

Retain

Even when you have maximized your share of wallet with a customer, your job is not yet done. Your primary strategy for loyal customers is to recognize and appreciate them. With social media and the Internet, the power of word of mouth is stronger than ever. A loyal brand advocate can bring yet more customer revenue by referring you to their friends or family, or by raving about you publicly and influencing strangers to also buy from you. Not all churn is created equal. It is especially important to retain your high value customers. Loyalty appreciation and lapsed customer reactivation are just two of many strategies you can use to proactively retain your customers. Chapter 13 will introduce various retention metrics and methodologies.

In France, the telecommunication company Orange developed a comprehensive strategy to preserve its customer base, when a new entrant disrupted the market by introducing plans 50 percentage cheaper than the existing ones. The marketing strategy included actions at every stage of the customer life cycle:

From an acquisition standpoint, the operator created new, more attractive plans to adapt to its new competitor. On the one hand, the company built a new low price brand to target the digital and price sensitive segment (specific target of the new entrant). On the other hand, fierce competition of the other existing operators pushed the company to reduce its standard plans by 20 percentage. The average revenue per user (ARPU), revenue and margin were at risk, since the existing customer had the opportunity to massively migrate to cheaper plans.

To limit value destruction, the firm developed a massive "Personalized Customer Program," in which it contacted proactively customers every 6 months with the promise to adapt their plan to their actual voice, text, and data consumption. Treatment was adapted to customer lifetime value: VIP customers were contacted by call centers whereas medium value customers received an email and low-value customers a text message. Algorithms were used to develop personalized recommendations depending on the customer consumption, ARPU, and other factors. For instance, if a customer was paying more than the actual price of the plan due to international communications, the company recommended a more comprehensive (and expensive) plan including international communications. Cross-selling campaigns were also launched to equip mobile clients with Internet subscriptions in an attractive "quadruple play" bundle. This program resulted in a decrease in the ARPU of only 10 percent in a year.

Proactive retention was the most challenging program, since the company had a large customer base, hence a high risk of revenue attrition. The first step was to categorize the root causes for churn by customer segment and to deploy retention actions for each one of them. Models were developed to estimate the likelihood to churn by segment. The company analyzed the best time to reactivate a client: a customer was considered at risk between the three months prior to the end date of her subscription and the three following months. For price sensitive clients, top churn root causes were related to the price of the plan, in which case they were offered to migrate to the low-price offers. Digital high-value clients were leaving to buy the most recent smartphone at a significantly lower price when they churned to the competition (operators commonly offer large discounts on mobile phones to new customers, in order to increase their customer base). The company solved this issue by adjusting the smartphones' prices for premium clients, while decreasing the subsidy rates for lower value clients. Besides, it included a new feature in its premium offers: one new smartphone for free every year. While it lost more than 700,000 customers in the first two quarters of the year, the operator preserved its customer base and reached more than 800,000 net adds (acquisitions minus churns) in the two following quarters. (*Source*: www.orange.com/en/content/download/10703/237238/version/5/file/FY+2012+EN+VDEF.pdf; http://satisfait.orange.fr/maitrise_budget_bilan_conseil_personnalise.php.)

Increase Customer Lifetime Value for All Customers

Now let's put all we have learned about customer lifetime value together in one framework. As a company you don't just have one customer. To optimize enterprise value you need to optimize total customer equity—or the sum total of the lifetime value of all customers.

An easy way to think about optimizing customer equity is to think of your customer pool as a physical pool full of water. Think of increasing customer lifetime value across the customer portfolio as increasing the water level in a pool. The pool is filled with the money spent by the active customers of your brand. Active customers are those customers who have spent money with you in the past 12 months. Higher value customers spend more money and fill the pool up faster than lower value customers. Water is draining as customers leave you and stop spending money with you. Some customers are coming back after a hiatus. How do you increase the water level in your customer pool? You can: add more (valuable) customers, prevent churn (and value migration), or reactivate inactive customers. Figure 4.2 summarizes this methodology of optimizing customer equity across your portfolio using this pool cycle analogy.

Add More (Valuable) Customers

You need to add at least as many customers as you lose in a year, preferably more. Therefore, how many customers you need to acquire in a given year to at least stay stable depends on your churn rate and on your rate of value migration. If you lose more customers, or if you lose more of your valuable customers, you will need to acquire more revenues to

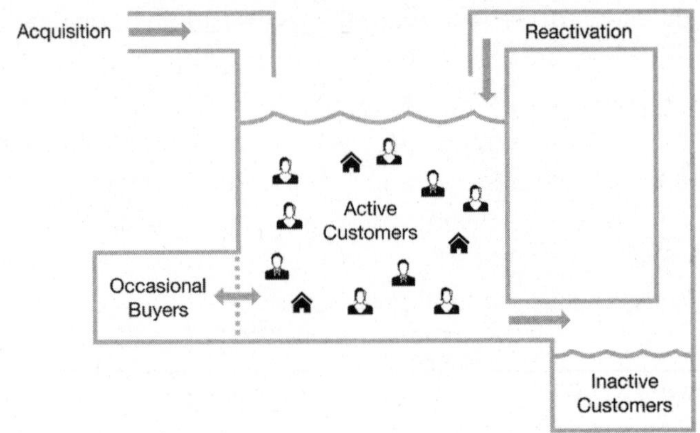

Figure 4.2 The Pool Cycle Management Framework

compensate for this. The opposite is also true. If you can find a way to acquire more valuable customers, you don't need to acquire as many of them. We talk about marketing spending optimization in Chapter 5 and give examples of specific marketing strategies to acquire more valuable customers in Chapter 11.

Prevent Churn

When a customer leaves you it may be too late to get him or her back. Your chances of gaining a customer for life are much greater if you proactively reach out to a customer than if you wait for that customer to leave you and try to get them back later. We elaborate on strategies to grow customer value in Chapter 12.

Engage Inactive Customers

When a customer leaves you, not all is lost. On average it is 10 times cheaper to reactivate a lapsed customer than it is to acquire a new one. Reactivation programs for lapsed customers therefore are a low-hanging fruit for marketers looking for new revenue streams. It is even better to engage a customer to prevent a customer from lapsing in the first place. We focus on programs to retain and reactivate customers in Chapter 13.

PART 2

Nine Easy Plays to Get Started with Predictive Marketing

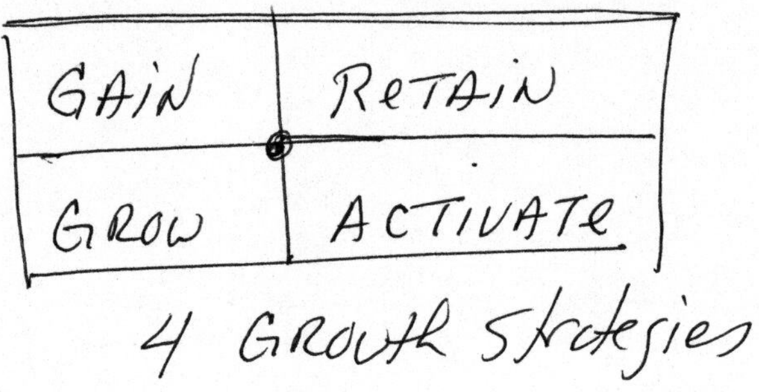

CHAPTER 5

Play One: Optimize Your Marketing Spending Using Customer Data

Optimizing marketing spend is a vast subject to cover on its own. However, most of the approaches lack customer behavior and predictions as their focal point, which leads to media response optimization, and not true marketing optimization.

When asked to allocate marketing budgets, most marketers immediately think about allocating budget to the most important sources of revenues, the best performing channels and the best performing keywords from a response perspective, ignoring the customer who responds to marketing. However, we want to introduce a different framework to think about marketing spending: the predictive marketing way to allocate spending is based on allocating dollars to the right people, rather than to the right products or channels.

As we have said in Chapter 4, your most important job as a marketer is to optimize the lifetime value of every customer, and the customer equity of your customer base as a whole. Therefore, you need to allocate your budget by taking customer into account. In this chapter we look at the following framework when it comes to allocating marketing budget:

- Create separate plans to invest in acquisition, retention, and reactivation.
- Differentiate your spending on high-, medium-, and low-value customers.
- Find the products that bring in the highest lifetime value customers.
- Find the channels that bring in the highest lifetime value customers.

Invest in Acquisition, Retention, and Reactivation

To an extent, it is cheaper to reactivate lapsed customers than to acquire new customers. It is even cheaper to retain customers than to reactivate customers. On average, according to AgilOne data, existing customers spend 83 percentage more and visit 60 percentage more often. It is therefore critical to be deliberate about retaining customers, such as converting one-time buyers as quickly as possible to repeat buyers.

When thinking about allocating your marketing spending, think about how to allocate budget to your acquisition, retention, and reactivation efforts separately. If you can, you may even want to allocate different marketing personnel to each of these efforts. Some companies are starting to organize around groups of customers and the objective to be achieved with each group: acquiring new customers, engaging existing customers, and reactivating lapsed customers.

In our experience, most companies are too focused on acquiring new customers when they could achieve growth more cost effectively by focusing more on retention and reactivation. Retaining existing customers requires more work but ultimately is more efficient from a cost perspective. Predictive marketing is a key enabler, as we outlined in this book to engage existing customers.

Let's look at the growth numbers of a fictitious company (see Figure 5.1). This company is consistent in acquiring new customers: it brings in about 175,000 new customers every year. However, every year it is getting better at bringing back existing or past customers. It brought in business from 266,000 existing customers in 2014, a 44 percent increase from the 185,000 existing customers it booked in 2011. The growth of this company is almost entirely fueled by existing customers. This is usually a very good thing, especially because in our experience reactivating existing customers is about 10 times cheaper than

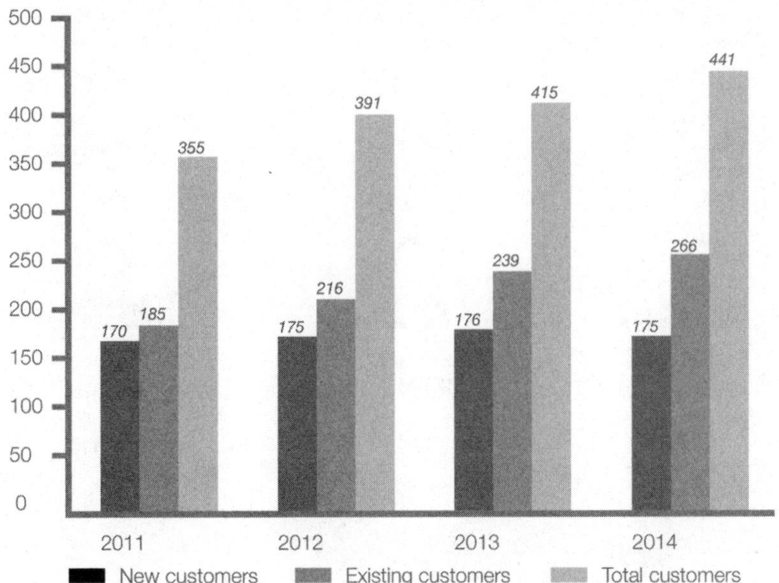

Figure 5.1 Growth from New and Existing Customers

acquiring new ones. So not only is this company growing its top line revenue, it is also becoming more profitable.

For the next year, the company can now project growth of its existing customers (see Figure 5.2). If growth of existing customers continues, then it may have 305,000 customers buying in 2015. That means it only needs to acquire 136,000 new customers to achieve the same revenues next year as it did this year. The numbers used in this example are typical for the retail industry, and if you are in that industry you can use these to do your own planning:

- About 40 percent of new customers will come back the next year as repeat customers.
- About 70 percent of repeat customers will come back the next year as repeat customers.
- Ten percent of past, lapsed customers can be reactivated to return as customers in the next year.

For most companies, acquisition requires 7 to 10 marketing touches and each touch is three to five times more expensive (due to lower

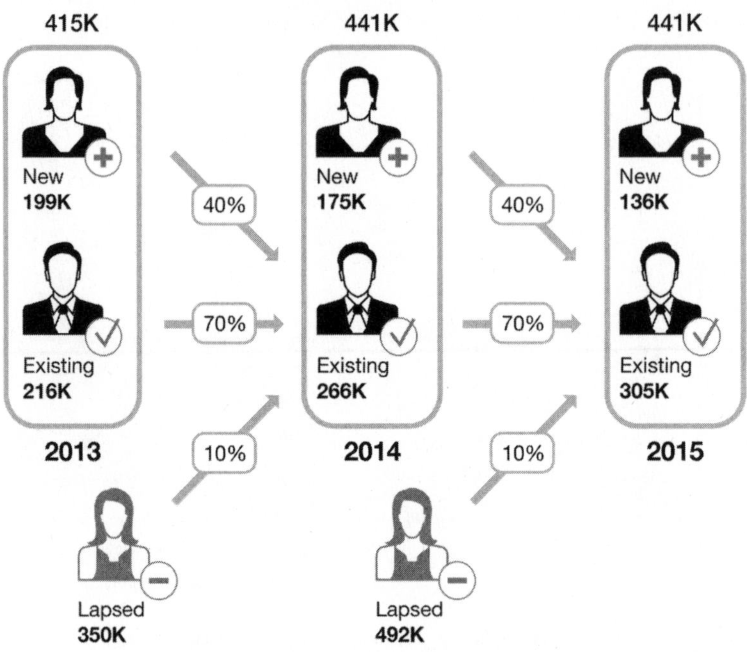

Figure 5.2 How Many New Customers Do You Need?

response rates) than for existing customers. Existing customers require only three to five touches. The resulting economics are 10–20 times higher costs for customer acquisition than for customer retention.

Perhaps the most important point here is that every percentage improvement in retention has a positive compound effect on growth, while acquisition starts from zero year after year and is very costly. Continue to focus on improving retention by measuring and improving retention over time, improving as compared to your peers, and by breaking down retention into its components and improving and benchmarking the piece parts. For example, retention by geography or by product categories might be very different and offer opportunities for improvement.

If we go back to the company in our example and benchmark them against their peers, it may no longer surprise you that they are outperforming their peers when it comes to existing customer growth rate (see Figure 5.3). They are, however, lagging slightly when it comes to new customer growth. Benchmarking against your peers is a powerful way to identify areas of opportunity for your company.

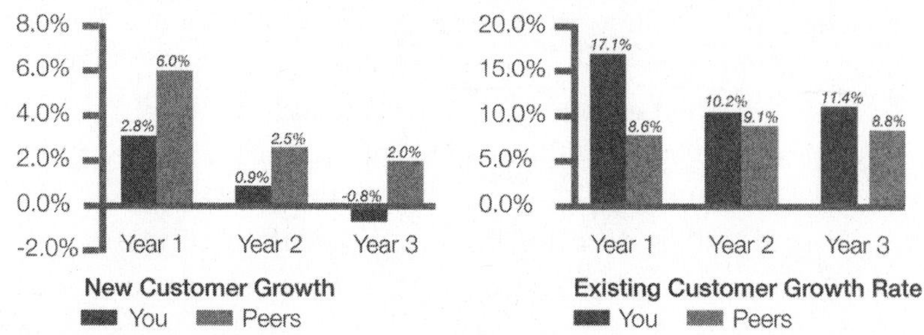

Figure 5.3 Benchmarking Your Growth

When you engage in benchmarking, compare each of the customer life cycle stages separately. For business marketing, this may be measuring the conversion in each of the stages of the customer funnel. You might find that you are doing better than average when it comes to converting prospects and suspects to leads for your company, but that you lag when it comes to converting leads to trial or first purchase (see Figure 5.4).

When you decide how much to invest in each of your life cycle segments, take into consideration that conversion rates for each group are very different. When advertising to existing customers, you may find that your conversion rate is 60 percent, whereas perhaps the conversion rate of advertising to brand-new customers is only 6 percent. This means

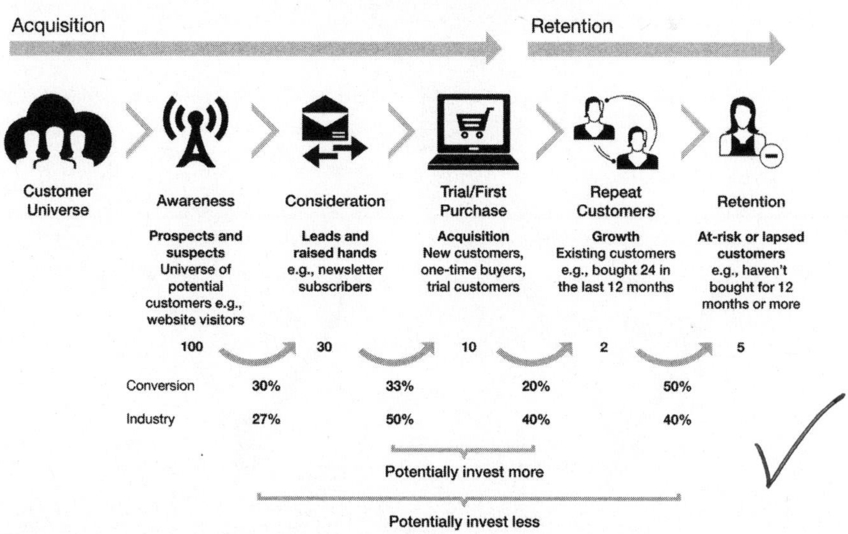

Figure 5.4 Engineering the Marketing Funnel

that you should be willing to spend more for a click from an existing customer than for a click from a new customer.

We give a detailed example in figures 5.5 and 5.6. In this example, let's assume you are getting 100 visitors to your website using pay-to-click advertising. For every 100 visitors, you are getting 20 new orders. However, of these 20 orders, 15 come from existing customers reactivated by your campaign and only five orders come from brand-new customers.

This scenario lines up with what we see across businesses. Most of your traffic tends to come from new customers, whereas most of your orders come from repeat customers. It may look at first like you are getting a 20 percent conversion rate from your campaign, whereas in reality you are seeing a blended conversion rate from new and existing customers, each with very different economics.

If you had to spend $0.20 for each click, you would pay $20 for the 100 visitors to your site or $1 per order. On the surface this campaign is making you money because you are making $2 in margin per order, so $1 of profit for each order. Because of the difference between new and repeat customers, however, the truth is much different.

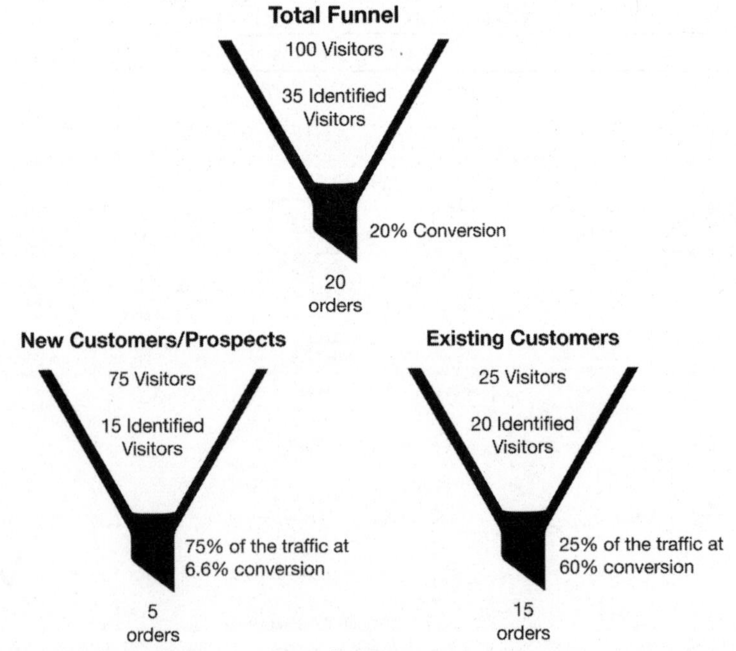

Figure 5.5 Marketing Funnel by Life Cycle

	Clicks	Cost per Click ($)	Marketing Spend ($)	Orders	Cost per Order ($)	Average Margin per Order ($)	VC Margin ($)
Overall	100	$0.2	$20.00	20	$1.00	$2	$1.00
New/ Prospects	75	$0.2	$15.00	5	$3.00	$2	($1.00) ←Acquisition Cost
Existing	25	$0.20	$5.00	15	$0.33	$2	$1.67 ←Net Profit

Figure 5.6 Marketing Spending Optimization Example

In reality, of the 20 orders received, 15 were from existing customers, which were reactivated with your marketing campaign, and only five from brand-new customers. Looking at it this way, it turns out that the new customer acquisition campaign is actually losing you money in the short run. Each new customer costs you $3 to acquire and brings in only $2 per order. This means you are losing $1 on the first transaction of each new customer. Losing money on acquiring new customers is not necessarily a bad thing as long as you know what you are doing. Most marketers are fine losing money on customer acquisition, provided that the customer has a lifetime value that will make the relationship positive in the long run. We look at that next.

Each existing customer is costing you only $0.33 to reactivate and is making you $1.67 in net profit. That seems pretty good, but perhaps you could have reactivated this customer with a well-timed email campaign and avoid the reactivation cost altogether.

The solution is to do optimization separately for your acquisition and retention budget. You can optimize your acquisition budget based on the time it takes to break even or the customer value achieved in the first 90 days. Optimize your retention budget based on net profit per order, cutting down on negative net profit activities. For each of these you can use either actuals from the past or predicted measures for the breakeven time period.

Optimizing Your Acquisition Budget

We recommend that you optimize your acquisition budget based on payback time or customer value (predicted or actual). Figure 5.7 illustrates the concepts of payback time and customer value. The payback time is the period it takes for you to recoup your acquisition spending. Let's say it

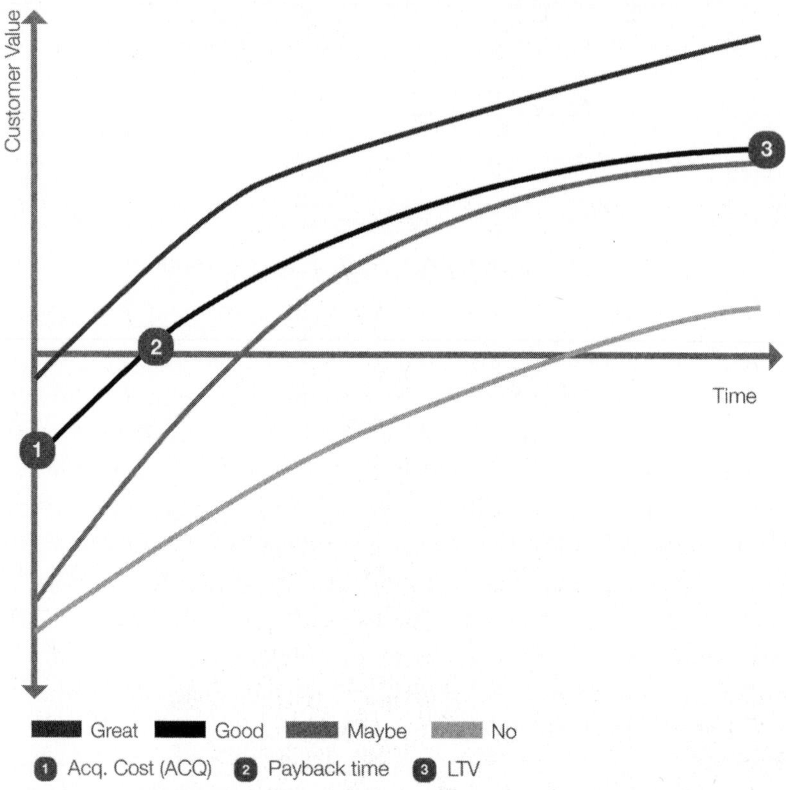

Figure 5.7 The Customer Value Path

costs you $5 to acquire a customer and it takes you one month to receive enough profit, or customer value, from that customer to recoup that investment. The payback time for the customer acquired from this particular activity is thus one month. You could rank all your acquisition activities based on payback time and pick the best ones.

The other way to optimize acquisition activities is to choose a time period, for example 90 days, and to see which acquisition activities lead to the greatest customer value at the end of the evaluation period. We picked a relatively short time period here, 90 days, because the acquisition landscape is very dynamic. Keywords that work one week may not work the other week, so looking too far into the future may not lead to accurate results. In other words, the acquisition activity that leads to great results this year may no longer exist one year later.

We recommend that for each of your acquisition efforts, you try to fill in the payback time and the return on investment (ROI) from customer value at the end of your evaluation period. You can use the template in Figure 5.8 to do this. Then simply pick the best performing activities for next year. Certain considerations go into play, such as the quantity of customers acquired, the variability over time, and the ability to invest more.

Some acquisition sources, such as banner ads on a high-fashion blog, may have extremely short payback periods and yield a profit on the first order, but are contributing very few new customers. The marketers goal is not only to be optimal in the profit sense, but in quantity as well. Acquisition sources that might be highly efficient might yield only a few customers, and hence are not impactful. In one case, a blogger was delivering very valuable customers to a brand, but could only deliver very few customers with no ability to scale with a larger investment.

Second, some sources deliver consistent performance over time, whereas others have more variability. Consistent sources are always preferred over highly variable ones. Lastly, you should look at your ability to invest more. Certain marketing investments such as search engine marketing (SEM) can be increased if performing well, whereas others might be supply constrained. Therefore, even though a source is performing, there might not be a chance to invest more in these sources.

Optimize Your Retention Budget

We recommend that you optimize your retention budget based on contribution margin and customer value. After optimizing for acquisition, marketers need to build profitable relationships with those customers over time. After a customer has placed her first order, the acquisition cost is already a "sunk cost." Therefore, the approach should no longer

Source of Acquisition	Acquisition Cost ($)	Payback Time (Days)	90-Day ROI (LTV-ACQ/ACQ)
SEM_Yahoo	12	43	15%
Banner_FB	19	123	−20%
Retargeting_SH	25	80	2%

Figure 5.8 Acquisition Sources Worksheet

take the acquisition cost into account, since those customers are already paid for and optimized for that cost. This requires careful understanding of the variable contribution margin. The variable contribution margin is defined as the gross margin minus the marketing cost to generate that order. You should perform this calculation for each source of marketing bringing orders from customers placing their second or subsequent orders. The contribution margin is going to be different for low-value, medium-value, and high-value customers. We look at allocating budget to each of these groups of customers next.

Differentiate Spending Based on Customer Value

Losing a high-value customer is much more costly than losing a low-value customer. Therefore, when allocating your retention budget think about different value-based segments and how likely they are to buy from you again. For this you will need to be able to calculate the likelihood to buy for each segment. The customers with a lower likelihood to buy are at greater risk of leaving you—and never make another purchase again.

You should allocate budget based on customer value and risk. We will walk through the example of Figure 5.9. Let's say you have 600,000 new customers with an average annual value of $100. In addition, your existing customers include 90,000 high-value customers that spend an average $400 a year, 540,000 medium-value customers that spend an average $110 a year, and 270,000 low-value customers that

	Number of Customers		2014 Value		Retention		$ at Risk	Risk
New	600,000	×	$100	×	25%	=	$15M	17%
High	90,000		$400		90%		$32M	37%
Med	540,000		$110		60%		$38M	44%
Low	270,000		$20		20%		$1M	2%
							$87M	100%

Allocation based on value at risk.

Figure 5.9 Spending Based on Value and Risk

spend only $20 a year. Losing one of the $400 customers is more costly than losing a $20 customer.

The historical retention rate for each of these groups may be different as well. Perhaps your high-value, loyal customers have a 90 percent retention rate as compared to a 20 percent retention rate for the low-value, discount shoppers. If your retention rate drops, you have $32 million at risk with your high-value customers, $38 million at risk with your medium-value, and only $1 million at risk with your low-value customers. Another way to look at it is that if you can further increase the retention rate of each group, you have $3.6 million of upside with high-value customers, $24 million of upside with medium-value customers, and $4.3 million of upside with low-value customers. So whereas the retention rate of high-value customers is high at 90 percent, still 37 percentage of all money at risk due to churn comes from this group. On the other hand, while the retention rate of your lowest value customers is only 20 percentage, only 2 percentage of all money at risk comes from this group. It would make sense to spend more money to protect the potential loss of medium- and high-value customers in this case. We share concrete tips and examples for campaigns to grow and retain customers in Chapters 12 and 13.

Find Products That Bring High-Value Customers

Now let's look at your product portfolio through the lens of customers' lifetime value. If you simply rank your products based on the revenue they bring in you may miss important insights. Let's assume you sell five different categories of products: category 1 through 5 as shown on Figure 5.10. Category 1 may bring in 25 percent of your new customer revenues as compared to only 6 percent for category 5–type products. However, if you could only look two years into the future, it would be clear that it is in fact a different product category altogether, category 2 that outperforms all other product types based on customer lifetime value. Some categories of products may have lower customer revenue in year one but over time will result in more repeat purchases and higher customer lifetime revenues. When deciding how much money to invest in each product category, you should take future revenues into account. You can also spend more money to acquire category 2 customers because those have a higher lifetime value over time.

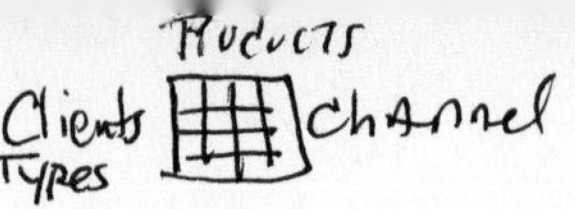

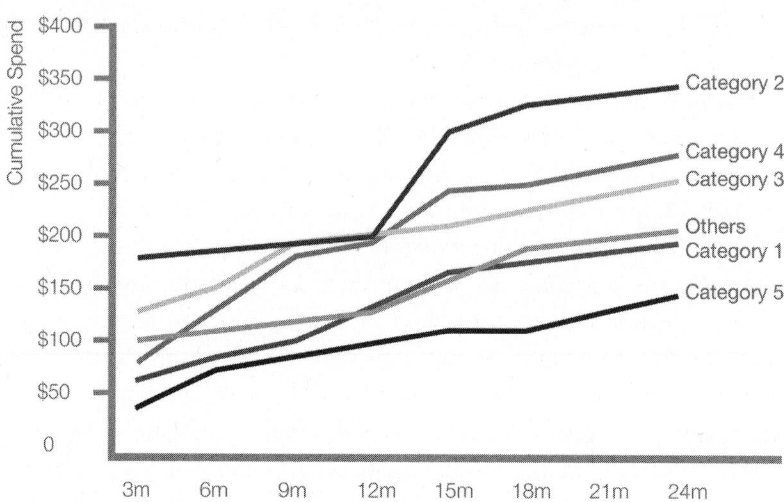

Figure 5.10 Lifetime Value by Acquisition Category

Find Channels That Bring High-Value Customers

Acquisition channels, too, can be ranked based on the types and value of the customers it delivers. Not all channels deliver customers of equal value. In one example, a company uses various outlets to acquire new subscribers. After 60 days, the customers acquired via the Spa channel and those acquired via DailyCandy or AdFusion are about eight times more valuable, on average, than those acquired via US Weekly.

Similarly, when Anne Swift, chief marketing nut at Nuts.com, an online retailer of nuts and dried fruits, had to decide how much money to spend on specific adwords. She was somewhat reluctant to bid much money for certain keywords. However, when she switched from looking at just the first order to looking at predicted lifetime value to determine profitability of a campaign, she found that many of her bidding strategies had been too conservative.

When Adam Shaffer worked for PCM, a billion-dollar electronics distributor, he had to decide which sources to spend on. He initially focused on adwords campaigns. However, he found that some of these campaigns were acquiring the same customers over and over again. Instead of spending one time to acquire a customer, customers were searching and clicking paid links each time they came back for a repeat purchase. These customers were not nearly as profitable as Adam had initially thought. On the other hand, when Adam looked at his direct mail campaigns he was pleasantly surprised. Although these campaigns were very expensive, for certain segments of customers, direct mail was a very profitable way to reach these high lifetime value customers.

In another example, we're working with an online golf retailer to review the performance of their Google Product Listing Ads (PLA). On the surface, it appeared that the Taylor Made and Adams PLAs generated the same number of buyers, with slightly more revenue and higher margin customers coming from the Adams PLA: Taylor Made and Adams each brought 67 buyers, with $11,453.18 coming from Adams

and $10,855.01 coming from Taylor Made buyers. So on the surface the Adams program is the more successful one by a small margin. By looking at the same information by customer order count, we can see that the Taylor Made PLA acquired 20 new customers and drove 39 incremental orders from existing customers. The Adams PLA, however drove 32 new customers and 26 incremental orders from existing customers. While Taylor Made drove fewer new acquisitions, it drove acquisition of highly profitable customers: revenue per new customer was $678.72 and margin $237.44 for each new Taylor Made buyer as compared to $326.48 in revenue and $174.29 per new customer for Adams. In conclusion, the Taylor Made program probably is the more important one to double down on. Existing customers can be targeted through other channels such as email, and while there were fewer new customers coming from the Taylor Made program, the overall new customer revenue and margin from this program outperformed the Adams program by a significant margin.

The Case for Last-Touch Attribution

The biggest problem when finding channels that perform is that multiple marketing efforts, in different channels, all assist in the outcome.

The sheer number of available channels, tools, and keywords have exponentially increased, leading to confusion and frustration from marketers as to what marketing touch is responsible for what customer action. For example, a customer clicked on a banner, three days later searched and came to the website through a Google Adword ad, then one day later, got an email and clicked. In such cases, all these marketing touches contribute to the conversion, but in a fractional manner. Understanding this fractional contribution is the domain of revenue attribution.

In order to do this, marketers needed to attribute gross margin and cost of the specific activity with each marketing touch. It was quite easy when touches were fewer and last-touch attribution worked quite well. With the advance of keyword advertising, retargeting, and various other online campaigns, marketers started to demand more sophisticated marketing attribution, such as multitouch attribution. Nowadays, many orders are touched by three-plus marketing events, which requires the marketer to sort out how much credit to give to each event.

Multitouch attribution can become complex very quickly, using techniques such as linear, time-decay, or time-window–based attribution. Each of these methods can be the right solution. For example, linear attribution—where each marketing activity gets equal credit—could be a good way to give partial credit to customers clicking on advertisements, but if you are sending them emails, direct mail, that is, outbound touches, the more you send the more credit they will get, hence reducing the effectiveness of all together.

There certainly is value in multitouch attribution for considered purchase items, such as cars, home goods, insurance, where the buying cycle is relatively long and the consumer is being educated and nurtured to make the right choice. For short sales cycle, impulse purchases, the problem is less important.

Many marketers obsess over accuracy of such calculations. The right approach is to find the attribution approach that is as simple as possible, yet accurate enough to sort through good and bad marketing investments. Test the following: How does the *order of performance* change between sources when you change attribution methods? If a marketing source is performing poorly, does it all of a sudden perform well when you switch from last-touch to linear attribution? Even if you do see changes in rank order of sources, the next question to ask is the importance of those sources in terms of the budget spent on them and their performance in variable contribution margin. If the order changes, but those specific channels contribute little in the grand scheme of things, then maybe investing in complicated attribution modeling is not worth your time after all.

In our experience, if you are marketing short decision-cycle products and services, such as buying a pair of headphones or a laptop case, last-touch attribution will be perfectly accurate enough. Because the decision cycle is short, consumers tend to make a decision whether to buy quickly, not requiring them to come back many times. Therefore, the last-touch attribution is more than adequate in providing the necessary accuracy compared to the marketing cost/benefit of using attribution and the cost of owning and operating a sophisticated attribution system.

Often the difference between last-touch and multitouch attribution does not make a good source perform poorly, or a bad source perform well all of a sudden. Rather the okay performers, or sources that are more or less zero, will flip-flop. We have tested the difference in ranking between last-touch and multitouch attribution and found only small differences. In attributed revenues in dollar terms the differences were less than 10 percent, and often much smaller given any specific channel. In terms of the rank order of the channels you can see the results of one such test in Figure 5.11. There were only two instances, both marked with ∗ in Figure 5.11, where two similarly performing channels were reversed in order when switching attribution methods.

One reason that last-touch attribution works so well in many cases is that the time frame from marketing touch to customer decision has shrunk from weeks to days, minutes, or even seconds. In the case of direct mail, consumers typically respond with a purchase within weeks after receiving the catalog. Catalog marketers call this the *matchback* or *backmatch* period. For most catalog campaigns, within four weeks 55 percent of all responses have come in. After eight weeks 85 percent of responses

Last touch attribution	Multi-touch attribution
1. Email	1. Email
2. Yahoo ads	2. Yahoo ads
3. Adwords	3. Adwords
∗4. CJ	∗4. Direct mail
∗5. Direct mail	∗5. CJ
6. Performics	6. Performics
7. Amazon	7. Amazon
∗8. FCBI	∗8. Skymall
∗9. Skymall	∗9. FCBI

Figure 5.11 Last-Touch versus Multitouch Attribution

have come in and after 12 weeks 99 percent of responses have come in. Given this, most marketers would use four weeks as their matchback window and only attribute responses that come in within the first four weeks to the direct mail campaign.

Modern marketing campaigns have much shorter matchback windows than direct mail campaigns. The timescales in digital marketing tend to be days instead of weeks. This is why last-touch attribution works well for digital campaigns because the customer action happens so quickly after the campaign. Using last-touch attribution can make finding the channels that bring the best customers significantly easier and attainable for all marketers, even those who have not invested in sophisticated marketing attribution solutions.

CHAPTER 6

Play Two: Predict Customer Personas and Make Marketing Relevant Again

As we saw in Chapter 2, clustering is the automated, machine-learning powered version of segmentation. Clustering is a powerful tool that allows us to *discover* personas or communities within your customer base. You segment customers to identify homogeneous groups that exist within your customer base, which can be used to optimize and differentiate marketing actions or product strategy.

An online retailer we work with is operating an e-commerce store where triathletes, hobbyists, and cyclists can celebrate and support their passions. The company wanted to cater to individual customer interests in a scalable and feasible way for its modest marketing team. It began by looking at the different personas that make up its customers and discovered certain distinct communities around its products: professional remote control racecar drivers; hobbyists building kits with their children; and remote control airplane enthusiasts. With this information, the company started to send out different newsletters to the different personas. Addressing each of these groups with meaningful personalized content immediately paid off: email click rates increased 66 percent.

This is very typical, as we have seen similar increases in response with many companies we work with.

Clustering is a means to an end and it is a tool to develop strategies. Strategy informs segmentation and not the other way around. The three example schemas we chose here are customer behavior around products, their shopping behavior, and their attitudes against various brands. Other schemas would depend on the business strategy you're trying to develop. Just like we're clustering customers, you could cluster keywords, products, stores, employees, and any other entity in your marketing ecosystem. For example one of our customers, Arcelik, a white goods and electronics manufacturer and retailer in Europe, wanted to improve store performance and understand the customer profile of its stores. Head of CRM efforts Bora Cetiner with direction from their VP of Marketing Tulin Karabuk clustered their stores and understood what made them different. Equipped with this, they were able to make changes to store layout, advertising, CRM efforts. Even the goals set for each store depended on which cluster they belonged to.

When you utilize clustering for customers, we call the outcome clusters personas, because it captures the underlying persona for the customer that belongs to that cluster. But how do you express personas in a way that the marketer can understand the persona? The easiest way to do this is using the same heuristics of how we humans do this. Humans are essentially difference engines that look for "edges" to detect a picture or highs and lows that are different and keep only this information. For example when we look at a landscape, we notice the horizon, the sun setting, and we don't pay attention to all the waves in the ocean. We use similar mechanism to display personas, and we express a cluster "DNA" to do this. Cluster DNA is not an industry standard term (yet), but we use it to describe the clusters to marketers. Cluster DNA depicts how a customer belonging to a specific cluster more or less likely prefers a product or behavior (or whatever the clustering schema is) versus any other one.

Types of Clusters

Let's look deeper into the three types of personas that we will use as our examples: Product-based clusters, brand-based clusters, and behavior-based clusters. These are three examples that we utilize on a frequent basis and informs a wide variety of strategies.

Product-Based Clusters

Product-based clustering models group customers based on what types or categories of products they tend to prefer and what types of products customers tend to buy together. Product-based cluster models are sometimes also called *category-based* clusters. A product cluster can be broad or very specific. In Figure 6.1 you can see people in one customer segment tend to *only* buy sweaters, whereas those in another customer segment buy different types of active wear. These people might buy swimwear and watches, but never kids' clothes, intimates, or jewelry. This is useful information when deciding which product offers or email content to send to each of these types of customers.

How could you use product clusters? A big sports retailer, which sells athletic gear and apparel across different sports to a range of ages, initially thought that the same female customers that were buying kids' soccer gear were also buying yoga clothes for themselves. The company began sending direct mail advertising yoga gear to the women who bought soccer products. However, when we ran our predictive clustering models, we quickly discovered there was no crossover between soccer moms and yoga moms at all. We found crossover shoppers in different categories at a much higher rate, which allowed the business to shift its focus away from marketing to what they thought were soccer and yoga moms to the newly discovered and much more qualified segment of soccer and baseball moms.

Brand-Based Clusters

Brand-based clusters tell you what brands people are most likely to buy. It groups customers together that prefer a group of brands more than other. For instance, you will be able to identify which customers are likely to be interested when a specific brand releases new products. The models can also offer broader insights into related brands that may be of interest to a customer by comparing her preference to an existing brand cluster. The results of the model in Figure 6.2 illustrate that customers who like Tahari by ASL also tend to like Calvin Klein and Nine West, but would not be interested at all in Desigual or 6126.

Many retailers we work with have discovered that the brand affinity of customers tends to be stronger than their product-type affinity. This means that if a marketer in the example of Figure 6.2 sends a promotion of Nine West shoes to a customer who has bought a lot of

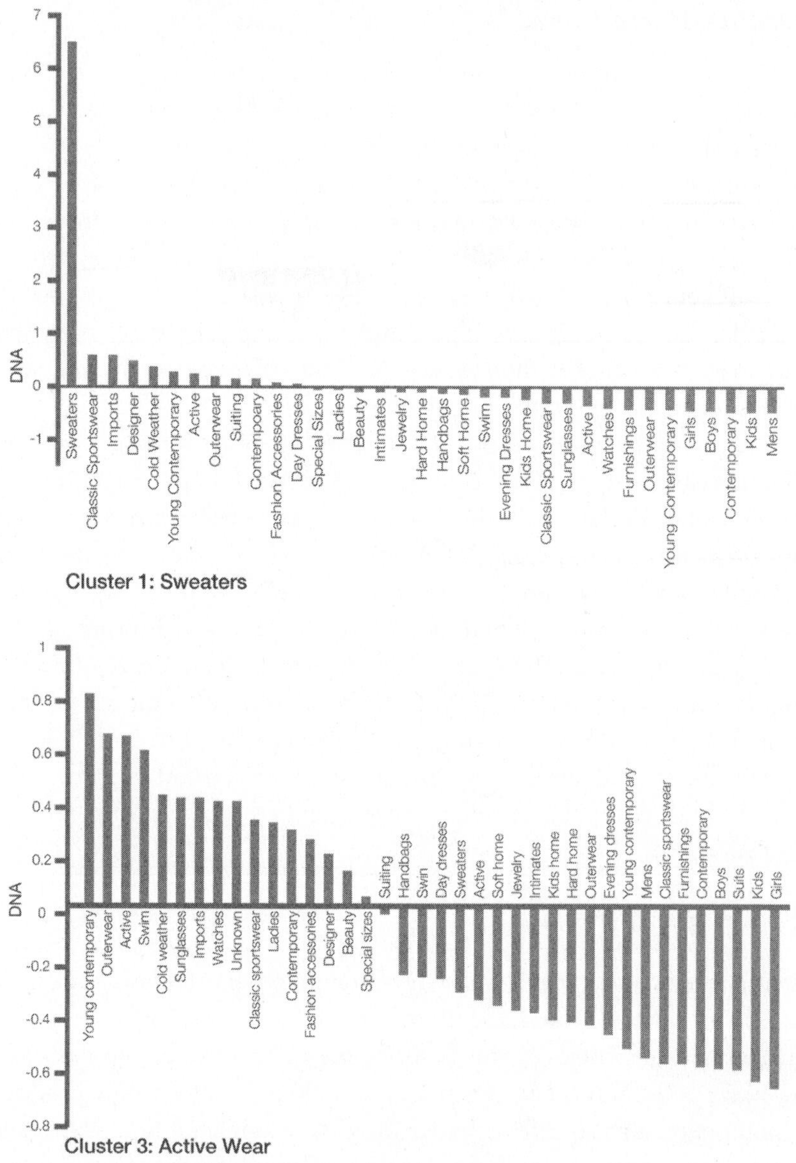

Figure 6.1 Example of Product-Based Clusters

Calvin Klein in the past, this promotion will likely generate a lot of sales. It will probably generate more sales than a campaign that is promoting watches to people who belong to the active wear cluster and have bought a lot of sunglasses in the past. This is a generalization and it is important to note that there are exceptions to every rule. This type of affinity is a

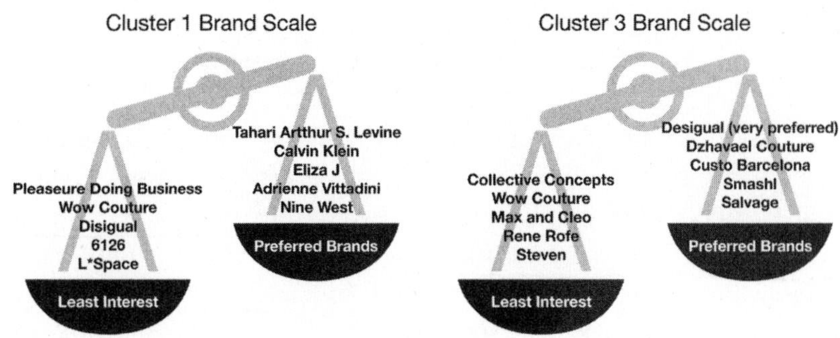

Figure 6.2 Example of Brand-Based Clusters

broader stroke affinity uncovering larger-scale patterns in your customer base than product recommendations we will cover later.

Behavior-Based Clusters

A behavior-based clustering model groups customers based on how they will behave while purchasing: Do they use the website or the call center? Are they discount addicts? How frequently do they buy? How much do they spend? How much time will pass before they purchase again? This algorithm helps set the right tone for contacting the customer. For instance, customers who only buy with heavy discounts may be great targets for inventory-clearing sales, whereas customers who typically pay full price would be better targets for a sneak-peek promotion of a new product line.

Behavior-based clustering can help identify completely new clusters you didn't know you had before. A clustering algorithm looks at a large number of variables including, but not limited to, average order size, days between orders, first order revenue, order variety, discount sensitivity, order frequency, total number of items purchased, total number of orders placed, number of returns, products bought in the first order, and order seasonality. Algorithms can look at hundreds of variables at the same time and discover which variables and attributes actually matter. Typically a clustering algorithm will find six to eight statistically significant personas in your customer data.

Every behavior-based cluster will have a cluster DNA that will reveal to the marketer which customer attributes are most differentiating and relevant in order to group customers. Algorithms are able to segment customers based on many more variables than a human being could. An algorithm will start with hundreds of dimensions and finally may pick 20 or so to define a certain behavioral cluster or persona. The example in Figure 6.3 shows some of the factors that could make up a cluster's DNA.

Let's look at an example from business marketing. Let's assume you are selling tools to small homebuilders and contractors. Your behavior-based clusters could reveal that you have some customers who only purchase from your call center agents, but always after spending a considerable amount of time doing research online. You may have another cluster with customers who stock up only once a year in your store, after receiving your direct mail postcard announcing your annual sale. And you have a third cluster, which also buy in your store, but basically come in once a week and always buy full price. Your marketing strategies for each of these three clusters would be very different. If you had only one customer behaving in this way, it would not be a cluster and not worth building a strategy around. However, the whole idea of clusters is that there is a statistically significant group of customers who behave in the same way.

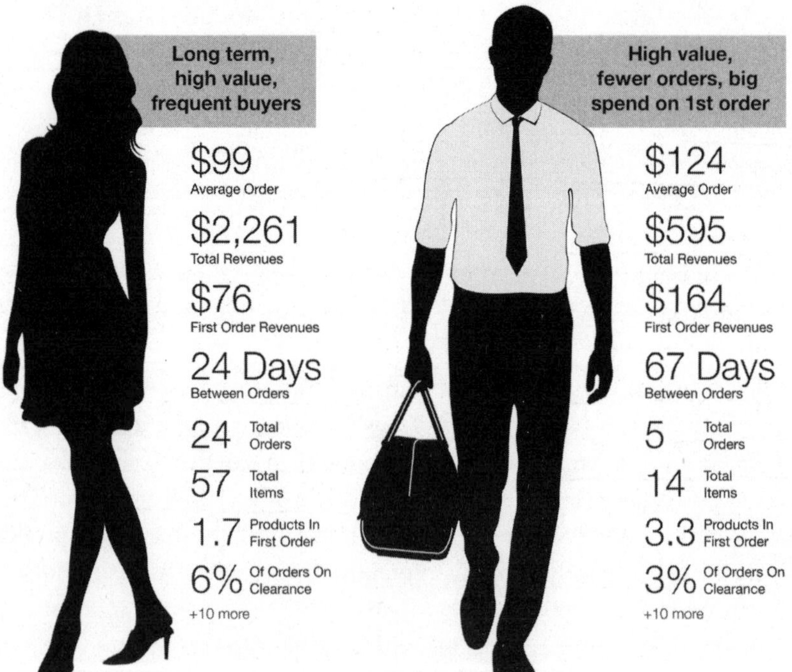

Figure 6.3 Example of Behavior-Based Clusters

Airlines' behavior-based clusters take into account factors like order frequency, days between orders, order seasonality, and discount sensitivity to help differentiate business travelers from leisure travelers. For airlines, this is a critical segmentation tool. Pricing and promotional strategies, as well as customer service strategies, can now be differentiated and tuned based on the types of customers being served on certain routes and flights.

Retailers might encounter behavior-based clusters such as full-price infrequent buyers, buyers who return products frequently (the so-called "returnaholics"), buyers with few orders who mainly buy when there is a large discount (the "discount junkies"), and buyers with a high order frequency who are very likely also your VIP customers. These different customer groups will be attracted to very different promotions. Your whales might enjoy receiving frequent emails from you and will purchase almost every time. However, sending the same email and content to your full-price infrequent buyers may turn them off to the point that they opt out from your email list. You might be better off sending this group a postcard if and when you are releasing a new product.

Using Clusters to Improve Customer Acquisition

Clusters are not only useful to target existing customers with more relevant communications. Clusters can also be used to craft more relevant new customer acquisition campaigns. Everything from the creative design to the places you advertise is influenced by the persona you are looking to target and acquire. The better you understand the different customer personas that buy from you, the more accurate you can be in designing campaigns to attract more buyers just like it.

A leading vitamin and wellness brand used to collect data, like statistics on the best-selling products, and analyze it around the boardroom to make hypotheses about their business. For example, when a certain joint supplement became a big seller, they assumed it was because of an uptick in their senior-aged customer base. They leveraged this hypothesis to tailor their campaign artwork, print mailers, and their media ads to an elderly customer. However, when they started to apply predictive clustering models to their data, clustering instead showed that the increase in joint supplements was actually due to a completely different customer:

customers that identified as body builders. Imagine how this impacted their business decisions! To start, the brand's marketing agency made a swift change to the artwork and media plan to save the resources that would have been wasted marketing to an elderly customer. The company can now work with its digital agency to make better product recommendations on e-commerce, as well as develop lifestyle content around this audience that is highly relevant to them for the blog and social channels. The brand's store planners can merchandise the joint supplement alongside the protein powder in-store. Its PR firm can plan a highly targeted event and bring in the right influencers.

Clusters can also be used successfully in combination with lookalike targeting on social media and in display advertising. We will discuss this use case in more detail in Chapter 11.

Things to Watch Out for When Using Clusters

The biggest mistake that marketers make when it comes to segmentation is to use only one-dimensional segmentation. No person belongs to only one segment. Segmentation is very contextual. Depending on the situation, a customer belongs to a different segment. For example, from a product perspective, John could be a runner and Mary could be a swimmer, but John could also be a discount-sensitive buyer always hunting for deals from a behavioral perspective and Mary always buys the latest product when it first comes out at full price. Now these are two dimensions that we can segment on that cannot be combined in a single dimensional way because another customer, Jane, could be a swimmer and discount-sensitive as well.

It is also important to find a way to update and use clusters on an ongoing basis. Many companies spend a lot of time creating the perfect clustering algorithm, performing exhaustive analysis whereby to select the cluster that would bring the most value or action-ability. Building a cluster this way can easily cost $100,000 or more. What's worse, by the time the analysis is complete and in the hands of marketing, the information in the customer file is ancient history. Paying continually for re-scoring a customer file on a quarterly (monthly usually is cost prohibitive) basis is expensive and still leads to sub-optimal results. These days, there is a better way, and modern software can ensure that clusters are updated and ready to use on a daily basis.

Clusters in Action

A global manufacturer and distributor of high-quality vitamins and nutritional supplements works to enhance the well-being of its customers by delivering high-quality, best-value nutritional supplements and wellness products. The retailer's European operations, which have more than 1,000 stores, wanted to gain a deep understanding of both online and brick-and-mortar store transactions. In particular, the retailer wanted to learn which products customers buy, how frequently they buy, and how discounts motivate them to buy. They focused on what buyer behaviors are driving the business, tailoring email campaigns accordingly. The retailer learned that the most valuable shoppers, which account for only 20 percent of its customer base, drove more than 80 percent of its profit. It also learned that food drives customer frequency and attracts these high-value shoppers. Certain food lines were considered unprofitable before understanding this insight. Now the retailer continues to carry these products to encourage customer frequency and attract high-value shoppers.

The company also learned that the purchase frequency of most of its customers is very low. However, loyal customers will shop more often and spend about 30 percent more per transaction. Also, customers who buy the store magazine spend 50 percent more than those who don't get the magazine.

The insights helped the company make adjustments to its merchandising and marketing plans, increasing overall revenue by 1.5 percent and the revenue of a specific new product announcements by 4 percent. It was also able to record a rise in the number of customers, the average order value, the average transaction value, and number of units per shopping cart.

The most innovative and impactful use of clustering is always starting with the end in mind. Define and understand the problem you're trying to solve or strategy you're trying to develop, then find the most appropriate clustering schema that will help you tease apart personas to work with.

CHAPTER 7

Play Three: Predict the Customer Journey for Life Cycle Marketing

In Chapter 4 we recommended that you look to optimize the lifetime value of each customer. In this chapter we look at the life cycle of a single customer in more detail to see how our strategy should include all stages of customer life cycle from acquisition to growth to retention. We start by looking at a simple customer life cycle or customer journey and then see how segmenting customers based on their life cycle stage can yield great insights and opportunities for customer growth. We also give you an overview of life cycle marketing strategies.

The Customer Value Journey

The basic principle of optimizing customer lifetime value is the same for all stages of the life cycle and can be summarized in three words: *give to get*. Customers are much more likely to buy from you if they have a relationship with you. The best way to develop that relationship is to deliver an experience of value. So to *get* customer (lifetime) value, *give* customer value.

Figure 7.1 shows basic concepts of the customer value journey. Customers will disengage you if they are not getting value from the relationship. The definition of value is very different from company

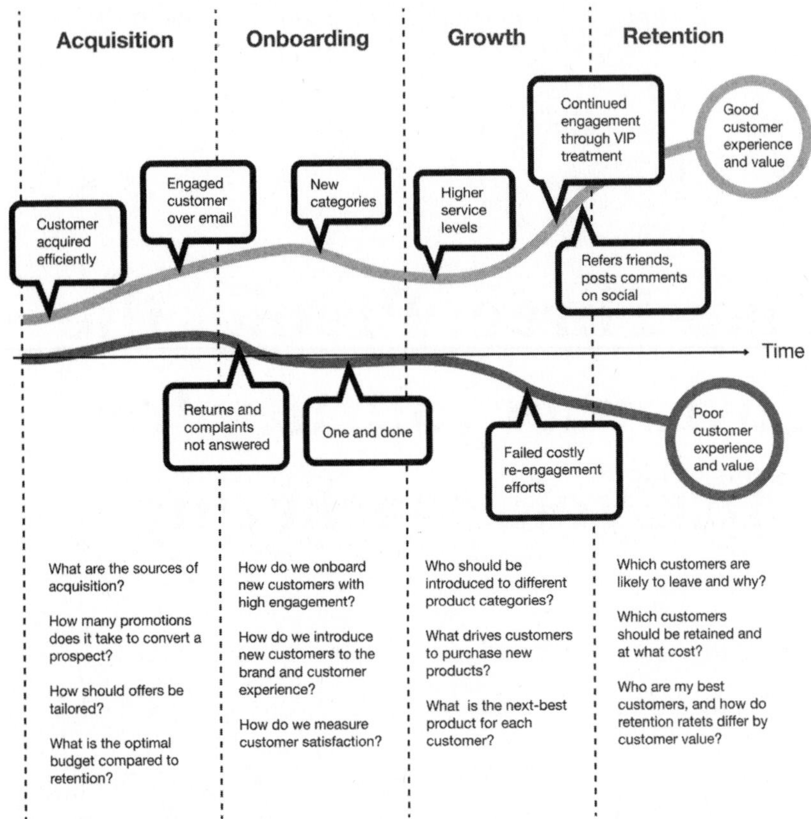

Figure 7.1 The Customer Value Journey

to company and it ranges from monetary value, especially in business marketing, to utilitarian value such as when using a great vacuum cleaner, to the self-confidence you may feel when wearing a designer dress. Whatever your definition of value, if customers are not getting it, they will look elsewhere.

There are three basic forces at work to create a relationship with a customer. First, does it make sense for the business to have a relationship with the customer, which requires thinking through size and type of transaction, future revenue streams, cross-sell, upsell opportunities, and cost of acquisition? Basically, will this customer deliver enough economic value to the business over time? Second, you need to think through whether it makes sense for the customer to have a relationship with you; this includes emotional attachment, risk of decision, follow-on products, or services required, involvement with the product, and so on. Basically, does our business offer what the customer is seeking? Third, to develop a relationship with a customer requires the business conditions to be right for the life cycle marketing to work. You need to be able to configure customer experience at a granular level and have the data to understand and predict customer behavior.

It is easier for companies selling certain products to develop a relationship with its customers than for others. For example, it is really hard for a deodorant brand to enable a life cycle relationship with a customer. Typically deodorant simply is not a high-engagement, high-risk product that makes sense for the consumer to provide information about and get something in return. On the other hand, for a camera brand or retailer, building a relationship with its customers is a lot easier. The camera buyer will engage with the brand starting from a camera purchase, continue to stay engaged with the brand for additional accessories, training videos, workshops, repairs, and so on. In this example, it really makes sense for both the business and the consumer to engage in a relationship, where it potentially benefits both and the business conditions are ripe to do so.

There are exceptions to every rule. For example, Secret is an antiperspirant/deodorant for women manufactured by Procter & Gamble (P&G) and first launched in 1956. In 2010 P&G launched the anti-bullying campaign "Mean Stinks" around the Secret brand. This campaign, now in its fifth year, has consistently drawn high engagement on social media and managed to really engage girls with the brand in a meaningful way.

First Value

As Confucius said: "Every journey starts with the first step," and this is true for the customer value journey as well. The first step in every customer journey is to get your prospective buyers to first value. We sometimes call this the "first wow." First value may occur after somebody has bought from you, but it is even better to try and get your prospects to first value before they have paid you a penny. This is truly "give to get" marketing.

Consider the many ways in which you can deliver value before somebody is technically a customer. In consumer marketing, you may be able to expose consumers to your brand via a great advertising campaign, viral marketing campaign, or other piece of content. Perhaps prospects first learn about your clothing line from your fashion blog or attend an enjoyable fashion show. Many yoga enthusiasts and runners first learn about active wear retailer Lululemon from the yoga classes and runs it offers at its stores. Marketers of time-share apartments are masters of designing first value experiences in the form of free events at exotic locations.

Dominique's daughter was recruited to a competitive soccer team using the "give to get" approach. While her parents had no intention of signing her up for such a time- and money-consuming activity, the club was smart and invited her daughter to participate in a free soccer clinic. From there she was invited to join the training of the team for a couple of weeks. Before long, she had made some great friends and was begging her mother to join the team. This is more than five years ago, and she is still playing (and her mom still paying).

Consumer goods companies have been using samples for a long time to get you to experience their product before buying it. The food sampling at warehouse club Costco is a popular pastime for many families. Retail companies are increasingly considering themselves content or entertainment companies first and retail companies second. Some retail CEOs even refer to themselves as editors-in-chief. The content is free, but the clothes are not.

Other brands are taking "give to get" very literally and engage in cause marketing. The Burlington Coat Factory partners with K.I.D.S/ Fashion Delivers, an organization that donates clothing and other products to underprivileged families across America. Every store opening is celebrated with a coat drive, making a charity event the first experience a prospective shopper has with Burlington Coat Factory.

There are plenty of examples in business marketing as well. When we were contemplating hiring a consultant, he first invited us to a free seminar, then offered a free one-hour consultation. He then sold us to a full group class and we eventually signed up for his services. Many business and consumer software companies now offer a free trial period or a freemium version of their software. Both allow prospects to use the fully or partially featured product for a period of time before committing to a purchase. When offering a free trial period, make sure customers reach first value before the end of the trial period. Again, the definition of first value is different for each company. If you are selling quality assurance test software, perhaps first value is defining your first test that runs with at least two different device types. If you sell marketing automation software, perhaps it is your customer launching her first successful campaign.

Recurring Value

But getting customers to first value is not enough to retain these customers long term. A single action does not a habit make. In retail marketing, we find that 70 percent of first-time buyers never come back. Perhaps they did not have a good experience or, more likely, they simply forgot about you. The same is true for many business products, including software. There usually is a honeymoon period just after purchase where users are very excited about trying out a new product or tool. However, if using the new software does not become a habit within the first months, much of business software ends up as "shelfware." Shelfware is software that was paid for but never used.

It is not always apparent that companies have lost these customers. If you are a magazine, you may only discover your subscribers have stopped reading your magazine when it comes time to renew. However, by then it is too late to create a habit of reading your publication. The same is true for other products.

In retail, customers are usually not considered lost or lapsed until one year after their first purchases. However, our research shows that for most products, if a repeat purchase does not happen within the first few months it probably will never happen. This window of recurring value is different for each company. If you are selling cars, the repurchase time frame could be years. If you are selling pet food, it is probably a month or less. In flash sales on fashion sites, it is weeks.

Whatever the length of the honeymoon period, just after a customer's first value experience with your brand, you have a lot of goodwill and an unique opportunity to convert this customer from a one-time buyer to a repeat buyer. Your job is now to deliver recurring value.

If you get a retail customer to buy a second time, the churn rate drops from 70 percent to 30 percent. In other words, whereas only 30 percent of one-time buyers come back to buy again, a whopping 70 percent of second-time buyers will return for another purchase.

Predictive algorithms help predict the repurchase window for your company. They can help you drill down to predict the repurchase window by clusters or by individual customer.

Let's say that you determined the honeymoon period for your company is two months and if a second purchase does not occur after two months, it will likely not happen. There are a couple of actions you can take with this information.

First, provide helpful information to the customer immediately after the first purchase and offer a thank you note for the initial purchase. This is also a good time to make recommendations for what the customer might want to purchase next. We speak more about recommendations in Chapter 10.

Second, if your product is something that is typically replaced periodically, such as face cream, water filters, or pet medications, send a friendly reminder a week or more before their supply is likely to run out. Most customers will find value in the reminder itself: They will consider it good customer service that you send this reminder. Waking up one morning to discover that you ran out of face cream or pet food is no fun, so a courtesy reminder is very welcome to most consumers.

If after 60 days no repeat purchase has occurred, it is time to step up your game. You have nothing to lose at this point, so you might want to consider creating additional incentives to get the customer to buy again.

In business marketing, you similarly want to see recurring use of your product within the first months after purchase. For instance, if you are selling marketing automation software, you want to see customers set up a second and third campaign or landing page shortly after their first. Declining usage or nonusage is a sure sign your customer may not renew at the end of their subscription period.

New Value

Even recurring value and repeat purchases are not the end of the customer journey. If you have established a good pattern of recurring value, you may not lose this customer any time soon, but you are still leaving value on the table.

In Chapter 5 we talked about the difference between predicted lifetime value and upside lifetime value. Predicted lifetime value accounts for the future revenues you can expect from customers if they continue to buy from you, as they do now. We gave the example of a customer buying hockey tape from a sports store and the retailer trying to market complimentary products to her that she is currently buying elsewhere in order to capture new value.

If a customer is already going to the Disney theme parks every year, new value for Disney would be to get her to go on a Disney cruise vacation next. In business marketing, new value means getting customers to pay for more features of the same product, or buying more products from the same vendor. In our marketing automation example, new value could be going beyond installing simple email campaigns and configuring on-site personalization. If you are not experiencing the full value that a product or vendor has to offer, your chances of churn are higher. On many of our customer studies, we've found that given everything else being equal, customers with the higher number of categories or distinct products used, have higher future value. Engagement over multiple products is a strong indicator of future value.

Life Cycle Marketing Strategies

Now let's look at some high-level strategies to give customer value in order to get customer value. Figure 7.2 gives you an overview of life cycle marketing strategies. We will discuss these strategies at a high level in this chapter. For details on specific campaigns, read Chapters 11, 12, and 13.

Prospective Customer Strategies: Can We Help?

We have described many examples of what first value could mean for prospective customers. Whatever it is for your business, experiment with different ideas and measure the results. Measuring results also means listening to your non-buyers. Perform an exit poll on your website, or institute loss interviews for all lost deals in business marketing. Monitor your prospects in whichever way you can. Using the behavioral data such as email signups, form fills, web browsing behavior, keywords used, marketers need to predict and trigger campaigns to prospect to convert efficiently to become customers. Campaigns based on behavioral data make the experience personal and increase conversions significantly. For example, a prospect who searched for "red shoes" on the website after

Life Cycle Segment	Definition	Marketing Objective	Marketing Strategy
Prospective customer	Somebody who has never bought from you before.	Get the prospect to convert to a paying customer.	Deliver first value or first wow.
New customer	A brand new customer within the first 90 days of her first purchase.	Get your new customer to come back soon and buy again.	Welcome new customers, get customers to recurring value. Understand why they became a customer and whether and how they are different from existing customers.
Repeat/active customer	Somebody who has bought at least twice from you.	Keep these customers engaged, get them to refer others.	Continue to delight, introduce new value. Find ways to encourage them to refer friends. Introduce these customers to new categories or services that they haven't engaged with yet.
At-risk/ Inactive customer	Hasn't bought (or used) product or service for 90 days or not highly likely to buy.	Reengage these customers.	Investigate satisfaction; give a reason to try again.
Lapsed customers	Haven't bought in a year, or very low likelihood to buy	Reactivate these customers.	Give a reason to try again.

Figure 7.2 Overview of Life Cycle Marketing Strategies

signing up for the email newsletter should get best sellers in red shoes. These triggered campaigns are highly relevant and therefore effective.

Zendesk, a provider of cloud-based helpdesk software, generated most of its new business through a free self-service trial. Because Zendesk doesn't speak to its prospects in person during the buying process, it decided to monitor exactly what features free-trial users touched. Using this information, it was able to identify which parts of the software customers were not using and reengineer the onboarding process. These changes resulted in a more than 100 percent increase in engagement during the trial period.

It is also important to be helpful during the buying process. Many customers come into Apple retail stores with no intent to buy. Once children begin playing with free games and adults start experimenting with new phones and computers, it's only a matter of time before store associates ask customers how they can help. Before long, a customer might ask about the cost of upgrading a phone and a sale might ensue.

The same can be done with digital marketing. If you see that people are visiting your website but not completing a purchase, stretch out a helpful hand. The digital equivalent of "can we help" could be an online chat box, a pop-up, or a friendly reminder after visitors have already left your site. We speak more about remarketing campaigns such as cart abandonment, email, or display retargeting in Chapter 11.

In business marketing, you may want to pick up the phone and call a prospect with a simple "can I help."

New Customer Strategies: Thank You

We have established that if you don't convert the one-time buyer quickly, you won't ever convert that customer. So the actions you take in the first days, weeks, and months after you have acquired a new customer are extremely important. A good place to start with new customers is a simple thank you.

Nonprofits are masters at sending thank you letters. By including information about the donation's impact, nonprofits make the donor feel good and ensure future donations. The SmileTrain is a nonprofit that funds cleft lip operations in developing countries. When you donate to the SmileTrain, the organization responds by sending before and after pictures of a child who was physically transformed through your donation.

So few companies do a good job at a proper thank you that it is easy to stand out and make a big impression. When you order from Moosejaw, a retailer that sells outdoor gear and apparel, your order arrives in a box with a sticker that says: "Sealed with a kiss by: Matt" and the hand-written name of the packer who closed your box. You can find many pictures online of customers who were so impressed by this gesture that they posted praise about it online. The boxes also come with other stickers such as "No knife. Use teeth." and "Don't be surprised if you have seen this box before. We recycle." Moosejaw's CMO Dan Pingree says this allows the company to deliver customer experiences that people remember, not just products or transactions.

After your thank you, make sure to provide new customers with helpful hints on how to use or maintain their new products. This could be a list of tips on how to use, wash, or maintain the product. Perhaps a customer service representative could even pick up the phone and ask the customer if everything is okay with a first purchase.

We have found the same is true in business marketing. If a customer experiences problems with your product, nothing is more powerful than a customer service representative reaching out proactively. If you know your product is difficult to use, perhaps offer customers a free course or regular phone calls with a customer service representative.

Beyond getting customers to use your product or to come back and buy more, postpurchase is also a good time to make upsell or next-sell recommendations. Home improvement stores found that shortly after customers bought wood to build a deck, they were in the market for a new barbeque or grill. And shortly after customers bought a new wood-pellet grill, they typically would buy grill accessories, a grill cookbook, and refill wood pellets. Predictive analytics can help you find these correlated products and help you make the customer journey in greater detail. Once you know what products are usually bought next, you can send customers recommendations proactively.

If you fail to convert a customer during the honeymoon period, don't give up. Instead, step it up. You have nothing to lose so you might as well provide a more aggressive offer. The longer you wait, the lower your chances of bringing the customer back. You still have a much better chance than to wait for the customer to lapse.

Repeat/Active Customer Strategies: We Love You

There is a popular misconception that if customers are actively using your product or service and coming back to buy time and time again that you should leave them alone. Nothing could be further from the truth. There is still much to lose and to gain from these customers. You always want to stay top of mind with customers. There are so many brands out there that it is easy to be forgotten. Once out of sight, it is likely that your brand will also be out of mind. Plus, repeat customers often still have upside lifetime value if you can get them to buy other products from you. If nothing else, repeat customers are also prime candidates to become brand ambassadors for your brand and to refer their friends.

A simple campaign to appreciate your best customers can be powerful. For instance, when LinkedIn reached 200 million users, the company sent an email to its top 1 percent, 5 percent, and 10 percent most-viewed profiles in different geographies. Many of the top users proudly posted the digital letter they received online, and the simple gesture became one of the biggest viral marketing campaigns in LinkedIn's history.

Likewise, in the early years of Amazon, the e-commerce retailer sent coffee mugs to loyal customers around the Christmas holidays. We received such a mug and 15 years later remember it well enough to write about it in this book!

For repeat customers within customer life cycle management, creating treatment strategies would involve understanding customers from a value, behavior, engagement, product, and brand perspectives, similar to what we outlined in the chapter where we discussed clustering.

Inactive Customer Strategies: Remember Me

Don't give up on inactive customers. Just because they haven't bought anything for a while doesn't mean they won't ever buy anything from you. The first thing to do is to investigate if there is a specific reason why this customer stopped buying or using your product or service. You can do this by picking up the phone or via an email survey. Don't make assumptions. One vendor we do business with was trying to be ultra customer-centric by proactively unsubscribing consumers from their email list if they hadn't opened these emails for a while. Many customers who were unsubscribed automatically were upset. Even though they hadn't bought for a while, many said they still enjoyed reading the newsletter and had every intention of buying again.

The sooner you act on inactive customers, the better. Don't wait for them to lapse. Offer constant gentle reminders of the great past experiences they have had with your brand and provide a gentle nudge to come back again. Just like a simple "thank you" and "can I help" goes a long way, a simple reminder can work wonders for inactive customers.

Music app Shazam found the best way to re-engage subscribers that hadn't logged into the service for a while was to send personalized recommendations for songs or concerts via email or mobile push notifications.

If recommendations don't work, send reminders with a simple "we miss you" and start to give your customers specific reasons to come back. For consumers, perhaps a discount will get them to buy again. For businesses, perhaps you offer up a free tune-up or training. The messaging and offers for inactive customers and lapsed customers are very similar, but you should increase the value of the offers as time goes on. It will become more and more difficult to convince customers to come back.

You should take into account the personalized repurchase window when doing this. Certain products have a longer time between two purchases, and certain customers have a longer time between purchases. No point to remind me every month to come back if you know from my past behavior that I am the type of shopper who comes just twice a year to stock up.

Lapsed Customer Strategies: We Miss You

Lapsed customers are those that haven't bought for more than a year or those that let their subscription or service lapse. Here the guiding light is "what have we got to lose?" These customers may or may not respond to your emails, but there is a greater chance than with inactive customers that they are tuning out your communications. A strong offer is more important here than personalized recommendations and reminders.

Whereas most of the strategies of reminders, escalating offers of help and reasons to come back, and simple "I miss you" still apply for this customer segment, you may need to try different channels to reach these customers. If a customer hasn't opened an email from you for a year, it doesn't help to continue to send emails. Instead, you may want to try direct mail or Facebook custom audiences advertising to reach these customers. Perhaps the customer will actually look at the postcard offer and be inspired to return to your store.

PetCareRx sent postcards to reactivate lapsed customers. Postcards are expensive so they only sent these to customers with a relatively high likelihood to buy. Also, the incentive for coming back to PetCareRx was different for customers with different lifetime values. Those with higher lifetime values received a greater discount on their next order.

CHAPTER 8

Play Four: Predict Customer Value and Value-Based Marketing

The days of one-size-fits-all customer service are long gone. Not all customers are going to be as valuable to you as others. For instance, the costs incurred from customers who frequently return things they purchase could outweigh the revenue from those customers. In Chapter 4 we defined customer lifetime value in detail. In this chapter we look at strategies to segment and target customers by their lifetime values, a practice called *value-based* marketing.

Value-Based Marketing

Any business will have those low-value customers, as well as medium and high-value customers. The trick is identifying which customers fit into which value buckets and crafting differentiated marketing and service strategies based on the value of each customer. That means keeping perks like unlimited free shipping and returns for high-value customers, rather than the low-value heavy returners.

Figure 8.1 summarizes the three key strategies depending on customer value:

- High-value customers: Spend money to appreciate and retain these customers. Pay close attention to retention metrics here.
- Medium-value customers: Upsell to migrate these customers to maximize their potential. Pay close attention to upside potential of these customers.
- Low-value customers: Reduce your costs of servicing unprofitable customers.

For simplicity purposes we broke down the customers into three segments, high, medium, and low value. We usually designate the top 10 percent of customers as 'VIP customers', since there should be very few VIP customers to pay attention to, the next 60 percent of customers as 'average' and the bottom 30 percent as 'low profitability' customers. This is easily done by ordering customers from highest to lowest revenue or profitability and choosing the top 10 percent, the next 60 percent, and the lowest 30 percent. The reason why we don't do this based on an absolute revenue or profitability break (for example, all customers who spent over $500 per year is in high value bucket). The reason is to always have the same proportion of customers in the value segments, and track

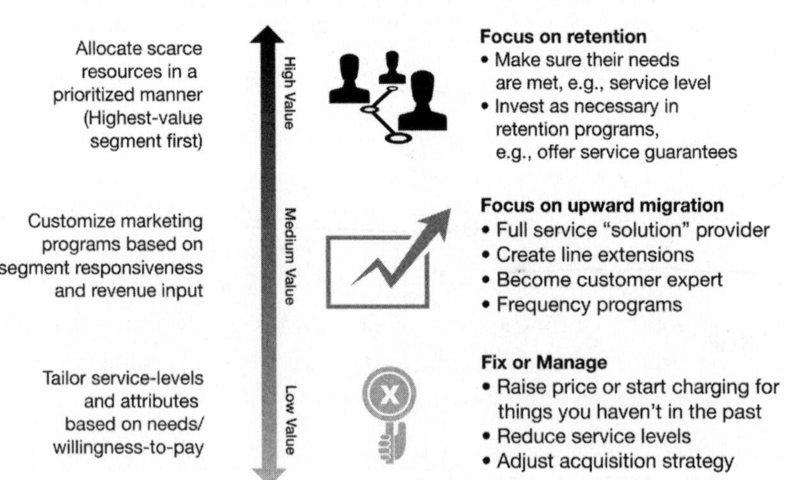

Figure 8.1 Value-Based Marketing Strategies

the average value of these segments. This way retention metrics can be calculated for the same portion of the population, and this approach is proofed against change in segment averages.

The reason for choosing this 10/60/30 is more of a business choice than mathematical. You can also choose to find the right split by looking at the histogram of value and decide on the right split in a more mathematical way. At an apparel retailer we worked with, within active customers, high-value customers spent $600 on average, whereas medium-value customers spent $120, and low-value customers spent $30. This is not atypical; in many cases we've seen top 10 percent high-value customers contribute close to 30–40 percent of all profits, medium-value customers contribute 60–70 percent and low-value customers contribute anywhere from 0–10 percent.

For any mix of customer value segments, you need to pay attention to how the mix changes over time, making sure that retention and acquisition for each of these segments trends favorably. The concept behind value-based marketing is to understand the mix of customer value over time. Figure 8.2 shows how this works by looking at the value breakdown of customers over the last 12 months (or if you're using predictive metrics, you would use predicted next 12-month value against last 12-month value) and cross-tabulating this against the prior 12-month value status of the customer. For example, if a customer was a high value in the prior 12 months and hasn't placed an order in the last 12 months, this is defined as a lapsed customer. However, there are three lapsed customer segments as shown, ranging from a high, medium, to low value segment. High-value customers lapsing is much worse than low-value

Last 12 months value status (rows) / Prior 12 months value status (columns)

	No orders	High Value	Medium Value	Low Value	Prospect → New
No orders	1	4	4	4	
High Value	2	3	5	5	7
Medium Value	2	6	3	5	7
Low Value	2	6	6	3	7

ID	Name
1	Inactive customers for both periods
2	Reactivated customers
3	Stable customers
4	Lapsed customers
5	Growing value customers
6	Declining, at-risk customers
7	Prospects who became new customers

Figure 8.2 Value Transition and Definition of Value Segments

customers (which you might even be better of without in some cases where low-value customers contribute negatively to profitability).

The transition matrix shown in Figure 8.2 can be used to calculate many useful metrics. The seven segments depicted in the figure describe important patterns in your customer data. Segment 1 describes customers who have been inactive for a long time (24 months or more in this example). These are not only lapsed customers, but customers you failed to reactivate. Most marketers have a growing number of these customers over the years and provide a pool of opportunity to reactivate from the past. Segment 2 is customers who have existed in your customer database and were inactive and recently have been reactivated. The importance of reactivation is that it counterbalances efforts of lapsed customers. Segment 3 is customers who stay within their segment of value over time. Segment 4 is customers who lapsed in the recent period who used to be active. Segment 5 is customers who are migrating upward in value, which shows they are increasing their loyalty and value. Segment 6 is the opposite of 5; these are customers who are migrating downward in value and signal attrition risk. Segment 7 is customers who are recently acquired and which value they have or are projected to have.

As we mentioned before, you can either use actual historical value or predicted future value when utilizing this framework.

Figure 8.3 shows an example of this framework. For example, we can see that 1,000 customers who used to be high-value customers have lapsed. It also shows that of the 21,000 customers acquired, 3,000 of them were high-value customers.

	Last 12 months					
	Prior 12 months					
	No. Orders	**High Value**	**Medium Value**	**Low Value**	**New Customer**	**Total**
No. Orders	20,000	1,000	14,000	20,000		**55,000**
High Value	1,000	15,000	2,000	1,000	3,000	**22,000**
Medium Value	9,000	5,000	96,000	3,000	14,000	**127,000**
Low Value	2,000	2,000	18,000	38,000	4,000	**64,000**
Total	**32,000**	**23,000**	**130,000**	**62,000**	**21,000**	**268,000**

Figure 8.3 Example of Value Transition Framework

	Reactivation	New	– Lapsed	Net Change	Spend/ Customer	Value Gain/ Loss
High Value	1,000	3,000	(1,000)	3,000	$600	$1,800,000
Medium Value	9,000	14,000	(14,000)	9,000	$120	$1,080,000
Low Value	2,000	4,000	(20,000)	(14,000)	$15	$(210,000)
Total	12,000	21,000	(35,000)	(2,000)		**$2,670,000**

Figure 8.4 Net Loss/Gain from Acquisition, Reactivation, and Lapsed Segments

In Figure 8.4 we show a practical usage of this framework for tracking performance of a customer base. We know that for every lapsed customer, we can either acquire a new one or reactivate an existing customer. This framework also deals with an important factor; are we acquiring and reactivating customers of same value compared to lapsed customers. This shows the retention in a more granular way to uncover what we call silent attrition, that is, we could be acquiring/reactivating the same number of customers, but of lower value, therefore losing enterprise value. In the example given in Figure 8.4, it shows that the active customer count (total net gain/loss, which is -2,000 customers) went down; however, due to increased retention of higher value segments, the customer value increased by $2.7 million.

Retaining High-Value Customers

Until recently, many firms were unable to identify their high-value customers, let alone give them the white glove treatment. Although airlines, banks, and casinos know it pays to make big investments in retention incentives for high-value customers, too many midsize organizations still ignore their best customers.

Spending to retain high-value customers pays off. Often a small percentage of customers make up the majority of revenues. A cosmetics retailer we work with found that 50 percent of revenue came from just 20 percent of customers. When analyzing its best customers, a popular flash sales site found that some of its best shoppers spent more than $100,000 a year with the retailer.

When a popular home improvement website first started to calculate lifetime value for their customers, it was surprised to find that some customers spent more than 20 times more than the average customer. These so-called whales were so important to the company that the CEO began picking up the phone to get to know these customers one by one. From those conversations, new ideas emerged on how to better serve and attract more high-value customers. Similarly, a flash sales site decided to send a box of chocolates for Christmas to their entire top 1 percentage of customers. This was well worth the money as their top 1 percentage made up 20 percentage of their revenues. Technology companies Wufoo and Stripe are well known for sending handwritten notes to wow their customers.

In the *Harvard Business Review* article "Manage Marketing by the Customer Equity Test," authors Robert C. Blattberg and John Deighton recount the experiences of McDonald's. The corporation's managers noted that the value of what they call *super-heavy* users—typically males aged 18 to 34 who eat at McDonald's an average of three to five times a week—account for a whopping 77 percent of its sales. Naturally, retaining these customers and getting them to eat at its restaurants more often is a priority. As a general rule it is much easier to get a current customer to use you more often than it is to get a new customer.

Another example of value-based marketing is airline loyalty rewards programs that are based on the dollars you spend with the airline, rather than the miles you have flown. This way, higher paying customers automatically get a greater reward than lower paying customers.

Marketers should use their retention budgets in order to proactively retain high-value customers. If you have an accurate projection of future customer lifetime value, you can experiment on what it takes to retain this customer. Some organizations might consider crafting separate marketing plans or even build separate marketing teams to focus on acquisition and retention efforts. Titles containing "customer marketing" and "customer success" are increasingly popular across many verticals.

We discuss retention strategies in greater detail in Chapter 13.

Growing Medium-Value Customers

Your main strategy for medium-value customers is to nudge them into the high-value customer bucket. In addition to selling these customers more of the products they are already buying, start predicting what other products and categories these shoppers might like. A customer than who spends $1,000 across three categories, say furniture, clothing, and kitchenware, has more future value than a customer who spends $1,000 on furniture only. Your strategy should always be to try and get customers to buy from you across multiple categories.

Customers who already like a company's products and services are less expensive to serve with new products and services. For that reason, you should be recommending different products to existing customers, as well as adding new products and services to meet your customers' evolving needs.

Companies that fail to use their knowledge of customers to promote or develop the products or services those people will need next are leaving the door open for another company to lure those people away. Although it is tempting to use new products to win whole new markets, it almost always makes better sense to stick with existing customer segments.

Mavi Jeans has been very successful with migrating customers to higher value segments. For example, the company found a segment of jean lovers who also had an affinity with certain tops but had never been marketed these tops. Adding campaigns based on these insights increased customer lifetime value by 36 percent.

In his *Harvard Business Review* article on loyalty-based management, Frederick F. Reichheld tells the stories of Entenmann's of New York, a leader in specialty bakery products, and the car company Honda. When Entenmann's saw its sales leveling off, it discovered that as its core customers aged, they were looking for more fat-free and cholesterol-free products. So instead of trying to find new customers for its existing products, Entenmann decided that it was more economical to launch a new fat- and cholesterol-free line of products to serve its existing customers. The new line has been extremely successful. Similarly, Honda figured out how to increase a Honda's owner repurchase rate to 65 percent, versus the industry average of 40 percent, by launching new cars that accommodate its customers' evolving needs. For example, it successfully marketed the Accord wagon to previous owners of the subcompact Honda Civic. The wagon was designed to accommodate the evolving needs of customers acquired in their early twenties who were now married with children and needed a larger car.

We discuss strategies to grow customer value in detail in Chapter 12.

Reducing the Costs to Service Low-Value Customers

Every brand will find itself with a segment of unprofitable customers. It is best to try to reduce the costs to service low-value customers, rather than firing these customers outright and leaving the door open for competitors to gain strength. In any business scenario, this is a fact of life. When acquiring customers, it is impossible to reject low-value customers. However, keeping it in check, that is, understanding, measuring, and monitoring the size and value of this segment over time, is extremely important. Once you know who is in this segment and why, you can focus on formulating strategies to reduce the cost to serve/market to this segment. Fortunately, it is now possible to differentiate the level of service offered to different customer segments.

A fashion flash sales site found a particular customer segment returned more clothes than they kept and therefore were very unprofitable. The company then decided to market only jewelry to this customer segment because online return rates on necklaces and earrings are much lower than on clothes and shoes. Other retailers have started to differentiate by offering free shipping to some but not all customers. If you return a lot of products, you will likely not receive the free shipping privilege in the future.

To that end, First Union Bank has a system called *Einstein*, which automatically assigns a green, yellow, or red flag to each customer. Service representatives are instructed not to waive fees for red customers, waive them for green customers, and use discretion for yellow customers. They have generated an estimated $100 million in incremental additional annual revenue based on this differentiated strategy.

Likewise, First Chicago Corporation imposed a $3 teller fee on money-losing customers (3 percent of their customer base). By identifying loss-making, high-volume users and sending them notices of fee increases, the company reduced its 11 million customer base by 450,000 in six months.

CHAPTER 9

Play Five: Predict Likelihood to Buy or Engage to Rank Customers

Propensity models, also called *likelihood to buy* or *response* models, are what most people think about with predictive analytics. These models help predict the likelihood of a certain type of customer behavior, like whether a customer that is browsing your website is likely to buy something. In this chapter we examine how marketers can optimize anything from email send frequency, to sales staff time, to money, including discounts, when armed with information about likelihood to buy or likelihood to engage.

Online pet pharmacy PetCareRx has served pet owners for more than 15 years. It sells many products that customers have to reorder at varying times from 3 months to 12 months. Like most retailers, PetCareRx took a one-size-fits-all marketing approach, offering a set calendar of discounts and promotions to all customers. But not all customers are alike and many are looking to buy at different times of the year. Using predictive analytics, PetCareRx was able to differentiate discounts across customers, leading to higher sales and retention without increasing costs. Customers were ranked according to their likelihood to buy. Based on that ranking, PetCareRx was able to determine which discounts would obtain the optimal response from each customer and offer minimal discounts through email or mailed postcards to customers who were already deemed likely to buy and offer larger discounts for customers who were less likely to buy. The surgical promotions drove incremental margin from customers who were already motivated to buy and incremental revenue from customers who previously felt no incentive to buy. Thanks to this and other predictive marketing campaigns, quarterly sales increased by 38 percent from the year before, profit rose by 24 percent, and customer retention increased by 14 percent. Plus, the changes allowed PetCareRx to more than double its campaign response rates without increasing the marketing or promotional budget by a single dollar.

Likelihood to Buy Predictions

To predict which prospects are ready to make their first purchase, a likelihood to buy model evaluates nontransaction customer data, such as how many times a customer clicked on an email or how the customer interacts with your website. These models can also take into account certain demographic data. For example, in consumer marketing they may compare gender, age, and zip code to other likely buyers. In business marketing, relevant demographics may include industry, job title, and geography.

Here's how it works: the models compare the prepurchase behavior of prospective buyers to the prepurchase behavior of thousands or millions of previous customers who ended up buying, comparing attributes like what emails they opened and what products they spent the most time looking at. The prospects that behave most like the previous buyers are tagged as "high-likelihood buyers" and marketers can then alter the way they interact with them to increase the likelihood of closing a sale. Once you're armed with this data, you can prioritize your investment in each prospective customer.

Likelihood to Buy for First-Time Buyers

For consumer marketers, likelihood to buy predictions allow you to decide how much of a discount you might allocate to a certain customer because people who are already more likely to buy won't need as aggressive of a discount as customers who are less likely to buy. The models then get better over time, as companies collect more data and automatically test whether predictions actually become reality.

For instance, the large European household appliance manufacturer Arcelik maintains a call center where employees are given a list of customers who are likely to be ready to buy a new washing machine within the next few months. Agents then make calls to these customers with offers such as a year of free detergent with the purchase of a washing machine. The tactic works well for considered purchases, such as refrigerators or cars, and larger-ticket items such as high-end fashion apparel.

A high-end shoe brand provides store associates with lists of customers to call too. The store associates have already developed strong relationships with their customers but they can be even more successful when armed with predictive analytics. Employees can now see which customers are likely to be interested in a certain style when a new season's shoe comes out, based on customers' past behavior or how similar their purchase habits are to other customers. Employees can then reach out to customers with that information. A call could go something like this: "Hi Joe, it has been a while since we've spoken. I just wanted to let you know that there is a new cross-country running shoe I think you might like. It's similar to the shoes you bought two years ago, but in a new material. I have put a pair aside for you in your size. If you have time, perhaps you could stop by on your way home from work to have a look?" Who would not want to receive a call or an email like that from their personal shopper?

As reported by the *New York Times* and others, President Barack Obama used propensity models, specifically propensity to vote for the Democratic Party, to help him win reelection in 2012. His staff of volunteers could not possibly meet with every voter in the country so the challenge was to find the undecided voters. There was no point spending time or money trying to woo diehard Republicans who would not change their minds anyway, or diehard Democrats who were already likely to vote for Obama. Rather, using propensity models, Obama's team of data scientists found those voters who were undecided but could still be persuaded. They then focused on finding already strong Obama supporters in the undecided voter's social circle and asked them to spend time with the undecided voter to explain their views.

Likelihood to Buy for Repeat Buyers

What good is spending money to acquire new customers if they only buy once and do not return? Therefore, it is not only important to predict likelihood to buy for first-time buyers, but it is equally important to predict likelihood to buy for repeat buyers. Your goal is to keep customers coming back time and time again. It is happy and loyal customers who have a large lifetime value, and many customers with a large lifetime value make for large revenues and profits for your company.

Predicting likelihood to buy for repeat buyers is a lot easier than predicting likelihood to buy for first-time buyers because there is a lot more information to go on. The likelihood to buy model for repeat purchases evaluates earlier transactions as well as other interactions similar to the model for prospects. However, the added information derived from the first purchase can significantly improve the accuracy of the likelihood to buy model for repeat purchases, as compared to a similar model for prospects. Unlike the first purchase predictions, repeat purchase predictions utilize all interactions of the customer, such as past purchases, returned purchases, and phone calls to customer service.

Choosing the Right Level of Discount Using Likelihood to Buy

There are two main uses for likelihood to buy predictions: which customers to focus on and how much money, including discounts, to spend on each customer.

Choosing your audience carefully is important if you want to optimize marketing ROI, because reaching customers can be expensive. For instance, a direct mail or call campaign that costs $1 per customer interaction and has a 2 percent purchase rate could cost $50 a person before a discount is even given. If you can target your audience and make the communications more relevant, the purchase rate could be significantly higher, say 10 percent, reducing the cost to reach each buyer significantly. In addition to choosing the right people, you can increase purchase rates by including relevant recommendations or content and to communicate with customers at the right time. Focusing on relevancy will allow companies to reduce their dependency on high discounts. Using this strategy it is possible to significantly reduce discounts as a part of their customer acquisition strategy. Figure 9.1 shows how a large U.S. retailer was able

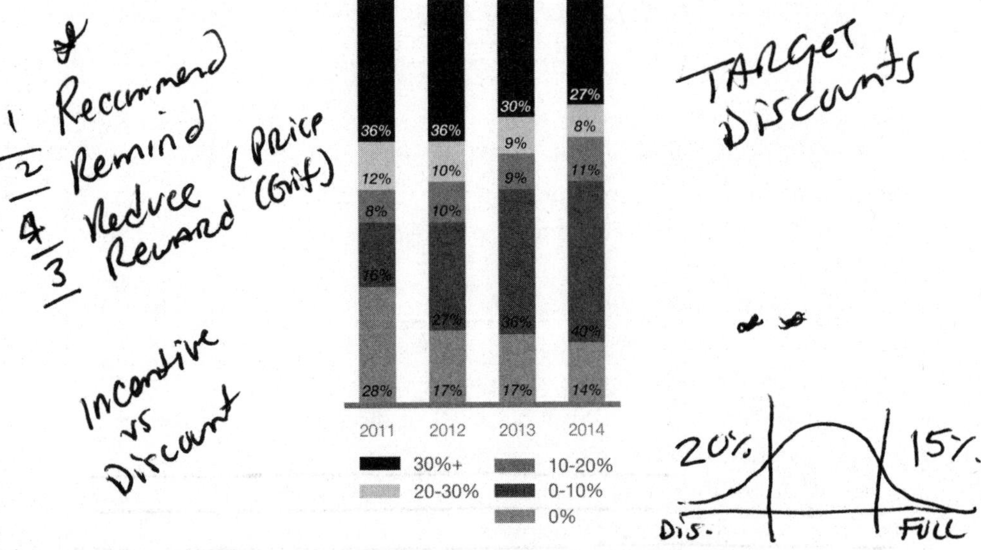

Figure 9.1 Percentage Customers Acquired with Discounts

to reduce the number of customers lured by high discounts from 36 percent to 27 percent, well below the industry average of 31 percent.

Discounts and other incentives can still be used as a sweetener in necessary cases, such as targeting a customer who has abandoned her cart. However, we recommend you do not give out discounts to everybody or else you will train your customers to get used to discounts. Instead, start with recommendations and reminders and use discounts only if you need them. The lack of understanding of the individual customer leads to blanket discounts, which reduces overall profit margins considerably. Only about 20 percent of customers are "discount junkies," people who will only make purchases when given a discount, according to an analysis of 150 retailers. About 15 percent generally pay full price for most of their products, while the majority of customers fall somewhere in between, the data show. By analyzing their customers' behavior, marketers can determine which customers may need more encouragement in the form of a gift or discount. It can also help marketers flag customers who will come back and buy anyway, so no additional monetary encouragement is needed. This model helps to maximize both revenue and profitability from each member of your customer base.

Targeting discounts is good for business and good for customers. By surgically targeting discounts, retailers avoid margin erosion, which in turn reduces the price increases retailers would normally have to take to make up for the lower profit margins. That practice effectively lowers prices for all customers. This is a simple but very powerful paradigm shift for marketers who traditionally focus on product lines, merchandising, and one-size-fits-all discounting. Behavioral and life cycle data available at the customer level combined with the predictive insight about likelihood to buy allows marketers to surgically discount to maximize margin and customer lifetime value.

Also, if you are going to include an incentive or discount to acquire, retain, or reactivate a customer, there is no need to go beyond the level of discount that customers are used to seeing. Predictive analytics allows you to tailor offers based on what level of discount triggered past customer purchases. Customers with a high likelihood to buy may get a lower discount but perhaps other perks such as early access to products to drive more purchases. Customers with a low likelihood to buy or those who only buy on discount (a behavior-based cluster) might get a higher discount.

A multichannel retailer of sports goods used to send all of its customers a 50 percent clearance discount at set times during the year. This campaign was motivated by its desire to clear old inventory. In other words, it was a product or merchandising-centric campaign, not a customer-centric campaign. This campaign trained customers to wait for the big annual sale and brought in few dollars for the retailer. Using predictive analytics, this company analyzed the likelihood to buy and discount sensitivity of all of its customers. If a customer is likely to buy with an offer of 25 percent off, you don't need to give them a 50 percent discount. Using predictive analytics, the retailer identified the right discount level for different groups of customers. Now the retailer still sends discount emails at set times, but it will send different levels of discounts to different groups of customers. It sends just enough to get the customer to buy, but not too much to give away unnecessary margin. Using this approach the retailer was able to achieve an overall increase in revenues of 20 percent.

Predictive Lead Scoring for Business Marketers

If you are in business marketing you can equally prioritize your investment using likelihood to buy models. You can ensure that your sales team spends most of their time with the prospects that have the highest likelihood to become buyers. This can have an enormous impact.

Consider the following example in marketing business software. Let's say you have a free trial for your software. Not all people who sign up for your free service have a serious intent to buy. It is not uncommon that 70 percent of free-trial signups are made just out of curiosity without an immediate need or budget to buy. Another 20 percent are serious evaluators and 10 percent are on the fence: they could go either way. If you randomly call people from a list, perhaps based on company size, it is easy to see how you may end up wasting your entire day on prospects that aren't serious. It is especially important to prioritize your time if you are serving small- and medium-size businesses, of which there may be millions.

The main difference between predicting likelihood to buy in consumer and business marketing is due to the nature of the purchase decision process. In most business marketing, the decision process is long and complex. Figure 9.2 compares the considered and quick decision processes.

With a considered purchase, which most business marketing falls under, the decision process is longer and includes many interactions between the marketer and the buyer. This requires special attention to focus on all prospects within the decision funnel. Hence business marketers turn to all interactions and signals from prospects to determine who is most likely to buy and therefore worthy of time and attention.

Because the replacement and delivery cycles for vendors, deals, services, and products can take a long time, most B2B marketers are hyperfocused on acquiring new customers, rather than getting existing customers to come back, where likelihood to buy first purchase models take greater importance.

	Considered	**Quick Decision**
Decision Cycle	6 months	1–7 days
Interactions during sales cycle	10	2
Average order value	$30,000	$200
Replacement cycle	1 year	1 month
Users impacted	Many	1
Functionality	Complex	Simple

Figure 9.2 Considered versus Quick Decisions

Basic	Point system: Each activity has specific points and these are added to create a score, which becomes the lead score. The score for each activity is arbitrarily determined. For example, a document download is 5 points and an email click is 1 point.
RFM-like	This is similar to Recency-Frequency-Monetary (RFM) scoring used in catalog marketing, where the leads get a composite score based on not only activity, but also size of the opportunity, deal size, and engagement metrics such as email opens, web visits, webinar attendance, and so on.
Predictive lead scoring	Predictive lead scoring builds on the first two basic models by learning from the past in a statistical manner. The predictive model learns from successful deals closed in the past and looks at the prospect behavior prior to deal closing and learns from those behaviors to help come to a decision.
Next action scoring	The best models not only predict a lead score but also the next action that could increase the overall likelihood of closing the deal. These are highly complex models that are mostly custom-built. However, these models take into account specific sequences of events rather than mere event occurrences.

Figure 9.3 Lead Scoring Methods for Business Marketers

Predictive models are not the only way to prioritize prospects for business marketers. However, predictive models are by far the most accurate and relatively easy to use. Figure 9.3 gives an overview of lead scoring methods beyond predictive methods.

Likelihood to Engage Models

Likelihood to engage models predict how likely it is that a customer will open or click on your emails. High email engagement is a strong predictor of buying intend. On the other hand, if likelihood to engage is low, subscribers may opt out from your list. Many consumers no longer bother to unsubscribe from your list, but simply stop opening your emails. For all intents and purposes this has the same effect, and cost, as a true opt out. When a customer unsubscribes from your mailing list, you will no longer be able to reach this consumer with promotions. Every retail marketer knows that email campaigns mean sales and cash for the retailer: with every promotional email sent out, new orders flood in. Email marketing works well to drive revenues. However, when it comes to email, you need to balance the short-term revenues it can yield, with long-term revenues. If you send too many emails, you may receive short-term revenues from some customers, but lose the long-term revenues of those who unsubscribe.

The challenge for most marketers is to send as many emails as possible in order to generate as much engagement and purchases as possible, without causing a subscriber to opt out or ignore you. By using a likelihood to engage model, you can potentially send fewer emails to each customer, drastically lower unsubscribe rates, and achieve higher customer engagement. If a customer isn't going to open an email, there is no point in sending it. That email may seem free, but in reality opt outs cost big bucks. In fact, our research shows that every opt out costs your company about 60 percent of that customer's future lifetime value. Let's say a customer's future lifetime value is $1,000, because you expect that customer to make 10 purchases of $100 each over the course of the next three years. Now if this customer unsubscribes from your email list, they will not be notified about new product offerings. Without an email to remind them, they may place only four orders, instead of 10, over the next three years. In other words, their potential future lifetime value just went down from $1,000 to $400—a reduction of 60 percent.

When Uncommon Goods, an online retailer of unusual gifts, adjusted its email contact frequency, results were amazing. It was able to lower its unsubscribe rates by 50 percent without hurting sales. It achieved the same results with fewer emails, because the customers were delighted that emails were just with the right frequency, and the frequency adjusted automatically when customers increased their engagement. The key to the Uncommon Goods success was to vary email frequency by customers, depending on their level of engagement and their likelihood to unsubscribe.

In our experience, email subscribers typically fall into five separate groups based on their likelihood to engage: Enthusiasts, Mainstreet, Sleepies, and Phantoms, and one special group, the Newbies. Enthusiasts are the subscribers that have the highest likelihood to open and click your emails. Figure 9.4 summarizes the open and click rates for each of these segments. The click rate of Mainstreet subscribers is about half that of Enthusiasts and a fraction of the open rate of the Enthusiasts. Sleepy subscribers have very low engagement predictions, and Phantom subscribers are ones with virtually no engagement, receiving your emails but rarely opening them. Newbie subscribers are a special group: they are

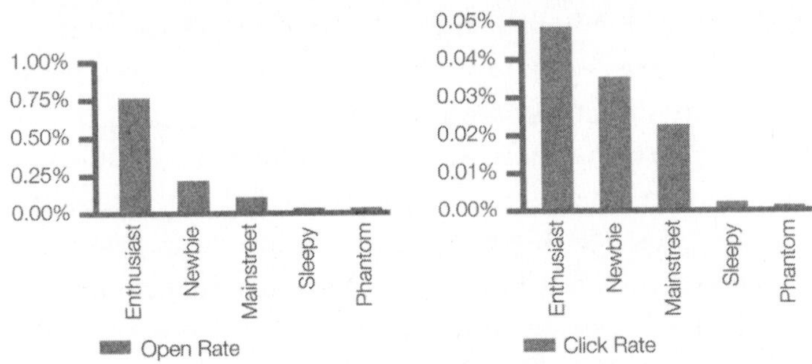

Figure 9.4 Open and Click Rates of Different Email Segments

the ones who have recently signed up for your email list. Their open and click rate tends to lie in between Enthusiasts and Mainstreet subscribers.

We found that email subscribers who most frequently open and click on emails also generate the most money—not because they buy more expensive items but because they buy more frequently. For every $1 spent by email Enthusiasts, Mainstreet subscribers spend $0.58 and Sleepy subscribers, who rarely open email, spend only $0.34. Enthusiasts bought 1.75 times more frequently than Mainstreet customers and 2.9 times more often than Sleepies.

Interestingly, once you get a customer to buy, they buy for a similar dollar value regardless of their engagement level, which can be an opportunity for the savvy marketer: your email enthusiasts already love your brand and buy often. You can try to nudge them toward higher-value products with the right incentives.

Newbies, which are email subscribers who have recently graduated from their email welcome campaign, are very lucrative customers: in our example they spent $1.24 for every $1 spent by Enthusiasts. Newbies also have very high open and click rates. In this respect they can be thought of as "baby Enthusiasts." But they differ from Enthusiasts in one major way: they also have the highest unsubscribe rate of all segments. So Newbies are very engaged yet very reactive: they are opening and clicking your emails but are quick to unsubscribe if they don't like what they see. We usually see that more than 60 percent of unsubscribes from a new email subscription come within the first 90 days of subscription. This is an important takeaway: realize that new subscribers are almost always starting out very enthusiastically. They are basically yours to lose, and almost all behave like your best customers.

Another behavioral difference between different groups of email subscribers is the sales channel mix for the different email engagement segments. Email Enthusiasts buy primarily from email click-through referral. At the other end of the spectrum, email Sleepies buy primarily through search engines or directly on your website (without referral). This suggests different behavior patterns. Customers that are less engaged with your emails are more utilitarian shoppers: they have a need and seek you out (either through a search engine or by coming directly to your website) and then they buy. Customers who are highly engaged with your emails are also strongly influenced by these emails. You might say that they are more impulsive: they might not have planned to buy, but were tempted by your irresistible email!

How Often to Email Your Customers

Finding the correct email cadence is tricky. You are looking to strike a balance between maximizing short-term email click-through revenue (typically by sending more emails) and minimizing long-term loss due to email opt-outs. The answer varies by customer segment: email Enthusiasts may not mind hearing from you every day, whereas those who rarely open your email cannot be emailed more than a couple of times a month. What is at stake is for customers to unsubscribe and the risk of losing future revenues that comes from being able to email relevant offers. As Figure 9.5 illustrates, there is a magical point that optimizes the

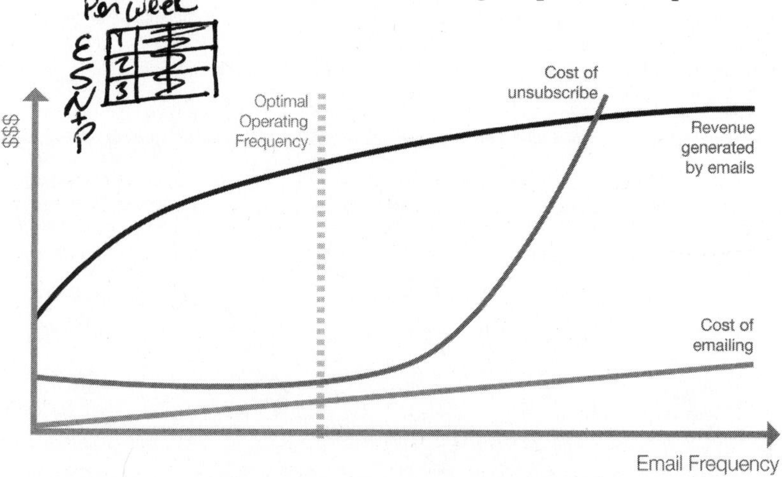

Figure 9.5 How to Balance Short- and Long-Term Email Revenues

net revenue from your email campaigns as deducting the cost of sending as well as the lost, future revenues due to unsubscribes.

So how to find that magical sweet spot? No surprise here: Testing! But be careful because email frequency testing needs to be done right. In order to truly test the effect of reduced frequency, you must design your test to remove other factors that might lead you to wrong conclusions. For example: let's say you typically send two emails per week to your entire contact database. On Mondays you send a "hot deals" email and on Thursdays you send a personalized product recommendation email. Now you want to test a 50 percent reduction in email frequency on a test group. You sample your test group randomly (so far so good) and send them only the Monday email for one month and measure the response. The problem is that the response you get actually measures three confounded factors: (1) reduced frequency, (2) day of the week, (3) email content type.

Instead, we recommend measuring both the cumulative opt-out rate as well as the purchase rate during the test period. Figure 9.6 walks you through the thought process. Purchase rate is defined as the percent of customers in the test group that made any purchase during the test. This is a better sales metrics than purchase dollars, which can be very noisy. The interplay of these two metrics will guide you in your decision whether to reduce frequency or not. The key is to run a reduced email frequency test against a control group: for some of your email

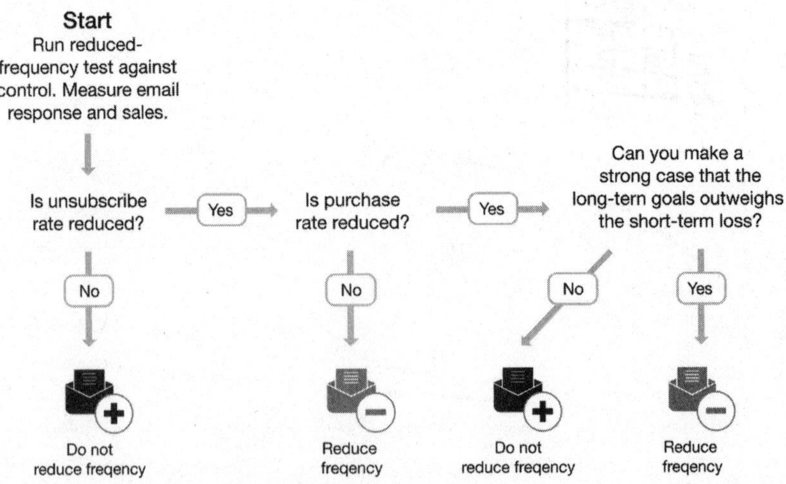

Figure 9.6 When to Reduce Email Frequency

subscribers continue as you usually would. For another group reduce your email frequency by 25 percent or even 50 percent. Run the test for as long as it takes your control group to receive at least 10 emails, but 15 is even better (yes, waiting is painful).

Now compare the two groups and ask yourself: Is the unsubscribe rate for the "reduced email frequency" group lower? If not, you don't need to change anything, because the main incentive to reduce frequency is to reduce unsubscribes. However, if the unsubscribe rate went down, the next question to ask is whether the purchase rate is also reduced. If the unsubscribe rate went down, but the purchase rate is unaffected, then reducing email frequency is a no-brainer. It will give you the same short-term revenue while preserving a lot of future revenue upside (by retaining these people on your email list). If, however, the purchase rate is reduced when you send fewer emails, then you need to ask yourself whether a strong case can be made that the long-term revenue gain outweighs the short-term revenue loss. This is a very hard question to answer—you need to estimate the cost of an unsubscribe in terms of loss of future revenue relative to the short-term email revenue you get per customer from the extra emails you send.

Most marketers err on the side of caution and make decisions based on the short-term revenues. I can't blame them. Fortunately, in our experience, some clients can reduce email frequency by as much as 50 percent without hurting immediate revenues (purchase rate). Reduced frequency may have other benefits: reduced send cost and potential increase in deliverability—but these are secondary considerations only after you convince yourself that you can reduce opt-outs without reducing revenue.

It is possible to reduce the unsubscribe rate without hurting revenues. Figure 9.7 plots the trajectory of one company following this strategy. They were able to maintain the cumulative margin per customer over time, while at the same time reducing the cumulative unsubscribe rate from 1.5 percent to 1.1 percent.

If you want to get started right now with frequency control, rather than waiting for the full test cycle, here are some final recommendations:

Newbies In the first 60 days from opt in do not send regular emails to this segment—only life cycle and triggered emails—Newbies are quick to opt out if they get a lot of nonrelevant emails.

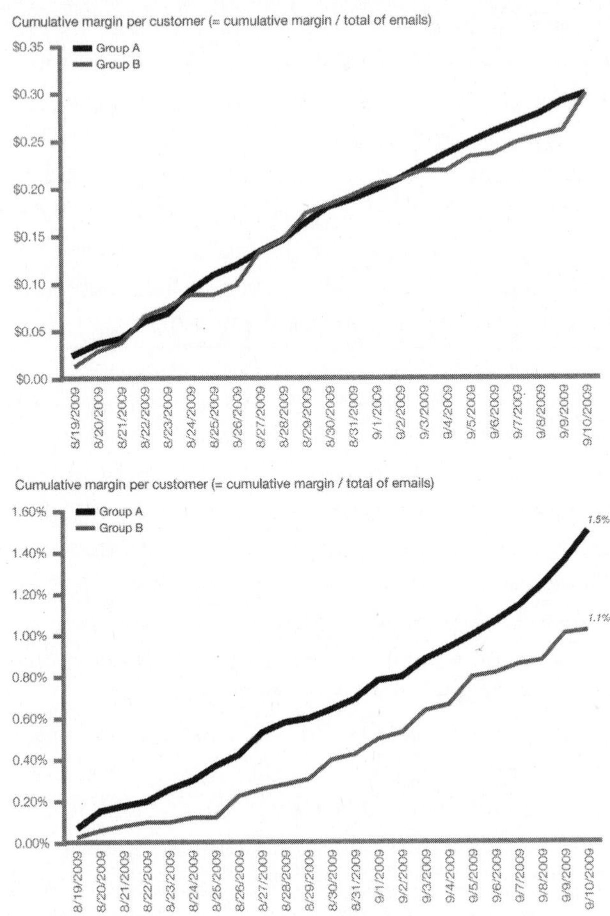

Figure 9.7 Reducing Opt-Outs with Equal Margin Dollars

Phantoms and Sleepies Send general emails at much lower frequency than your normal cadence. Example: if you typically send customers one email a week, this segment should only receive one email a month. If you send three to seven emails a week, they should receive only one a week.

Enthusiasts Do you have the ability to produce additional content? If so, consider sending an extra email to your Enthusiasts to see if you can get them to buy even more.

CHAPTER 10

Play Six: Predict Individual Recommendations for Each Customer

A North American beauty and cosmetics company with hundreds of stores was looking to personalize its communications to hundreds of thousands of customers and ensure that every online interaction between the brand and its customers was consistent with its messaging. It wanted to shift the mind-set from being discount-driven to improving customer service and satisfaction. The company chose to combine cluster-based targeting with personalized recommendations to send customers more strategic, personalized offers. The company first used predictive analytics to organize its customers in product-based clusters such as "bath and beauty" and "face cream." Then it emailed each of these customers content and recommendations that were based on their cluster. Clearly customers liked the emails and the company was able to increase revenues per email by six times.

In this chapter we learn all about making recommendations to customers. Recommender systems have been around for almost 20 years, Amazon being the primary example that started using this early on. There are three parts to making personalized recommendations: sending recommendations to customers at the right time, understanding the context, and sending the right content.

First generation recommender systems used simple rules configured by human beings based on things like keywords or titles. In other words, a merchandiser or content marketer set up a rule so that everybody who bought shoes would get a recommendation for protective spray shortly thereafter: "if browsing for shoes, also recommend spray." These first-generation systems used people, rather then predictive algorithms, to make recommendations.

Especially in categories with large selections, such as books, videos, and content, recommender systems utilizing the so-called wisdom of the crowd are more effective. Actual usage data or review data from users has more information than metadata like title, description, and keywords that describe the content. When we are trying to find a restaurant, book, or a movie, we tend not to trust canned descriptions of the product we are looking to buy. Instead, we ask trusted friends and colleagues what they think. The same logic is used with recommender systems, which can figure out which customers are most similar to an individual user and use behavioral data (usage, reviews, purchases, views, downloads) to recommend other content for that person. This strategy will allow for more relevant recommendations, rather than just trying to recommend products based on certain labels or content. In mathematical terms, these user-based recommendations are called *collaborative filtering*.

Choosing the Right Customer or Segment

The first question to answer is who to make a recommendation to and *when*. Good times to make recommendations are either during a purchase or after a purchase—and at certain times during a customer's life cycle, such as when you have not heard from a customer for a while. These recommendations are referred to as upsell, cross-sell, and next-sell recommendations, respectively.

Recommendations Made at the Time of Purchase

Upsell and cross-sell recommendations can be made to customers *during a* purchase, served on a website's product page, or during checkout.

A basic example of upselling is asking a McDonald's customer if she wants to supersize her meal, but similar instances can be found in all industries. You could suggest a higher-end version or a multipack of the same product, perhaps at a better price. Upsell recommendations are typically tied to a specific product: each product has other suggested products that can be used as upsells.

Cross-sell recommendations are also made at the time of purchase. Rather than recommending buying a larger or better version of a specific product, cross-sell recommendations are made to suggest other products that are typically bought alongside this specific item. The recommendation could read: "customers who bought a printer also tend to buy printer ink ..." and you could offer a modest discount if the customer decides to buy your cross-sell bundle. Like upsell recommendations, cross-sell recommendations also tend to be tied to specific products: every product has suggested products that can be used as cross-sells.

Upsell and cross-sell recommendations are a great way to increase average order value. Most upsell and cross-sell recommendations are tied to the product, rather than to a specific customer.

Of course recommendations do not have to be product recommendations. The online fare comparison engine Kayak developed a price prediction tool to advise the shopper on whether they should buy or wait, depending on the confidence of a price drop. Kayak uses this competitive advantage to improve customer experience and retain customers: "We want [travelers] to get to the best decision for their needs as easily as possible," said Robert Birge, Kayak's chief marketing officer in an interview with *USA Today*. (*Source*: www.usatoday.com/story/travel/flights/2013/01/15/kayak-advice/1834225/.)

The European eyeglass retailer Alain Afflelou revolutionized the optic market by launching the "Tchin Tchin" offer: when the customer bought a pair of corrective glasses, she could buy corrective sunglasses for only 1 additional euro. Used as an acquisition tool, this cross-sell recommendation at the time of the purchase presented limited upsell opportunities but enabled the company to grow its customer base by 50 percentage in three years according to the CEO in an article on the marketing strategies website www.strategies.fr. (*Source*: www.strategies.fr/actualites/marques/155836W/tchin-tchin-alain-afflelou-recidive.html.)

Recommendations Made After a Purchase

Next-sell recommendations are typically made *after* a customer has already made a purchase. This type of recommendation could be included in a thank you page or in the confirmation email.

The best next-sell recommendations are specific for each customer and take into account more customer data than just the most recent transaction. By the time somebody has completed a transaction, you know who this person is and should be able to make a more personalized recommendation. The more you know about a person, the better the recommendation. So if you can analyze all the purchases that a person has made, both online as well as in-store, your recommendations will be more accurate than if you are only looking at online transactions. So, as we discussed in Chapter 3, make sure to base your recommendations on complete customer profiles that tie all customer actions back to the same person.

Remember the home improvement store that found that people who build decks tend to be in the market for a grill shortly thereafter? A marketing program was devised to capitalize on this knowledge. Similarly, the grills company who found customers need wood pellets after their initial purchase of a grill now sends regular pellet replenishment reminders.

Recommendations Made During the Customer Life Cycle

You can try to use recommendations to reengage or reactivate lapsed customers. In this case, first you use predictive analytics to identify a group of customers at risk of leaving. Then you can reengage these customers with a personalized email. The recommendation can be a product, content, or relevant person. The power of recommendations is that they can be dynamically inserted into a web page or email and create an entirely personalized experience without having to redo the creative for each customer. The web page or email design is the same for every customer. Even the text in the page or email could be the same, telling lapsed customers "we miss you, please come back soon, we have these products waiting for you" but include person-specific recommendations.

Be careful using product recommendations if the customer has not bought for a long time. The product recommendations might be obsolete and the context of the customer might have changed completely: it is a new season, the customer might have picked up new hobbies, or life events might have occurred. Make sure you base your dynamic content on the latest information you have on the customer, and in some cases it might be better to use recent content, rather than products, to entice the customer.

Understanding Customer Context

Beyond the right time to send a recommendation, there is more context to take into account when making recommendations. For example, if a user who generally likes documentary movies is trying to find a movie he can watch with his children, the context needs to be recognized and the recommendation made relevant for that context. Likewise, a retailer might recognize that a shopper, who usually purchases work clothes, might this time be shopping for a special occasion and make a contextual recommendation, upselling or cross-selling jewelry and shoes to fit the occasion. Context could also be what products a customer has bought in the past. If you are going to recommend accessories for an electronic device, you better make sure that the accessories are actually compatible with the device the customer has purchased in the past.

Basic recommendations are "people who liked this product, also liked…" type recommendations. We call these *product-to-product recommendations* because a recommendation is generated with a specific product as the starting point or context. This could also be content-to-content or person-to-person type recommendation. By looking at what customers frequently buy or read together, you can make recommendations even if you do not know anything about the person looking at the page. These recommendations are often added to a product page. While you are looking at a specific book, you also see the other books people who bought that book liked. If you are looking at a person's profile on LinkedIn, you may receive recommendations for other profiles to check out. If you are reading an article on your favorite news site, you may be recommended other content to check out.

The problem is that perhaps you have already bought some of the books that are being recommended to you, or read some of the articles that are being displayed. Also, there may be very different personas or clusters considering the same product. If a school teacher and a student both look at the same book, they may have very different reasons or interests in considering the purchase. This is where person-specific recommendations come in. If you also know a customer's demographic profile, past behavior, and location, you have more personal context to make accurate recommendations about companion products. We call these *user-to-product recommendations* because the starting point for making a recommendation is the information you have about a specific person. Person-specific recommendations require you to both recognize the customer as well as have a history with this customer rich enough to generate recommendations.

Making irrelevant or out-of-context recommendations is probably worse than not making any recommendations at all. A well-known Forrester analyst received an email promising her the latest shoes in just her size. She eagerly clicked the email link but was redirected to a page with oversize shoes (rather than her size X). She was so disappointed about the experience that she tweeted about it. A happy customer tells 5 friends, but an unhappy one tells 20! So make sure your customer data is complete and accurate before you start making recommendations based on customer profiles.

Also, have you ever received an email or an advertisement with recommendations specifically for you, only to find that when you clicked on the email or advertisement it took you to a generic web page? Here the retailer is offering the promise of personalization but then does not follow through. The problem here is coordination across channels. Clearly this company's email and web systems are not coordinated. Again, an incomplete personalized experience may deliver more disappointment than delight.

As we mentioned in Chapter 7, the freemium business model relies heavily on the use of relevant and contextual recommendations to transform active users into paying customers. The online music platform Spotify manages to keep a steady ratio of 25 percentage paid to free users (15 million paying users in January 2015), even after the early adopter wave. In an article on TechCrunch the company's top management team explains that their mobile application drives much of this growth. Indeed, in Spotify's mobile free version, users can listen to an artist, but they have to listen to advertisements regularly and they cannot pick a specific song. If they try to do so several times in a row, a recommendation of the premium version at $9.99 per month pops up in the application. Spotify makes sure to emphasize all the advantages of the premium version when the user's frustration reaches its paroxysm! Recommendations in the right context are key to the success of Spotify here. (*Source*: http:// techcrunch.com/2015/01/12/spotify-now-has-15m-paying-users-60m-overall/ and Spotify app.)

Content—What to Recommend

Recommendations, whether for products, people, or content, make for great relevant and personalized content in customer communications. In fact, relevancy trumps the creative quality of the content. In tests comparing the performance of super-creative and meticulously designed emails against the performance of more basic, dynamically created emails with personalized recommendations we found that the click-through rates of more relevant emails are three to four times greater than the click-through rates of the more beautiful emails. Clearly customers preferred relevancy over design—although there is nothing to say you can't have both.

Increasingly, customers are demanding control over the products or content that companies are displaying. Perhaps the most famous example of recommendations gone wrong is when Target began sending baby and pregnancy-focused marketing mailers to customers they had identified with a high likelihood of being pregnant. In one instance, Target was spot-on but the customer had not informed her parents about the pregnancy and thus the recommendation was highly unwelcome and considered a violation of her privacy. We predict that over the next decade, most marketing interactions with the customer will become two-way, where the customer will be able to provide input and gain control over their own data.

This example has practically become synonymous for all that is good and bad about predictive analytics. In response, retailers are trying to give consumers more control over the purchases brands take into account when making recommendations. For instance, you likely don't want that lice shampoo you bought last week to continue generating recommendations going forward. We get back to privacy in Chapter 17 of this book.

As a marketer you want a level of control over the products that will be recommended as well. You don't want your predictive algorithms to recommend products that are out of stock, or very low priced items that are strictly accessories or refills to other products. There are merchandising or exception rules that you should configure before relying on automated algorithms to populate recommendations on your website or emails.

Recommender systems know when a product is new, whether it's gaining traction, or being viewed more or less over time, and are able to adjust recommendations accordingly. For example, when Apple releases a new iPhone, the new model iPhone is viewed less frequently than the old number in absolute numbers because the old phone has been around longer, but because the latest model is new and trending higher, a recommender system will identify it as more relevant when a user searches for an iPhone. Recommender systems take these factors into account and use temporal knowledge to learn and forget, so recommendations are up-to-date and relevant.

Beyond Recommendations

Recommendations are most frequently associated with website personalization. However, you can deliver recommendations in any channel: email, mobile, social, web, phone, or via display advertising. Recommendations thus can be a driving force for both inbound and outbound communications.

At the same time, there are many other ways to personalize an experience—on the website or other—beyond delivering product recommendations. In fact, all the concepts discussed in this book so far, from value-based marketing to life cycle marketing, are opportunities to personalize customer experiences—on the web and others channels. What if you could greet a high-value VIP customer on your website with a special message? Or if you could welcome back a lapsed customer after a long absence. Think what the barista would say if you walk into your local coffee shop after a long absence. Would he say "hey, you are a woman?"—No! Much better would be: "Hi Omer, it has been a long time! I'm so glad to see you back! Can I serve you the usual—a nonfat, decaf latte?" Just addressing customers by their first name alone can have a big impact. A software vendor, Do Inbound, found that simply addressing people by their first names in the thank you page of a walkthrough video increased the conversion rate from the walkthrough video to account sign-up by three times.

CHAPTER 11

Play Seven: Launch Predictive Programs to Convert More Customers

Now it's time to put it all together. In these final three chapters of Part Two we look at a number of strategies and campaigns you can use to deliver value throughout the customer life cycle. First we look at how you can use predictive analytics in order to convert more prospects, and we look at how to use look-alike targeting, a predictive technique in its own right, in combination with clusters and other customer segments to acquire better customers.

Predictive Remarketing Campaigns

Retargeting or remarketing, which are used interchangeably here, enable marketers to reengage people who have previously expressed interest in a brand, product, or service by interactions like visiting the brand's website or reading one of its emails. Retargeting is usually associated with visits to your website, and the subsequent reminder to come back is usually directed at you via display advertising. Remarketing programs work in shorter timescales, in hours or days, because their primary objective is to increase conversions within a specific context created by the consumer.

You probably have experienced these advertisements: after you look at a pair of shoes on Zappos, and after leaving the site, the pair will follow you around the web. Whether you are on your Facebook page or browsing another website—you will often see an advertisement with the specific pair show up in your feed or sidebar.

The trigger of retargeting however does not have to be limited to a visit to your website. It can also be an email you have clicked, a visit to the store, or a call to the help desk. Similarly, the reminder doesn't have to be delivered via display advertising. The reminder can equally come via email or phone call. When channels other than display advertising are used, this marketing technique is usually referred to as *remarketing*. It seems that some channels are more effective than others when it comes to remarketing. A November 2014 survey of 3,000 consumers in the United Kingdom and the United States by research agency Conlumino discovered that 66 percent of American consumers appreciate an email offer related to something they looked at online previously, but only 24 percent appreciate receiving this same offer in the form of an online advertisement. When using remarketing strategies, every marketer needs to consider privacy and the "creepy" factor. This is a very delicate balance that we cover in more detail in Chapter 17.

When customers visit your website, they directly and indirectly share a lot of information about their interests and intents with you. You can analyze not only the number, time, duration, and frequency of their visits, but also look at the search terms used to find your site, the specific pages of your site visited, the items looked at, any on-site searches conducted, and potentially items abandoned in a shopping basket on your site. All of these pieces of information can be used to do personalized outreach to these visitors in follow-up communications to try to bring them back to your company. A simple reminder can often help bring customers back to your site.

If the person you are retargeting has been to your website before, and perhaps has even bought from you before, you have even more information to personalize the reminder. For return visitors you can calculate their likelihood to buy and the clusters that they belong to, among other things. Armed with this information, you can further customize the outreach, increasing your chances of bringing that customer back. For example, if the person who abandoned a search session or a shopping cart is a high-value shopper with a low likelihood to buy, you might as well include a discount to try and get that customer to come back. You have little to lose when the likelihood to buy is low and a lot to gain when the predicted lifetime value is high.

You can reach consumers with retargeting reminders using display advertising, search advertising (Google Remarketing Lists for Search Ads), Facebook advertising (Facebook Custom Audiences), Twitter (Twitter Tailored Audiences), email, direct mail, or phone calls.

You can only retarget consumers if you can recognize them. You could identify a user based on personally identifiable information such as an email address, or a cookie, a small text file that stores information on your hard drive and helps advertisers track you as you move across the web. If all you have is a cookie, then all you can do is target display advertising to follow this user around the web. However, if you can recognize a user's email address, from current or past browsing sessions, then you have better options. You can now target this customer using email, Facebook advertising, or, if you can tie the email to a physical address, even a postcard.

There are some techniques you can use to recognize more anonymous visitors to your website. For example, you can tag and capture a web visitor's email address upon account creation and subsequent login, or tag and capture their email address on any forms that collect emails on the site—the most typical of which are newsletter sign-ups and guest checkout (customers provide an email there for confirmation purposes). A lot of the web traffic comes from email clicks, so a major boost in identification can be gotten when the client includes the user identity in the email links, so that the identity is passed in the URL (either as raw email address or as some encrypted ID) or puts code on the site to parse and decode the user ID from the link. Basically your goal is to capture the identity whenever possible and associate it with the cookie, so you can identify subsequent anonymous sessions by that user. Using these techniques and others, some brands have been able to recognize half of the visitors to their website as compared to the industry average of only 10 percent of known visitors.

Examples of predictive remarketing campaigns follow.

Predictive Abandoned Cart Campaigns

Abandoned cart campaigns consistently rank among those with the highest ROI. The Baymard Institute tracks cart abandonment rate statistics and finds that an average of 68 percent of shopping carts are abandoned on average. Considering this high abandonment rate, all online retailers should have an effective abandoned cart reminder campaign in place. An abandoned cart email sees an average open rate of about 30%, as compared to 14 percentage for broadcast emails. The click rate is about 8% as compared to 1.5 percentage and the revenue per email sent for an abandoned cart campaign in retail is about $2.50 as compared to $0.05.

A January 2015 AgilOne survey among 132 retail-marketing executives revealed that slightly more than half of retailers have completely implemented an abandoned cart campaign. This was up from 39 percent of online sellers in the same survey the year prior.

For most companies and industries, email is the best format for an abandoned cart campaign. For some large-ticket items, a postcard reminder can be effective. When designing your email, don't make it too complicated. Simply remind the potential customers of their abandoned cart and include a link to easily bring them back to their cart or checkout page. You want to get them to the checkout page with as few distractions as possible.

Experiment with timing. Measure the response rate to find out how long after the cart is abandoned to send the message. There are different schools of thought here. Some technology vendors recommend that you send a reminder as soon as possible. However, in our experience, faster is not always better. There are several reasons why you might want to wait a couple of hours, or preferably a full day, to send an abandoned cart campaign. First, some consumers find it creepy that you remind them right away. It strengthens the feeling that you are "watching every move of your customers." That is exactly what most marketers are doing, but you may want to be a bit subtle about it. Second, if you have multiple channels it is very possible that some customers abandon a cart but subsequently buy the item using another channel, for example, your call center. Unless your call center software is synchronized in real time to the system that sends the abandoned cart reminders, you may want to wait a couple of hours. This is especially true if you decide to include a discount in your abandoned cart reminder. Nothing is more disappointing to a customer than to realize they could have gotten a discount on the item they just purchased. Third, if you send a discount offer too quickly you may train your customers to expect a discount every time. If customers can get a discount just by placing an item in a cart and waiting for five minutes then every customer might do this going forward. That would have disastrous effects on your margins. Finally, some shoppers don't appreciate to be bombarded with marketing messages. Whereas they might have bought from you that day, if you contact them one too many times, you might scare them away. As always, it is best to test what works in your situation.

The essence of a predictive abandoned cart campaign, as compared to a regular abandoned cart campaign, is the use of predictive algorithms to differentiate the offer you send to customers. For customers who have a very high likelihood to buy you send a simple reminder. However, for customers with a very low likelihood to buy you can safely include a discount. You have little to lose because these visitors would not purchase otherwise anyway. You can go one step further and differentiate the level of discount based on a customer's historical sensitivity to specific discount levels. Test the impact of different levels of discount or gifts as part of the campaign to determine whether offering a discount can increase your revenue and purchase rates, or if it simply eats into your profit margins.

Predictive Abandoned Search Campaigns

Unlike abandoned cart campaigns, which are somewhat specific to online commerce, search and browse abandonment campaigns apply in all industries. AgilOne research shows that visitors who use a website's search functions are six times more likely to make a purchase than visitors who do not. These visitors are more than just casual browsers. Don't lose these potential customers to competitors. You can set up an abandoned search campaign to remind these customers to return to your site, to give you a try or to get in touch. Abandoned browse emails have open rates very similar, or even higher than, abandoned cart emails, typically in the 30 percent range. Click through rates are about 8 percent. The difference between abandoned cart and abandoned browse tends to be the conversion rate: about 4 percent for abandoned browse and anywhere from 20 to 60 percent for abandoned

cart campaigns. As a result the revenue per email that you can expect from abandoned cart campaigns is about $2.50, but for abandoned browse campaigns it is only $0.50. Of course revenue numbers are highly dependent on your average order value and the numbers quoted are specifically for retail, where the average order value is about $100.

An abandoned on-site search campaign works just like the abandoned cart campaign. If a website visitor is logged in, an email or Facebook advertisement can be sent to the address on file offering recommendations similar to or complementary to the searched for items. If the visitor is not a logged-in user, cookies can be used to retarget them with ads for relevant items.

Abandoned search campaigns also work for people who come to your site using a Google AdWords search. Google AdWords is often one of the most expensive marketing channels. Once you have paid for a potential customer to click through to your site via an AdWords query, it makes sense to do everything possible to convert him or her into a customer. The best part about a visitor coming via AdWords is that you already have a good idea about what she is interested in buying. Similar to the campaigns above, abandoned AdWords searches can be followed up with targeted offers enticing the potential customer to come back to make a purchase.

The same recommendations we discussed for abandoned cart campaigns apply also to abandoned search campaigns, with respect to capturing site visitor information, timing abandonment campaigns, and including an offer based on predictive insights. We recommend you limit yourself to personalized recommendations and a friendly reminder for customers with a very high likelihood to buy and that you include an offer or discount for those with a very low likelihood to buy. As with abandoned cart campaigns, you may want to wait at least 24 hours before sending your reminder or offer, to give customers a chance to complete their purchase first and to avoid training them to wait for discounts.

Predictive Abandoned Browse Campaigns

Even if you do not have on-site search or if a visitor does not use your site's search feature, you still have the potential to collect data through a visitor's browsing history. AgilOne data shows 96 percent of all website visitors leave your site without buying something. Most of these could be targeted with reminder advertisements or emails. Compare this to the number of people who abandon a shopping cart, which is only 8 percent of all website visitors, or the number of visitors who end up buying something, which is on average only 4 percent. In other words, there are 12 times more people you could target with an abandoned browse campaign than with an abandoned cart campaign. For some companies an abandoned browse campaign generates even more revenues than an abandoned cart campaign. Whereas the likelihood to buy is much greater for abandoned cart shoppers, the volume of abandoned browse shoppers can, in some cases, more than make up for that.

When an electronics retailer started to experiment with triggered emails, they first focused on abandoned cart and post-purchase emails. They sent about 3,000 post-purchase recommendations daily to those who had bought something and about 4,000 abandoned cart campaign emails. The campaigns were very successful. Abandoned cart campaigns had an open rate of 55 percent and drove an incremental $10,000 in revenue every day. When this company launched abandoned browse campaigns they were pleasantly surprised that this campaign was even more successful. By comparison, they were able to send 100,000 emails each day! Surprisingly, the emails had an even higher open rate than the abandoned cart campaign, with a whopping 60 percent of recipients opening the offer. This abandoned browse campaign alone drove $40,000 of incremental revenue each day. This is a good example of predictive marketing in action! Full disclosure: the numbers of this example have been changed from the original to obfuscate the company, but the ratios are based on an actual case study.

Needless to say, the same rules apply to abandoned browse campaigns as to abandoned cart and abandoned search. You can make these campaigns even more profitable by differentiating your offer based on likelihood to buy.

Using Look-Alike Targeting

Remarketing only works for known visitors. Remarketing can help you convert more browsers into buyers and get past buyers to come back and buy again. However, remarketing cannot help you find and acquire new consumers for your products, services, or content. This is where look-alike targeting comes in.

Look-alike targeting is a predictive analytics technique to find people who look just like an initial "seed audience." For example, if you feed a look-alike targeting system, such as Facebook's look-alike audiences, a list of your existing customers, it can find you prospects that have the same characteristics as your existing customers. You can now use this "look-alike audience" to launch an advertising campaign. The principle is not limited to customers. You could feed a look-alike targeting system a seed list of people who have liked your Facebook page, and it will go out and find people who have a high likelihood to also "like" your page. You can also use this principle to find audiences that behave like a specific subset of your customers. For example, perhaps you export a list of your best, most valuable customers and then advertise only to those prospects who "look like" your best customers. Or perhaps you define a cluster, which likes leather clothing, and now look for prospects that "look like" your leather cluster so you can target very specific advertising featuring leather-clad models to this look-alike audience.

Figure 11.1 illustrates the concept, using Facebook as an example. Facebook look-alike targeting is increasingly popular, but Facebook is not the only network that gives advertisers the ability to use look-alike audiences. Many advertisers, including Twitter, Google Display Network, and others also offer look-alike audience capabilities.

On Facebook, you start by uploading a specific list of customers to Facebook custom audiences. This can be the list of customers who prefer leather products, or perhaps the list of your best customers. Facebook will now try to match these records to its user database. Matching happens

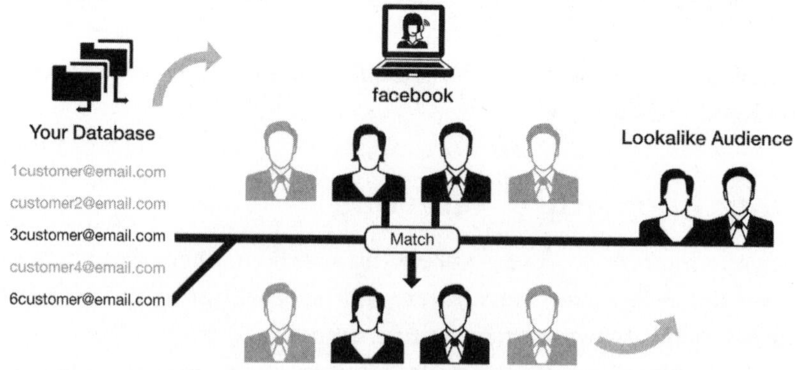

Figure 11.1 Facebook Look-Alike Targeting

based on email address. The list needs to contain at least 100 records that match to a Facebook account. After matching at least 100 users, Facebook now uses their internal algorithms, which also use predictive analytics, to go out and match your segment to other new people in the Facebook database that "look like" your original list.

Look-alike modeling is a powerful tool that enables marketers to go out and target people who have similar traits or behaviors to their existing customers or website visitors. Look-alike algorithms typically need to be fed a list of at least 100 or more existing visitors or customers as a "seed."

Look-alike audiences can be used to support any business objective: targeting people who are similar to sets of customers for fan acquisition, site registration, purchases, and coupon claims, or simply to drive awareness of a brand. It can also be used to find audiences who put an item in the basket of your website but didn't pay for it.

Before using look-alike targeting, make sure your seed audience is clean and well selected or else the look-alike targeting algorithms will not work. Look-alike targeting is only as good as the inputs are. Remember, here, too: garbage in, garbage out. Make sure your seed audience converts really effectively before you expand the seed audience with look-alike targeting. Go for quality before quantity for your seed audience. We recommend that you start with a look-alike campaign that is based on your best customers. These are customers that have bought from you several times and therefore you are sure that these are quality customers.

Optimizing for Similarity or Reach

Marketers can optimize their look-alike campaigns for "similarity" or "reach." When optimizing for similarity, marketers are looking for impressions with tight accuracy—and presumably better results. You could say, for example, "with 90 percent certainty, I know that this person will buy from you." There will be fewer of these customers than customers who have, say, a 60 percent chance to buy from you. When optimizing for "reach" the match is hazier and the ROI lower, but you might acquire more customers overall.

On Facebook, you can choose to optimize your audience for "similarity" or "reach" automatically, or to customize something in between.

When optimized for similarity, a look-alike audience will include the top 1 percent of people in the selected country who are most similar to the seed custom audience. The reach of the new audience will be smaller, but the match will be more precise. When optimized for reach, a look-alike audience will include the top 5 percent of people in the selected country that are similar to the seed custom audience, but with a less precise match. Instead of using the types (explained earlier), you can manually set a ratio value that represents the top x percent of the audience in the selected country. The ratio value should be between 1 percent and 20 percent and should be specified in intervals of 1 percent. A North American Beauty Company used product-based clusters to launch specific look-alike advertising campaigns on Facebook. They first uploaded a list of all existing customers who were part of a bath and body cluster. Then they designed the creative for a Facebook advertising campaign specifically to appeal to this type of bath and body customer. This combination of clustering and look-alike targeting turned out to be highly profitable. For the North American Beauty Company, these campaigns delivered between 2 and 10 times return, when comparing revenues generated to the investment made in Facebook ads.

As said, look-alike targeting works on many other advertising networks, not just Facebook. The mechanisms for selection and purchasing media are similar across networks, and new options become available every year.

CHAPTER 12

Play Eight: Launch Predictive Programs to Grow Customer Value

In this chapter we cover examples of programs that can grow customer value and revenues after the initial purchase. We cover specific campaigns including post-purchase programs, replenishment and repeat purchase programs, new product introductions, and customer appreciation programs, and we take a look at loyalty programs and omni-channel marketing in the age of predictive analytics.

The Secret to Growing Customer Value

The secret to retaining a customer is to start trying to keep the customer the day you acquire her. As we discussed in Chapter 7, the most important concept in marketing is to "give to get." This applies both before and after the purchase. The key to creating customer loyalty is to build value for the customer right from the start of the relationship. This means the customer must have a great experience from the very first interaction.

The initial transaction is just the beginning of a long relationship that needs to be nurtured and developed. Engagement with customers should not stop when you convert a prospect into a buyer. If you are able to convert new customers into happy customers, you can expect future upsell and referral revenues. Expansion revenue—done correctly—can be very high-margin revenue because it's typically lower cost to deliver. Referral revenue, too, can be very high margin. Acquiring new customers through referrals is cheaper, faster, and more effective than through any other means. Referred customers have a shorter sales cycle and a higher conversion rate than other customers.

The concept of growing customer value during the entire customer life cycle, both before and after the initial purchase, is visualized in the expanded customer funnel of Figure 12.1. Remember, it's a lot easier to get more money from a customer who is happy *and already paying you* than it is to get money for the first time from noncustomers. At a high level, the path to customer value is: engagement ==> investment ==> offer ==> conversion ==> rinse and repeat.

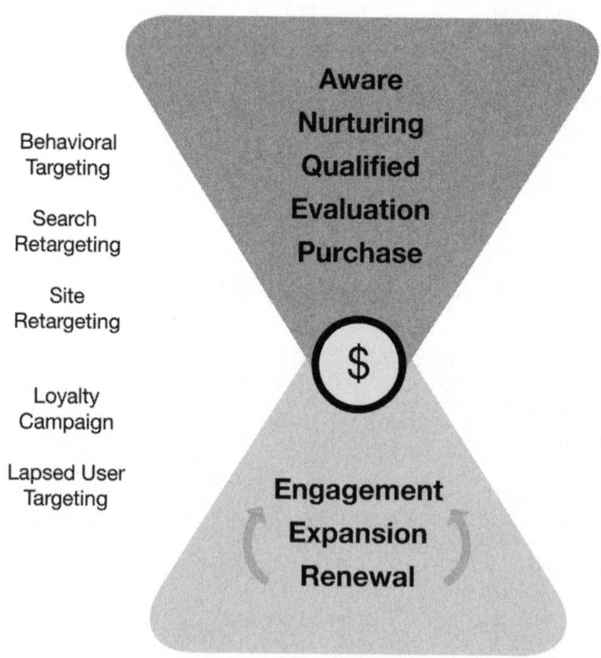

Figure 12.1 The Complete Customer Funnel

Predictive Post-Purchase Programs

One of the programs you can use to grow customer value from the start is a predictive post-purchase program. A post-purchase program is a marketing program triggered by a recent customer purchase. Examples of post-purchase programs are customer welcome campaigns, post-purchase recommendations, replenishment campaigns, and repeat purchase programs. Post-purchase programs are effective since data shows most customers make a follow-on purchase within a short period after a purchase when there is a similar need or the brand is still fresh in the consumer's mind.

Customer Welcome Campaigns

The simplest form of a post-purchase program is a new customer welcome campaign. In retail, our research shows that if a customer buys only once, the chances that they will come back a second time are only 30 percent on average. However, if you can get that customer to buy a second time, the odds increase significantly. Seventy percent of two-time buyers will come back again. This means that marketers need to act quickly to reengage new customers and to get one-time buyers to become two-time buyers. A new customer welcome message—either via email or direct mail—is an easy and effective way to build loyalty with new customers and build on their early excitement to encourage them to make a second purchase. A welcome email can see open rates of 35 percentage or greater and purchase rates greater than 10 percentage. These rates are right in between abandoned cart and abandoned browse campaigns discussed in the previous chapter.

The new customer welcome campaign should thank the new customer, welcome them to your brand, and should include a personalized offer to encourage a subsequent purchase. Free shipping for a limited period of time or a free gift with the next purchase can work well with certain segments of customers. Engaging customers in reviews and sharing with friends and colleagues are also effective ways to start building relationships.

A more sophisticated version of a new customer welcome can involve a series of emails over a period of time. For instance, a company might send welcome, thank you, or follow-up emails one day, one week, and one month after purchase. The optimal timing and messaging of each campaign can vary by company and industry, so be sure test which combinations provide the best results for your company. Introducing them to other categories, additional services, or even uses and care for the product they just bought are all great ways to continue to build relationship with the customer.

Predictive analytics can be used to improve the success of your welcome program. If you can predict the future value of a customer at the time of their first purchase, you can tailor your welcome campaign with personalized offers geared to different segments. For high-potential or high-value buyers, it is worth a lot of money to get them to come back, so you need to carefully craft a set of communications and offers and pay special attention to this segment. These customers expect a higher level of service, and for most brands it is important to differentiate treatment of this segment specifically.

Online services companies—like California-based online home cleaning service company Homejoy—excel at providing best-in-class first experiences and welcome messaging to increase customer loyalty renewal. Homejoy developed a comprehensive welcome program to ensure "100% Satisfaction Guaranteed" and drive people who tested the services to their second booking. The company sends a series of personalized campaigns at key moments in the customer journey: a traditional welcome email right after the first online booking, a text reminder on the customer's mobile phone three days before the appointment, a text with a special service phone number during the appointment, and a feedback email. One month after the appointment, a personalized follow up email is sent with the first name of the client and the name of the house cleaner with a special offer. By using different channels to reach customers, Homejoy goes above and beyond the client's expectations and increases the customer's likelihood to stick to the brand.

Direct mail is also making a comeback for welcome campaigns. Lilly Pulitzer sends oversized postcards on high-quality matte paper to every new customer who bought through their e-commerce site. The creative is personalized using the first name of the customer. Variable printing techniques are now available to allow for text or images to be changed piece by piece without slowing down the printing process. In the case of Lilly, the offer of the welcome campaign is a "present with your next purchase" to get the first-time customer to make that coveted second purchase.

Post-Purchase Recommendations

Not only new customers should get a follow-up message after their purchase. The same is true for any purchase, whether made for a first-time or a returning customer. After each message, send customers a thank you note and use the opportunity to suggest tips to enjoy the new product or service. You can also present them with relevant offers or product recommendations for future purchases at this time. Post-purchase emails are just as successful as welcome emails, and much more successful than any kind of blast message you send. Open rates tend to be over 30 percent and the conversion rate is close to 8 percent.

For consumers, the decision whether to include an offer in the post-purchase message could be based on the value of the customer. You should invest more in getting higher value customers to come back. For business marketing, the post-purchase program should not focus on the next sell, but rather on providing guidance and advice on how to get the most out of their initial purchases. Remember, the customer will only choose to buy more from you if the initial purchase delivers its expected value. Therefore, until business customers have received value from your solution, focus on getting those customers to value, rather than making next sell recommendations.

Replenishment Campaigns and Repeat Purchase Programs

If your company sells products that have an expiration or natural replenishment cycle, such as trash bags or printer toner, send a message to remind your customers to renew or replenish. You may have noticed that Amazon now has a "buy it again" button and prominently features products with short product lifetimes on your personalized homepage. Amazon and other retailers also give shoppers discounts for recurring orders and offer subscription services. Replenishment reminders are among the most powerful marketing programs out there because consumers perceive well-timed reminders as great customer service, and our research shows that purchase rates can be four times that of any other campaign. Replenishment campaigns are the best performing of any life cycle marketing campaign. This means that open rates are between twenty and fifty percent and purchase rates may be as high as thirty percent as well. For many customers, replenishment reminders are a welcome customer service.

Timing really matters when it comes to repeat purchase reminders. There is likely an average repeat purchase time frame for each of the products and services you carry. However, to increase repeat purchase conversion further, you would need to *predict* the repeat purchase window for every customer. Products like packaged food items may be consumed at different rates by different customers, but by tracking the rate of purchase for each customer, you can predict the best time to send reminders for different groups of customers. Replenishment timing can be set in a combination of three ways: manually set by the merchant, wisdom of the crowd looking at average replenishment timing across all customers, or by looking at individual replenishment cycles from the past. Manual and wisdom of the crowd are good approximations but are no substitute for customer level data because customers may use your product at different rates. For example a beauty salon buying a specific shampoo might need to refill every week, whereas a regular consumer only needs a refill for the same item every three months. Therefore, the most successful strategy is to use customer data when available, then resort to wisdom of the crowd, then ultimately manual entry by the merchant, who can make an educated guess.

An international shoe retailer tested replenishment campaigns on its top-selling products. At first glance replenishment fits better with consumables than shoes, but it turns out that shoes wear out at fairly predictable times and loyalists can be persuaded to buy from the brand again. In one such "shoe replenishment campaign" the brand recommended shoes to clients who had purchased exactly 18 months ago, and to a random control group. The open rate of the repurchase email was 5 points higher for the test group, visits to the website per email sent were 15% higher and product views per visit were 19% higher. Replenishment email campaigns proved to be very effective for this brand to create upsell opportunities and to reactivate customers with relevant content. The same retailer sent a successful campaign to parents who bought shoes for their children also, a specific segment with a frequent need for new pairs as they grow up.

New Product Introductions

When companies release new products or features, they often forget to advertise these new products or capabilities to their existing customer base. By using customer segmentation and predictive algorithms, marketers can now predict which of their existing customers would be interested in more niche products or feature introductions. And nothing creates a more compelling reason to buy than new product introductions.

The same strategy can also be used to promote leftover merchandise or broken inventory. Let's say you have only sizes 6 and 12 of a popular dress that has sold out of other sizes. There is no point in sending a promotion for this product to your entire database. However, if you could pinpoint those consumers who are interested in such dresses and wear a size 6 or 12, you have a highly relevant and powerful campaign.

A New York–based publisher wanted to improve the results of its New Releases Newsletters with better targeting. The original segmentation this client used was based on genre preferences that customers declared when they subscribed to the newsletters. The company then created dynamic clusters that were based on the actual purchasing and browsing activity of the subscribers. The question: which will turn out to be more accurate, what consumers *say* they are interested in (preferences), or what they *show* they are interested in through their actions (clusters). It turns out that deciding which genre newsletter to send to whom based on clusters had a two-time better open rate, a four-time better click-through-rate and a seven time higher click through rate than those sent based on the consumers' self-stated preferences. The conclusion: it is equally, if not more, important to observe what people *do* as compared to what they *say*.

Customer Appreciation Campaigns

It is easy to forget your best customers. These best customers can make up a significant portion of revenue and nearly all of your profits. On average, we have seen 60-plus percent of revenue and 90-plus percent of profits come from about 20 percent of customers. We've met some forward-thinking CMO's who focus exclusively on their best customers. These customers are the lifeblood of the company, and there are many things you can do to reward your high-value customers. These rewards don't always have to involve money. For instance, you could give high-value customers a preview of your new collection or invite them to your headquarters for a tour. Likewise, your CEO could recognize them with a personal email, call, or handwritten note, or you could give VIPs access to a special customer service phone number or section of your store.

It might also be wise to recognize these customers more formally such as with a token gift during the holidays. One of our customers had a company event where they had a famous singer give a concert. They also invited their platinum customers to this event. It was exclusive and provided their customers an amazing benefit that money cannot buy. They talked about this in public forums and encouraged other customers to become brand loyalists.

Before you can reward valuable customers, you first need to deeply understand them. Not all valuable customers are created equal. Customers can be loyal in at least four different ways:

1. Customers have been doing business with you for a long *time*.
2. Customers *spend* significantly with your brand.
3. Customers buy from many different categories.
4. Customers *refer* or influence a friend or colleague.

Although all of these customers are valuable, each is loyal in a different way and would require a different program to engage with them.

Similarly, when a retailer of outdoor goods and apparel wanted to better understand its most valuable customers, it used software algorithms to find different types of valuable shopping patterns that people might have missed. It identified four very different high-value personas that all behaved very differently:

1. *Big-big-but-do-not-return*: One group of customers made single, large orders, but never returned to buy more after the initial purchase. This group likes adult outerwear, as well as high-ticket items like tents and strollers. They buy high-end brands and tend to live in wealthier states like New York, California, or New Jersey. These customers tend to be acquired through advertisements featured on vendor websites during busy shopping times such as the holidays.
2. *Reward addict*: The second group of valuable customers has a reasonably large average order value but not as large as the big-big-group. However, this group buys much more frequently, almost once every two months like clockwork. These customers are high revenue but lower margin because they use a lot of rewards points, will not hesitate to return things, and will frequently buy items during clearance

sales. These customers buy from the website and tend to be male, young (30–40), and live in less-populated states. These customers buy outerwear, sleeping bags, tents, and climbing gear.

3. *Old school*: Old-school customers like to buy from stores, come shopping on weekends, and will often buy items on clearance. Old-school buyers have an affinity to the footwear category. They like different brands than other valuable segments, and for the most part live close to the company stores. The old-school customers tend to be acquired first in December through pay per click campaigns.
4. *Fallen from grace*: The last valuable customer segment discovered is called "fallen from grace." This group of customers typically starts out amazing with more than three orders in their first two months and a great average order value that is almost double the average for the company. However, these customers often stop buying after a few months and have a higher propensity to return items.

Once you understand the different types of valuable customers, you can start to design campaigns to keep these segments engaged. For the old-school customer segment, you may want to invest in a direct mail or even clienteling campaign whereby VIP customers receive a postcard or phone call alerting them to new footwear models they might like. For the *Big-big-but-do-not-return* segment, perhaps you can send an annual Christmas gift that is an add-on to their tent or stroller, such as a high-quality water bottle they can take on walks or camping adventures.

Loyalty Programs in the Age of Predictive Analytics

Loyalty programs are designed to turn customers into loyal advocates who support and recommend your brand. Consumer marketers have long used loyalty programs to try to move customers along on the customer loyalty continuum.

Retail loyalty programs evolved when progressive retailers recognized that without a "customer identification tool," they were unable to recognize individual customers and reward them for desired behavior. While retail loyalty programs have many purposes, the greatest value that is created for retailers is this ability to identify individual customers and to measure and understand their individual behaviors. This consumer behavior data far outweighs the currency value of providing consumers the opportunity to build a reward opportunity by shopping at one particular store. This opportunity is often misunderstood.

Bolstered by the initial success, Mavi—the apparel company featured in Chapters 1 and 3—also used predictive analytics to bolster its loyalty program. Mavi implemented a loyalty card as early as 2008. Eighty-five percent of its revenues now runs through this loyalty program, and more than 90 percent of all products bought in the store can be traced back to a specific customer. This is very important to being able to see the complete customer picture. Mavi decided to use loyalty points to try and increase the average order value of a customer's first order. For example, customers spending an average of $100 would receive a message saying "come spend $150 and get extra points." To another group that normally spends $300 it would say, "come spend $400 and get extra points." Not only did the program increase the value of the first order, it also drove repeat visits. Customers now had points to spend and would come for a second visit to do this. Often they would spend more money than they had points for. And the average number of visits per customer increased from 1.2 to 2.1 as a result of this program. The program is so successful that half of the company's discount budget is now allocated to this card program.

Loyalty programs are making a comeback in ways that would not have been possible just a few years ago. First, online purchases and behavior can be tracked even without consumers signing up for formal loyalty programs. Zappos now recognizes VIP customers automatically and greets them accordingly on their website. You don't even have to wait for a VIP customer to spend a lot with you to recognize this group. Thanks to big data and predictive analytics it is only now possible to identify behaviors that point to a customer *becoming* a VIP in the future so you can treat them with white gloves from day one. To identify shoppers in the store, without enrolling them into a formal program, retailers have started to use e-receipts, newsletter signups or free wifi as ways to capture shopper information and later identify shoppers in the store.

Second, the days of one-size-fits-all loyalty programs are rapidly coming to an end. Instead of offering the same incentives to all customers, offers can and should now be customized on a person-by-person basis.

As the Mavi example showed, the best loyalty programs are tailored to drive specific actions from specific customers.

Third, although loyalty programs have historically focused on rewarding purchases of goods or services, marketers are increasingly looking to reward behaviors that they know will eventually lead to sales. For instance, the rewards program of online flash sale site Gilt awards points to customers who are browsing its website, referring friends, or connecting to its Facebook Timeline because it found that more browsing almost always leads to more buying. (*Source:* Gilt.com website Insider Program.) In a way, loyalty is both influencing and influenced by customer engagement. More engaged customers certainly means more loyal customers.

An example of a creative and modern loyalty program is the PowerUp Rewards™ program of the company GameStop, which sells new and pre-owned game consoles and software and is expanding into mobile devices. PowerUp Rewards members receive many perks that aren't "points," such as pre-owned promotional and trade programs, exclusive midnight launch deals, consumer electronics specials, and great prizes to solidify the company's position as the destination for all things gaming. Members are also automatically entered into monthly Epic Reward Giveaways™ when they make a transaction with GameStop. Epic Reward Giveaways are unique and exciting once-in-a-lifetime experiences that GameStop created based on their strong relationships with gaming publishers and other entertainment partners. GameStop hosted more than 5,000 PowerUp Rewards members at their second annual GameStop Expo in Las Vegas. With more than 200,000 square feet of video gaming excitement and innovation, customers experienced the features of the new Microsoft Xbox One and Sony PlayStation4 consoles before they launched, played the hottest new video games, entered to win great prizes, and met with top video game publishers and other celebrity guests.

Just three years since launch, the PowerUp Rewards program had 27 million members in the PowerUp Rewards program, approximately 7 million of which were paid members. The program's paid memberships may also include a subscription to *Game Informer* magazine, additional discounts on pre-owned merchandise in stores, and additional credit on trade-ins of pre-owned products. *Game Informer* digital edition has grown to over 3 million subscribers across 15 countries worldwide, making it the largest digital magazine in the world.

The program has been very successful for GameStop. PowerUp Rewards members shop with GameStop approximately 5 times more often than nonmembers, accounting for 71% of total U.S. purchases in 2013. Also, the consumer data that GameStop collects through the program allows them to make informed strategic decisions about anything from real estate selection, marketing programs, and efficient product purchasing decisions (*Source:* GameStop 2013 Annual Report.)

A Word about Omni-Channel Marketing

A growing percentage of shoppers engage with you using multiple channels, and many shoppers migrate from one channel to another over their lifetime to become multichannel shoppers. At least twenty-eight percent of shoppers who first buy online migrate to also buy in the store over time, and twenty-two percent of those who start in the store migrate to also buy online. These percentages are likely grossly understated as most marketers still struggle to identify in-store shoppers. Omni-channel behavior represents a special challenge and opportunity for marketers. As we discussed in Chapter 3, the challenge is to create truly complete customer profiles. The opportunity is to use customer data to drive in-store customers online and online shoppers into your stores. Also, when it comes to predicting customer lifetime value, the number of channels customers use is always a very important predictive variable, given everything else left constant.

The role of your various channels isn't always obvious. Let's look again at the example of GameStop. Rated as one of the top 25 retailers (ComScore Data), GameStop.com brings virtual store shelves to more than 9 million unique visitors to the site each month. Initially it was looking at its website as a source of direct e-commerce and revenues. However it turned out that more than 60% of store shoppers visit the GameStop web or mobile sites prior to making a purchase inside the stores, and for every $1 of online sales, the web and mobile channels influence ten times that amount in their stores. The company has launched other innovative omni-channel experiences as well that drive customer loyalty. The GameStop web-in-store service guarantees every game is in stock by giving customers the choice to order any product online while in a store and have it shipped directly to them for no charge. The pick-up@store service allows customers to shop for games, systems, and accessories online and pick them up at their local store (*Source:* GameStop 2013 Annual Report.)

As long as you have the physical address of a customer in your database, you can use direct mail, email, web, or social campaigns to alert all your customers, online and offline, to new store openings, in-store events, or in-store promotions. A company that used this strategy successfully is 100% Pure, an organic cosmetics brand founded in 2005 as an online-only store and has since grown rapidly to 12 stores in three states. Last year the company sold more than 7 million products. This company's marketing team is small. 100% Pure interacts with customers across multiple channels, but its web sales account for nearly half its total business.

100% Pure used predictive marketing to promote its brand across channels: using customer data from its online store, 100% Pure was able to analyze every region in the United States to determine where most of its customers were located. It found that most customers were located in California, followed by New York, Florida, and Texas. This helped the company decipher where to open its next seven stores.

Once it opened the new stores, it needed a way to drive online customers into the stores. Using predictive analytics models, it targeted existing customers with a high propensity to buy with direct mail to drive traffic to its nearest stores. The company saw a revenue lift of 163 percent. For one specific store grand opening, the company sent invitations to select customers who lived within a 50-mile radius of the store and that it had identified as having a greater propensity to buy and a high lifetime value. It then sent an email reminder to those customers two days before the opening. The store saw sales increase seven times its average daily sales.

One of 100% Pure's greatest success stories with predictive marketing was a campaign around its best-selling coffee bean eye cream. Because the product is a 60-day supply, the company used AgilOne to trigger an email at 45 days to invite the customer to repurchase the item online or in store. The company saw a 200 percent average sales lift.

CHAPTER 13

Play Nine: Launch Predictive Programs to Retain More Customers

In this chapter, we will look closer at the definition of loyalty and churn, and cover specific customer retention strategies including customer appreciation campaigns, proactive and reactive churn management, and customer reactivation campaigns.

Understanding Your Retention Rate

The retention rate of your customers is defined as the percentage of customers that you retain during the measurement period. There are at least two ways to measure retention: you can focus on the percentage of customers you retain or on the percentage of dollars you retain. We recommend you focus on dollar value retention. This overcomes the challenge of having great retention metrics at a customer count level and still having an unhealthy business. The way you do this is by understanding the retention rate of your customers by value segment they belong to, as described in Chapter 8.

The Concept of Negative Churn

Negative churn is the concept of growing revenue from existing customers at a rate faster than the rate at which other customers stop buying your products or services.

When customers stop buying your products and can no longer be counted as customers, it's easy to think that the lost revenue will have to be replaced with sales from new customers and just focus on acquiring new customers. However, that approach doesn't take the whole picture into account. What you should really be looking at is the total value of all revenue going in and out of your business, rather than the number of customers you are gaining and losing. That's because certain customers could be generating more revenue by buying more products and using more of your services, boosting total revenue above the amount of lost revenue from lapsed customers.

To get to the concept of negative churn we have to move from counting the number of customers that leave us to counting the number of dollars that leave. You may lose some customers (and the revenue dollars that come with those lost customers), but if you do your job well you will gain many expansion or repeat revenue dollars from other, more loyal customers.

For example, if you lose $100 through customer attrition and nonrenewals, but you gain $150 for the same period or cohort through expansion revenue (upsells, cross-sells, higher usage, etc.) you have *negative* (net) churn of $50. On a customer-basis (but still considering revenue), if out of 100 customers you lose 10 (gross), but you are able to upsell, cross-sell, or drive additional usage from the 90 customers that are still there, allowing you to generate more revenue from the 90 than you did the original 100, you have a negative churn rate.

When a company is in early stages of growth with just a few million dollars in revenue, customer churn is not necessarily a big concern. It seems easy to replace customer revenue with new customers. However, as revenue grows, replacing revenue lost to churn often means tens of millions of dollars that need to come from new customers. The benefit of focusing early on customer retention and achieving negative churn (when upsell revenue is greater than lost revenue) is that the revenue from your existing customers compounds over time just like retirement savings.

Understanding Your Business Model

Some industries have inherently higher retention rates than others. In retail, retention rates tend to be very low, typically well below 30 percent. In automotive, no more than 40 percent of buyers ever purchase the same car on two successive occasions. In industries where the relationship between the customer and the firm is more complex, such as in business software or banking, retention rates can be well above 90 percent. It is no surprise then that the retail industry has been an early adopter of predictive marketing, in a quest to increase customer loyalty and customer lifetime value.

Figure 13.1 outlines some of the different marketing environments created by different business models. These environments have different requirements for customer programs, due to their unique nature of their products, supply chain, selling models, and customer decision cycles. For example repeat purchase and replenishment campaigns are more important for those products that have a short product lifetime and/or a short product replacement cycle.

Type of Business	Typical Industries	# SKUs	SKU Replacement Cycle	Product Usage Lifetime	Margin
Fashion	Electronics, apparel	High (1,000+)	Short	Medium (1–3 years)	Varied (10%–60%)
Replenishment/ Versioned	Food, drug, cosmetics, CPG	Low-Medium (50–2,000)	Medium	Short (<6 years)	High (35%–65%)
Considered	White goods, auto	Low (10–50)	Medium	Very Long (>5 years)	Low-Medium (15%–-35%)
Subscription	Subscription consumer services, home services	Very low (<10)	Low	Medium	High
Basics	Books, electrical tools	Medium	Low	Medium	Low

Figure 13.1 Business Models

Not All Churn Is Created Equal

When measuring customer retention, it is important to realize that not all churn is created equal. For example, churn on new customers is always higher than it is for customers who have already proven to be loyal and who have come back to do business with you more than once. It is important to understand these differences. Let's look at an example. You are the head of marketing for a hypothetical golf course called GolfGear. Your CEO has read some industry reports and shows you the following data: The churn rate of GolfGear is 15 percent as compared to 5 percent for competitors. She then adds that even though GolfGear's growth rate is satisfactory, retention rates are dismal.

Although this seems to make sense on the surface, the reality can be more nuanced. It turns out the retention rates of GolfGear are exactly in line with the industry average. However, because GolfGear is growing so quickly, a relatively larger percentage of the customer population is brand new. Because churn on new customers tends to be much higher than on older customers, the aggregate retention rate for GolfGear is lower (see Figure 13.2).

You could dig in a little deeper. When you are losing customers, who are you losing? Not all churn is equally bad. All brands have unprofitable customers. Losing an unprofitable customer is not nearly as bad as losing one of your best customers. Let us look at a large retailer. The retailer is experiencing a decline in the number of active customers and a decline in revenues (see Figure 13.3).

To truly understand the root cause for the decline this retailer decided to look at the churn by customer value segment (see Figure 13.4). The overall churn rate observed was 22 percent, but it turns out that the retailer is losing lower lifetime value customers. Churn is highest among those customers spending less than $1,000 at 34 percent. For customers

GolfGear			Competition		
Tenure	**Population (%)**	**Churn Rate (%)**	**Tenure**	**Population (%)**	**Churn Rate (%)**
0–4 months	30%	30%	**0–4 months**	5%	30%
5–12 months	25%	10%	**5–12 months**	10%	10%
1–2 years	40%	5%	**1–2 years**	50%	5%
3+ years	5%	2%	**3+ years**	35%	2%

Figure 13.2 Example of GolfGear Churn Rate Details

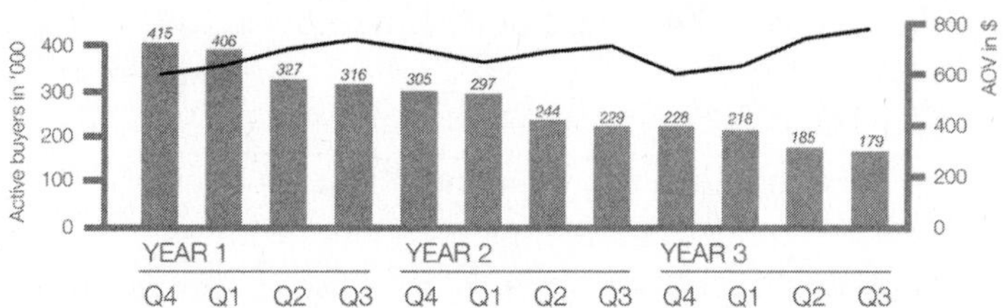

Figure 13.3 Declining Customer Count, but Increasing Aov

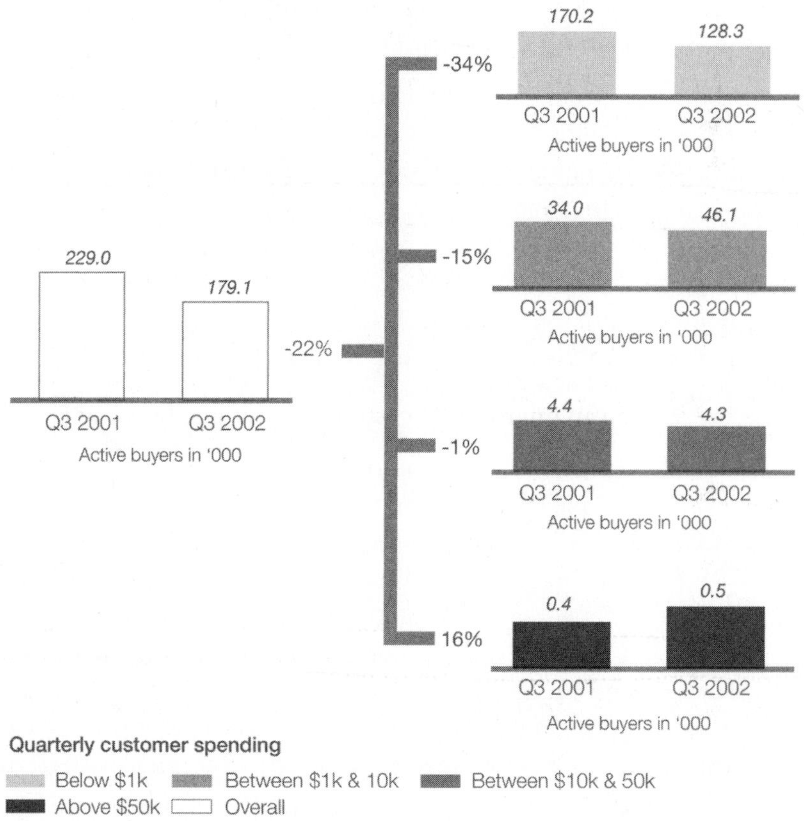

Figure 13.4 Decline in Low-Value, Not High-Value Customers

spending between $1,000 and $10,000 the churn rate is significantly lower, namely 15 percent. For medium-to-large spenders between $10,000 and $50,000, the customer base is fairly stable with a small decline of 1 percent. However, it turns out that this retailer is succeeding in attracting 16 percent more big spenders, who spend more than $50,000 with the company, which is 50 times more than the lowest value segment. As a result, this retailer may very well be increasing its profitability even though the number of active customers is declining and its revenue is decreasing.

Value Migration Is Also Churn

As we outlined in Chapter 8, you do not need to actually lose customers to lose money. The most overlooked aspect of churn is value migration. Value migration happens when customers spend less money with you in a given year than they did in the previous year.

Let's look at the example of a retail bank. This bank was measuring customer gains and customer churn year over year and found that both were stable over time with a growth rate of 5 percent and a churn rate of 4.1 percent. Yet this bank was experiencing a significant decline in revenue. It turns out that the average balance held in the bank by its 2 million customers was declining at 2 percent each year.

The management of this bank initially pressured the marketing team to focus on improving customer churn. However, a simple profitability analysis found that the effect of value migration, in the form of declining bank balances, was much greater than the impact of customer churn. In fact, of the lost revenue due to value, migration was three times larger than the lost revenue due to account closings. Once they understood the reasons behind the decline in revenues, the bank could take steps to turn the situation around. It focused the team on combatting value migration, not just account closings, and created a separate customer segment to monitor the behavior of the declining segment.

Churn Management Programs

Churn management programs can be untargeted, applying equally to all your customers, or targeted. Churn management can also be reactive or proactive. Untargeted churn management could be making general

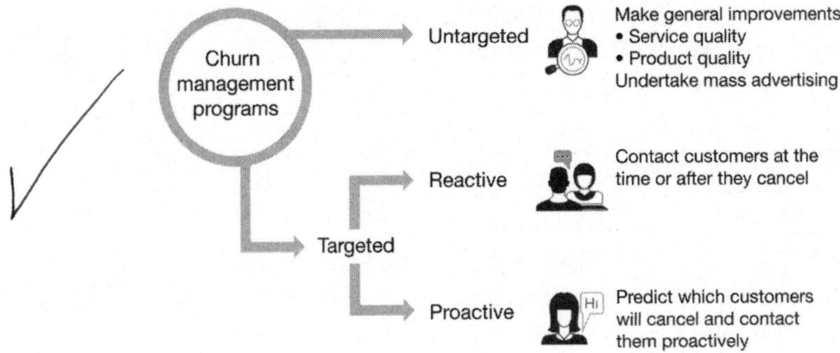

Figure 13.5 Overview of Churn Management Programs

improvements to service or product quality or undertaking a mass advertising campaign. Targeted churn programs can be reactive, triggered by a customer canceling their service, for example, and proactive, based on predictions of customers at risk (see Figure 13.5). Another name for proactive churn management is retention management.

The advantage of reactive churn management is that you only incur a cost for customers who are actually churning. The downside is that you may be too late. The advantage of proactive churn management is that you will likely save more customers because you reach customers *before* they have made their final decision to leave you. The downside is that you may train your customers to always be looking for deals.

Proactive Retention Management

It is much easier, cheaper, and more effective to try and prevent a customer from leaving than it is to save a customer last-minute or to reactivate that customer after she has already stopped shopping with you.

Central Desktop helps people work together in ways they never imagined possible through its web-based collaboration platform. Usage data was stored in disparate systems, making it difficult to identify customers who weren't fully using the software. Central Desktop's services team needed early visibility into thousands of accounts at a time so they could proactively reach out to those at-risk customers.

Mark Fordham, vice president of services, and Katie Gaston, community and operations manager, led the charge in implementing technology to uncover customer insights and become increasingly forward-thinking as a department. First, they pinpointed key indicators of accounts at risk of unsubscribing. For example, they uncovered five key features that indicate customer "stickiness" and retention. Customers who use at least two of these five key features turned out to have a 40 percent higher retention rate than customers who use none or only one of these features. Central Desktop now proactively promotes these specific product capabilities to all customers from day one to increase retention. Additionally, Central Desktop is now able to send highly targeted and personalized emails to the specific users who haven't used all capabilities of the company's collaboration tool.

Ultimately, predictive analytics combined with proactive customer outreach has proven to be a winning strategy for Central Desktop: its overall churn rate went down by *10 percentage points* in just more than one year. Predictive models can indicate which customers and contacts have a low likelihood to make a future purchase. Predictive models can also flag customers who are abusing the system. Rather than just letting these customers go, you can use preventative touch campaigns to check in with customers at risk. In consumer marketing that could mean sending a simple reminder, a relevant or compelling offer—a personalized recommendation, a discount, a gift, or an invitation to an upcoming sale or event. An example of a preventative touch campaign could be sending contacts with a low likelihood to buy but a high predicted lifetime value (LTV) an offer for 20 percent off their next purchase.

In business marketing, proactive retention management can be as simple as giving the customer a call at the right time to offer help. Let's say you are a vendor of online software. There could be many reasons that customers are disengaging. Perhaps the primary end user has left and the new team doesn't understand the value of the software, or doesn't know how to use it. Perhaps your customer is experiencing performance issues with your software but hasn't taken steps to call you for help. Perhaps the customer has a feature request. There are a thousand reasons, many of which are preventable and solvable, that a customer is dissatisfied. The problem is that customers may not always realize their problems are solvable, and you may not realize when customers have a problem.

If you use predictive analytics, you can watch for early warning signs that a customer is unhappy and check in accordingly. Warning signals could be declining visits to your website or email opens, or simply declining consumption of your products or services. For software products, if a customer logs fewer usage sessions than usual that could be a sign. By looking at the behavior of thousands of customers who have churned, software algorithms can identify what is common about customer behavior prior to canceling their service and alert you if new customers are exhibiting this concerning behavior. The end result can be magical. Nothing is more delightful for a customer than to receive a proactive call from a customer service representative when they are experiencing trouble. In fact, it is not unusual for these unhappy customers to be so thankful that they turn into lifetime customers once you have resolved their issues.

How Much to Spend to Save Customers?

When it comes to churn management, an important question to ask is what is the maximum dollar value of the retention incentive you can offer for the program to be profitable. How much money you can offer depends on the lifetime value of the at-risk customers, the targeting effectiveness (can you accurately identify the churn rate risk of a specific, target segment), and the program effectiveness (churn rate in a target segment).

Let's look at an example. A recent cellular network failure in a certain region has led to many complaints at your call center. You suspect this is having an impact on churn. You discover that in fact the churn is very high—around 10 percent—among customers who called to complain in the past month. So about 10 percent of customers who called in January ended up churning in February.

These churning customers are very valuable and carry a $250 average lifetime value. So you want to create a proactive program to lower churn among complaining customers. You design a program to call these customers who have recently complained and apologize for poor service. You also offer them a financial incentive to upgrade to a better service the next month. If you know the program can reduce churn from 10 percent to 5 percent, then you could spend up to $12.50 on the retention of each customer.

The general formula to calculate this is:

X = Y (%)∗LTV
X = the money you can spend to try to retain each customer
Y = the percentage of customers that you can save with your campaign
LTV = the lifetime value of each saved customer

The trick is that in real life you don't actually know what Y is, but you can find Y by testing your program at a smaller scale. All you know when you get started is that the maximum improvement in retention is 10 percent (the rate of churn) so the maximum amount of money to spend in this particular case is $25.

The right way to develop a proactive churn management program is to first find customers to proactively target. The way to do this is to develop hypotheses on customer variables that are related to churn. Then you design a test program for these at-risk customers. Make sure to split your target segment in two or more groups, including a holdout group that will not receive a retention incentive. Only testing can ultimately quantify how much churn reduction will result, or what level of redemption will happen on incentives. These learnings can be used to refine the program.

Retention and Share of Wallet

It appears that growing the number of products and services that somebody buys from you may also increase the retention rate of that customer. The more effort the customer invests to tell you about themselves, the greater their stake in making the relationship work. This is a well-known strategy for telecommunications providers. The churn rates on customers who are subscribed only to cable television services is more than double that of customers who buy their television, Internet, and phone service from the same provider, as outlined in a paper titled "Does Service Bundling Reduce Churn?" by Jeffrey Prince and Shane Greenstein (November 2011).

AgilOne data shows that the same principle applies across other industries: retail customers who buy different categories of products from a given brand have higher retention rates than those customers who just buy a single product type. Therefore, all marketers should aim to increase the number of product types customers buy as a proactive retention strategy.

Identifying the Root Cause of Churn

There may be several reasons the customers are not getting the benefit from the product or service they have bought. Identifying the root cause of churn is a best practice when it comes to proactive retention management. Perhaps customers are experiencing product issues: the product frustrates them—poor fit, bugs, data loss, slow performance, irritating user interface. If this is the case, you need to solve the product issues first, or update your merchandising strategy. Perhaps customers are experiencing poor customer service when they call in to get help. Perhaps the customer bought the right product and you are delivering good customer service but they do not know how to use it. In business marketing this often occurs when there is a change in the guard and the new users and sponsors are not familiar with your product.

Whatever the root cause, identifying underlying reasons and improving them can significantly increase your retention rates. Through predictive analytics algorithms you can score each customer's likelihood to churn, as well as identify and rank order the factors that contribute to the churn score.

A consumer services company was able to improve their retention by ten percent through following steps: First, build a model to predict which customers are likely to churn, and score each customer daily using this model. Second, inspect the model to understand factors that drive the churn score and strategize around actions to take. Third, test the effectiveness of different customer treatment methods. Some factors that were driving churn were the number of calls the customer had to make to the call center regarding trouble with their service, equipment, delivery time, and a sensitivity to price. Customers who were vocal about the issues they were having were then called back, treated courteously, and offered a discount on equipment maintenance or on service if they extended their contracts further. For the customers who were sensitive to price, but were longtime, loyal, valuable customers, the company proactively called them a few weeks before their contract ended. The call center representatives discussed their current contract price versus the market rate and worked with the customer to ensure they would extend the price they were comfortable with. Naturally—the amount of effort and discount spent to retain the customers was always proportional to how valuable the customer had been in the past; or if they were a new customer proportional to their predicted lifetime value.

A subscription-based research firm set out to improve retention of their customers. They needed to know the following: Can we predict the probability that a given customer will renew the annual subscription? More over, if a customer is at risk of churning, what are the contributing reasons (e.g., because the customer is not using x, and the firm didn't do y)? Lastly, what levers does the firm have to increase retention for each customer at risk, and which of these are the most cost effective? The company analyzed the interactions between customers and the firm's primary products, such as search activity and the consumption of online research by customers, email and phone conversations with the firm, etc. A major insight was that consistent engagement of the customer with the content was more important than just raw volume of content consumption. So a customer that consumes content in a few big bursts is less likely to renew than a customer who consistently consumes even small amounts of content. The firm now has a consistent effort to engage each customer at least once a month with relevant content. Delivery of relevant content recommendation by automated emails turned out to be a very cost-effective retention lever. These emails utilized automated recommendation engines to push relevant content—for example: a customer who read specific content would get an email with links to related content. Some high-cost levers (such as consultation calls with an expert rep) are very effective retention levers but should only be used for "premium" customers.

Customer Reactivation Campaigns

When a customer leaves you, not all is lost. AgilOne data shows that it is on average 10 times cheaper to reactivate a lapsed customer than it is to acquire a new one. Reactivation programs for lapsed customers therefore are a low-hanging fruit for marketers looking for new revenue streams.

Reactivation campaigns are for customers who have not purchased anything for an extended period of time. Typically, a customer is considered lapsed or lost after she has not spent money with you for twelve months. For subscription services, you can consider a customer lapsed or lost as soon as they let their subscription expire—whether after one month or three years. Lapsed customers can frequently be reactivated with the right offer or product recommendation. Since these customers have essentially been written off and are not expected to make any additional purchases, the most successful reactivation offers are typically fairly generous—such as a significant discount on a next purchase.

One company we work with noticed it had a large amount of customers who once loved the brand but hadn't engaged with the company for a while. It wanted to focus on customer loyalty and engagement by bringing enthusiastic customers back to the brand. The company used its knowledge of the type of products its customers enjoy to send smart product recommendations. These campaigns resulted in an eightfold increase in monthly revenue.

Reactivating customers builds on the investments you have already made and avoids the costs of trying to get new customers. These original customers are already aware of your brand and are more receptive, so reengaging them can lead to gaining significant incremental revenue.

In many measurements we made, most reactivated customers behave like a new customer, that is, they almost restart their life cycle. This also means that the early periods after reactivation are when customers are most vulnerable to lapse again and require special attention.

Reactivation Campaigns in Four Steps

So where do you start with reactivation? First, determine which customers you want to reactivate. Then determine the most receptive candidates, customize your message to this group, and reengage these customers using different channels.

Determine which customers you want to reactivate. Not all past customers may be worth bringing back. Marketers need to carefully determine which customers were profitable, interested in products they want to sell/grow, and other strategic factors. For example, you may want to exclude customers who returned more than 5 percent or had more than 30 percent discounting on their previous orders.

Determine the most receptive candidates. You may only want to approach past clients who are most likely or ready to respond—especially if your reactivation campaign is expensive such as in the case of direct mail or targeted display advertising. Even if you are using email, you probably don't want to send marketing messages to customers who are not ready—otherwise you risk seeming overenthusiastic and drive customers away.

Reengage customers using different channels. The shopping journey spans across many distribution channels. There is no reason your marketing message should not be omni-channel as well. After customizing a message using your customer's past data, try to reach customers at as many points as possible. A greater number of contacts usually correlate to a higher response rate. So don't forget to send that email, postcard, or app notification with personalized offers.

Customize marketing message using past data. Now that you know which lapsed customers are ready to respond, take a look at their purchase history. What have they responded to in the past? What type of products do they buy? What kind of brands do they like? Craft your messages according to their tastes and needs. By looking at past trends, you may be able to figure out why the customer lapsed and use this as an opportunity to address this reason. Perhaps the customer may give you a second chance.

PART 3

How to Become a True Predictive Marketing Ninja

CHAPTER 14

An Easy-to-Use Checklist of Predictive Marketing Capabilities

In order to use the predictive marketing techniques we discussed in this book, you will need to organize your business around the customer and acquire both the mind-set and the enabling technologies for predictive marketing.

Organizational Capabilities for Predictive Marketing

The mind-set shift required for successful predictive marketing includes a shift from campaigns to the customer life cycle, products to customers, siloed to omni-channel approach, and one-size-fits-all approach to contextual marketing programs.

Most marketing organizations are still run based on a calendar of marketing campaigns: an email blast, an event, a direct mail drop, a display advertising campaign, a store opening. As a consumer, you don't care about marketing campaigns. You are one person and you have one, continuous, experience—good or bad—with a brand. The marketing calendar needs to be replaced with the concept of life cycle marketing that tries to maximize lifetime value of customers over their entire engagement with the brand through a series of personalized, triggered campaigns.

Most marketing organizations still operate in silos. You might have an email marketing group, a store marketing team, a web manager, a direct mail manager, and so on—all working with separate vendors and marketing service providers. In many organizations the direct mail group doesn't know what the email group is doing and the email group might not talk to the display group. In the meantime, customers are receiving mixed messages from different channels.

We all have received multiple display ads, emails, and catalogs from the same vendor that were completely uncoordinated. You might have received competing offers from different channels that belong to the same organization. The ads may seem irrelevant and the suggestions for products had nothing to do with what you have purchased before and where you live. To make sure this doesn't happen, many companies are reorganizing their marketing teams around providing customers with a consistent message. They are creating omni-channel task teams and appointing heads of the omni-channel experience. Many companies also use an "integrated campaign planner" for the purpose of cross-functional coordination.

Some companies are starting to organize their marketing team by customer life cycle with a separate team focusing on new, existing, and lapsed customers, for example. Other companies assign marketing teams by customer personas, such as a publisher which organizes around "romance lovers" and "suspense aficionados." Whatever organization structure you choose, focus on the customer and the customer experience.

When Shazam, an online entertainment company, became serious about customer engagement, it decided to dedicate a team to this stage of the life cycle. Early on, Shazam realized that relevant communication keeps customers engaged, a key metric for a consumer marketing company. Shazam focused on understanding the engagement behavior of each of its users, such as how consumers interacted with its mobile application and how their music tastes differed. When Shazam enabled highly personalized engagement programs throughout its email marketing and app experiences, it increased its customer retention by a double-digit percentage in the first month of a new registered user, which is huge when you calculate the compounding effect on customer lifetime value.

By now, most people are pretty fed up with "batch and blast" campaigns where all customers get the same message at the same time. These sorts of campaigns lead to high opt-out rates and lower the efficacy of marketing campaigns. By contrast, precisely targeted campaigns can triple prospect conversion and customer engagement. These types of campaigns take into account the customer's preferences, interests, and propensities to buy so marketers can change their messaging based on the context of each situation.

When moving from batch and blast to more relevant customer experiences, think about these three dimensions for each program, whether triggered or scheduled:

1. Audience: The first and most well understood aspect of segmentation is deciding who is being targeted and why, what is the context? Are you reaching out because the customer has just visited your website, or purchased something in a store, or are you trying to re-connect with a customer you haven't heard from in a while.
2. The frequency of the communication: Part of being relevant is also knowing the right cadence of communication. The right amount of communication with your customer leads to higher engagement and ultimately higher retention. By reducing the frequency of emails to some customers, we have seen that marketers are able to reduce their unsubscribe rates by close to 50 percent.
3. The right content/offer: What is the best content for the customer at any point in time—keeping in mind where the customer is in their journey with you? In some cases, it could be an offer to entice someone to buy something she previously looked at, a reminder to come back or an interesting article related to something the customer is interested in. For instance, a sporting goods retailer now sends out snow reports based on the customer's location to people whom it knows like to buy ski clothes.

Technical Capabilities for Predictive Marketing

Beyond the organization aligned with predictive marketing, you also need to evaluate your technology stack and make sure you have technical capabilities to support predictive marketing. In this chapter, we will look at some of the technical requirements, and in Chapter 15 we will look at some of the options to satisfy these requirements.

The technical capabilities for predictive marketing include the ability to (a) aggregate and integrate customer data, (b) analyze and predict customer needs, and (c) design and execute customer experiences across all customer touch points. We will discuss each of these capabilities in greater detail. Figure 14.1 summarizes these capabilities.

Customer Data Integration

Data integration:

- ☐ Out-of-the-box connectors for ESPs
- ☐ Webtag for capturing key web events
- ☐ Standard integration packages (ERP, etc.)
- ☐ Turnkey Google analytics integration
- ☐ Enterprise grade integration framework

Data quality:

- ☐ Fuzzy Phonetic matching (partial match)
- ☐ Standardization (phone, email, address)
- ☐ Daily de-duping (individual & household)
- ☐ USPS DPV (delivery point verification)/ NCOA (national change of address)
- ☐ Genderization
- ☐ Geo tagging

Predictive Intelligence

Out-of-the-box predictive models:

- ☐ Likelihood-to-buy models
- ☐ Likelihood-to-engage models
- ☐ Clusters (brand, product, behavior)
- ☐ Predicted customer value
- ☐ Product recommendations

Built-in reporting:

- ☐ Turnkey business and marketing reports
- ☐ Turnkey, configurable dashboard
- ☐ Profitability measures (returns, discounts)
- ☐ Revenue opportunity reports (benchmarks)
- ☐ Option to connect data to Tableau, Excel or SQL

Campaign Automation

Campaign execution:

- ☐ Native e-mail execution (or via partners)
- ☐ Native web personalization
- ☐ Social campaigns (Facebook, Twitter, etc.)
- ☐ Offline (direct mail, call center, store)
- ☐ Mobile messaging
- ☐ Online advertising (display ad targeting)
- ☐ Web retargeting

Campaign design:

- ☐ Segmentation and campaign design UI
- ☐ Built-in audiences
- ☐ Built in e-mail creative templates
- ☐ A/B testing (measure results based on $)
- ☐ Measurable hold-out group performance
- ☐ List export (manual and via API)
- ☐ Attribution

Figure 14.1 Checklist of Predictive Marketing Capabilities

Customer Data Integration

In order to segment and target customers, you will need to collect customer data and integrate it into a single customer profile. In Chapter 3, we described the types of customer data you might want to collect and explained that data integration is the process of linking all customer data, including online and offline transactions and engagements, into a single customer data profile.

Many marketers start with just online or offline customer data. However, there are huge benefits to starting out with a view that integrates both online and offline customer behavior because half of all shoppers shop both online and offline. There are also many vendors that can help connect legacy systems like order management and enterprise resource management systems.

Connecting and bringing data together is relatively easy these days; the bigger hurdle is data quality and cleansing. As we discussed in Chapter 3, if you don't link your data you may think you have three unprofitable customers when in reality these purchases add up to one very high value customer. Data cleansing is an ongoing effort, and customer data ideally needs to be reconciled on a daily basis. The average American has three email addresses and moves twelve times in their life, so chances are you have a lot of duplications in your database.

One brand we worked with discovered its customer database was full of duplications, inflating its customer file threefold. Part of the problem was that the company had never integrated data from offline, online, and call-center channels. In addition, a long-term promotion it ran that gave discount to first-time buyers had inflated its customer file since clever consumers signed up with many different names, phones, email addresses. Although it was heartbreaking to see the number of customers decrease, the company now no longer had to waste a lot of money sending three times the amount of promotions to the same people.

Lastly, do not forget to protect any customer data from theft or accidental exposure. Identity theft and credit card breaches are fast-growing crimes, and unfortunately many companies have made headlines of losing customer data in recent years. You do not want to be one of these companies. We will address data protection and privacy in Chapter 17.

Predictive Insights

In Chapter 2 we discussed various predictive analytics models in detail, including propensity models, clustering models, and recommendations. Many technology providers only provide a workbench to *create* predictive models, but some vendors have developed standard models that come out of the box. If models come out of the box, ask what other companies in your industry have used and tested these models and what were the outcomes. Also keep in mind that the predictive analytics process is as much about data preparation as it is about the development, testing, and deployment of algorithms. Either you have to take care of these internally or your service provider or technology provider must do these things for you.

Whereas predictive models allow you to divide your customers into distinct segments, analytics reports will allow you to evaluate the efficacy of the programs you are running and discover new revenue opportunities in your existing customer base.

Reports can highlight opportunities, such as customers at risk of leaving you or a low repeat purchase rate. When a large retailer organized its data, it was surprised to find out how few customers came back to buy a second time. In fact, repeat buyers made up only 17 percent of its customer base. This finding led to discussions at the board level and ultimately to a new, companywide, customer relationship management strategy to entice first-time buyers to come back.

The more data you have, the more questions you will have as well. Make sure that marketers can access customer data instantly, using an easy interface, without the help of IT or professional services resources. For example, perhaps you discover you have a very low retention rate for high-value customers. You might want to perform some root cause analysis to understand this issue. Do these customers buy from different channels or buy different products? Is the return rate on those products higher than average? These are just some of the questions you might want to ask about your business.

Campaign Automation

Ultimately, the rubber hits the road when you, the marketer, design the experiences that deliver value to customers throughout their life cycle. So ask yourself how you are going to design and orchestrate customer experiences across channels and across different stages in the customer life cycle.

Just having insights is not enough. You need to be able to make customer insights available at each customer touch point. This means that customer insights should trigger customer engagement campaigns, preferably in real time or as real time as possible. Customer insights should also be used to personalize dynamic content such as emails or digital advertisements.

Campaign roadmaps, resource allocation, and project management shall not be forgotten in the equation for successful execution. Most marketers underestimate the bandwidth required to develop and automate more targeted campaigns. Make sure to define and assign clearly the different tasks required and phase the project with realistic timelines.

Questions to Ask Predictive Marketing Vendors

The questions you ask about predictive marketing technology will be driven by your business requirements. To help you get started, we've listed some questions that most companies should ask. The questions fall into the same three broad categories we have just discussed: Will you get a complete and accurate picture of your customers? What kinds of analysis will you get, and how can you use it in day-to-day campaigns?

Will I Get a Complete and Accurate Picture of My Customers?

What channels are supported? Different execution channels provide different types of data and require different types of output. Be sure the system can import data from the channels you use today and expect to use tomorrow and that it can feed data back to those channels in the formats they need. Find out if connectors exist for the specific channel systems you have in place and, if not, what's involved in creating them. If you'll need real-time interactions, such as helping to personalize web pages for individual visitors, ask specifically how this is accomplished. Pay particular attention to the support for offline channels such as direct mail, call centers, or in-store purchases.

What types of data are stored within the system? Every system starts with customer profiles. Most can also store transactions.

Systems designed for campaign management will store promotion history and responses. Some will capture different types of unstructured data, such as the contents of web pages visited, topics covered in news articles, sentiments expressed in public comments, and structured information extracted from such sources. Look for the ability to store and reconstruct data that may have changed over time, such as customer status. Ask whether marketers can add new data types and sources for themselves. If you sell to businesses, find out whether data is organized at the individual level, company level, or both.

Where does the system get its data? One source is your own systems. These include marketing automation and customer relationship management (CRM) and can extend to web analytics, email systems, and order processing systems or repositories. Some vendors capture digital behaviors directly through their own tags on web pages and emails. Several scan public web sites, social networks, and other sources for information that identify companies and individuals who are likely to be good prospects for their clients. Vendors may also load reference data about companies and individuals from compiled directories such as Dun & Bradstreet.

How does the system load its data? Most products offer a combination of direct real-time loads via application programming interface (API) calls and batch loads of files extracted from other systems. Real-time updates are essential if you want treatments in every execution system to reflect behaviors in all other channels. Be sure to find out if there are any limits to the volume of data that can be loaded, either in terms of response time (how many simultaneous interactions can the system handle?) or batch volume (will posting large files take many hours or incur high costs?).

Does the system provide data quality and enhancement? It is not enough to simply dump customer data into the system. Find out if the system can automatically cleanse entries (checking for standard formats, fixing misspelled names, and removing profanity), validate information (testing for valid email addresses and mailing addresses, check that the address is not registered as "do not mail" or that the owners have moved, and so on), append likely gender based on first name, geo-tag based on address, enhance consumer records with census data or cluster codes, and enhance business records with company size, industry, parent company, and so on.

How does the system link data that relates to the same customer? Linking related records allows you to remove duplicates and to group members of the same consumer household or business. This is essential to building a complete profile and to prevent multiple offers to the same customer. Linking capabilities vary widely, from sophisticated "fuzzy matching" of similar name/address strings to simply using identifiers provided by your operational systems. Systems may also use external reference data, such as directories of companies and lists of address changes. Ask how much control you will have over matching and householding rules, but bear in mind that most vendors have more sophisticated approaches than users could create for themselves.

What Kinds of Segmentation and Targeting Will I Get?

What kinds of statistical models can the system apply to customer data out of the box? Models may predict responses to a specified offer, recommend what information to present, classify customers into segments, or serve other goals. Systems vary in the types of models they build, the amount of human effort required to build them, whether the system provides its own model-building tools, and in reporting provided to explain model results. Ask whether the models are rules-based (requiring users to define them manually) or statistical (based on truly predictive or automated analysis such as clustering, collaborative filtering, and propensity models). Rules-based models take much more time to research and configure and are often less accurate than statistical methods. Check whether the models are standard or custom and what results other businesses like yours have seen.

What kinds of analytical reporting and dashboards are available? You'll want basic customer profiling, promotion analysis, and segmentation. Some systems offer polished dashboards to highlight trends and current activities. Look for data exploration features such as drill-downs and filters, custom reports in tables and cross-tabulations, data visualization, and trend analysis. Make sure you understand which data is available to the system's reporting tools and whether there are any limits on what can be extracted from the system for use by other tools.

How Easily Can I Take Actions on the Segments or Recommendations?

How does the system help to deliver customer treatments? Some predictive marketing platforms execute marketing treatments directly, most often by sending emails. But they primarily support external execution platforms by delivering data, scores, or decisions. They may do this on-demand via APIs, by allowing direct queries from external systems, or by sending file extracts. Beyond understanding capabilities, it's worth knowing which external systems are already integrated with a predictive marketing platform and what functions those connectors support.

In Addition to the Questions About Features, Ask Yourself Whether This Is the Right Vendor for You

What's the underlying technology? Technical information such as the type of database gives useful hints about likely strengths, weaknesses, and growth potential. You will certainly want to know whether the system is offered as a vendor-operated service in the cloud, as on-premise installed software, or both. Also ask about the scale and nature of existing deployments so you can judge whether your business is likely to make demands the vendor has not previously met.

What's involved in installing and running the system, and how long does it take? By definition, predictive marketing platforms are designed for nontechnical users. But it is still important to understand how the system is set up, how long the initial deployment is likely to take, what is expected of the client and what the vendor will do for you, and what kinds of training and support are available. Judge the skill level and time commitment you will need to operate the system on a day-to-day basis and to make occasional changes such as adding a new data source.

What help is provided to analyze data, segment customers, or run campaigns? The services and resources included in the subscription or license fees vary greatly. Find out which services are available for free and which involve additional charges. Does the vendor provide predefined campaigns or a playbook of recommended actions? Are there ongoing training and tune-up sessions? How many hours or many sessions with a customer success representative are included? Is the customer service staff trained as engineers or marketers? How much experience do they have running campaigns like the ones you are planning?

What will the system cost? Prices may be based on data volume, transactions, the number of customers monitored, user count, or other dimensions. There may also be separate implementation, training, and support fees. Get a detailed quote and be sure it is all-inclusive. Look at whether you will need to sign a long-term contract, whether pricing is related to performance, and what happens if service level guarantees are not met.

Who am I doing business with? The background of a system's developer often gives hints about its suitability for particular purposes, degree of sophistication, scalability, growth path, and likelihood of long-term survival. Information about funding, number of clients, and time on the market also addresses these topics.

Are you a consumer marketer or a business marketer? Most solutions are heavily specialized in either consumer marketing or business marketing, which will influence built-in templates, connectors, and even predictive models.

What is your business goal? Some solutions that claim to deliver predictive marketing are focused on helping you find new prospects or audiences for your products, whereas others focus more on optimizing lifetime value of your existing customers. Whatever your business goals are, make sure the solution you are considering supports them.

Do I have requirements for on-premise software or can I deploy a cloud solution? In some companies, security policies or other requirements dictate that only on-premise software can be deployed. On the other end of the spectrum, more and more companies find that choosing cloud-based solutions gives them more flexibility, faster time to deployment, and lower total cost of ownership.

Do you go with a turnkey or a customized solution? Some solutions are highly customizable and customized for each and every customer, whereas other solutions come with many default, out-of-the-box models, audiences, and campaigns.

Do you have true omni-channel requirements? Before you go too far, decide which channels are your priorities: advertising, social, mobile, web, email, direct mail, call centers, or in-store clienteling. All solutions will have strengths and weaknesses.

CHAPTER 15

An Overview of Predictive (and Related) Marketing Technology

You have three options if you want to build the technical capabilities outlined in Chapter 14: (1) build predictive models yourself using a predictive analytics workbench and somehow import these models into your campaign management tools, (2) outsource predictive analytics-powered campaigns to a marketing service provider, or (3) evaluate and buy a predictive marketing solution, such as a predictive marketing cloud or a multichannel campaign management tool. We will look at the pros and cons of each of these three options and also discuss related technologies, which may claim some predictive analytics capabilities.

Do-It-Yourself Predictive Marketing

Predictive marketing technologies have existed for many years in the form of modeling tools such as SAS, SPSS, and Matlab. Many large companies, ranging from Netflix, Amazon, or Best Buy, to many companies in travel and telecommunications have teams of data scientists who use these workbench-type products to develop predictive algorithms.

However, utilizing these tools has several important drawbacks: before you can use a predictive analytics workbench tool, you first need to translate your business requirements into technical requirements that data scientists could turn into algorithms. Most marketers are ill equipped to do this, and may not be able to accomplish this task without the help of external consultants. In some ways, you have to reinvent the wheel. From scratch, you have to define what type of models you need for which business problems, and—unless you are using an experienced data scientist—you don't get to benefit from the lessons learned by other companies in your industry.

Utilizing the workbench-type products requires a team of data scientists to collect and integrate data, prepare data, develop, test, and deploy models, and ongoing involvement from IT and data scientists to help marketers run reports, extract segments, and prepare lists for campaigns. Many companies have trouble automating predictive marketing using these modeling tools.

Most analytical efforts would yield great result if it could be made part of the workflow of a company. When Omer worked at McKinsey, he helped to create some powerful analysis and algorithms, but as soon as McKinsey walked out of the room, there was no way for the customer to repeat the analysis or provide the predictive scoring on an ongoing basis. One of the projects Omer was involved in was at Micro Warehouse, a company for which he later headed up marketing. He created powerful models for optimizing marketing spend and another model for estimating the upside potential of business customers. These models yielded extremely good results when tested during the project, but when the project was over, the company could not institutionalize these predictive marketing tools. This was one of the reasons the late Jerry York, who was the CEO of Micro Warehouse, recruited Omer to head up analytical marketing.

Outsourcing to Marketing Service Providers

Database marketing service providers (MSPs) provide a fully outsourced option for companies to outsource and analyze their customer database. Most MSPs evolved from providing data hygiene and processing for direct mail campaigns to offer full hosting and managing of customer databases as well as layering on additional services such as analytics and consulting. For the most part, MSPs focus on servicing larger companies.

Most MSPs will have predictive analytics capabilities, but these capabilities tend to be manifested in highly customized models that are built or tweaked on a per-customer basis by professional services teams. Therefore MSPs are a good option if you have the time and money for a longer-term engagement.

By using an MSP you can reduce your reliance on internal IT. There are, however, inherent disadvantages about outsourcing your customer database. You often have to pay per list or per campaign, and MSPs are not set up to provide customer insights that extend beyond a specific campaign. Omer has experienced firsthand that every report you want to run needs to be paid for and scheduled in advance, which often means waiting weeks or months for the answer to a question. If you keep customer analytics at arms' length in this way, it is unlikely that you will build a truly customer-centric organization. For those who are committed to build their company and strategy around the customer, our strong belief is that it is imperative to bring customer data in-house and to give all customer-facing personnel instant access to customer data.

Most marketing service providers are essentially consulting organizations. Most have the capabilities to deliver direct mail and email campaigns, but lack the product capabilities to deliver real-time, personalized experiences, such as real-time web recommendations or personalized advertising campaigns.

Campaign Management and Marketing Cloud Options

Campaign management products are focused on designing and executing marketing campaigns across channels, including email campaigns, web campaigns, social campaigns, and mobile messaging. Almost none of the campaign management tools execute all of these channels natively but will rely on third parties for some. Campaign management tools certainly can help you plan the right message to the right customer at the right time, via the right channel. Many of these tools started as email service providers and therefore have a strong focus around the email channel, rather than the customer. Customer profile capabilities are still very rudimentary in many of these systems, though all are certainly focused to improve these.

Most campaign management tools have a strong online focus, and quite a few have not yet built out the data hygiene capabilities to track and correct physical address information. Also, not all campaign management tools have robust data management capabilities such as online/offline identity resolution, fuzzy matching, deduping capabilities. Therefore, most campaign management tools cannot be used as a single source of marketing execution needs.

Most campaign management solutions are evolving to refer to themselves as marketing clouds, sometimes including some data management platform or content management and collaboration capabilities as well. Please note that at the time of this writing, the vendor landscape is in high flux. Many established software vendors are offerings a compilation of multiple products under one brand umbrella, not well integrated. There are many startups early- and late-stage funded by venture capital firms that are working to build solutions from ground up with the customer data being the key element for the connected omni-channel customer and marketer of today.

Business marketing–oriented campaign management tools are often referred to as marketing automation tools. Marketing automation vendors, too, typically started as email execution for business marketing but quickly added the ability to design web forms and track user engagement across web and email. Some marketing automation vendors can now also design and track social campaigns as well. Marketing automation tools can link customer data from different sources, but tend to lack robust data management capabilities and require matching to business information from various standardized data sources. Most marketing automation vendors have some built-in lead scoring, based on rules, but many are not using truly predictive models yet. In business marketing, predictive technologies tend to create less value, as the size of the customer base is smaller. Like campaign management platforms, marketing automation tools were developed from a perspective of campaigns, and the architecture therefore tends to be campaign-focused, rather than customer-focused.

Other Tools You May Have Heard About

There are several other marketing tools you may be operating or that you may have heard about that tout predictive or analytics capabilities. Most of these other technologies are not sufficient for predictive marketing, but can still play an important role in marketers' toolkits. For the sake of completion, we summarize these related technologies in Figure 15.1, which you can use as a reference to lookup "what's what."

Marketing Service Provider (MSP)	Full outsourced marketing analytics and database management	Optimization of direct mail and email campaigns	Customer database is outsourced, not accessible to the marketer	Advanced segmentation controlled by the outside service provider	Direct mail and email campaigns; no real-time web or advertising
Campaign Management/Marketing Automation	Design, orchestrate and execute omni-channel marketing campaigns	Demand generation and loyalty marketing; primarily for online channels	Ability to collect, but limited ability to deduplicate or cleanse; exact match only	Limited predictive models; often custom models requiring services	Direct or partner based ability to execute across channels; online and offline channels
Web Analytics	Measure both aggregate and user level data on owned website properties	Website and mobile performance optimization	Website metrics, can be tied to a person by matching user ID's with your database	Conversion trends, website usability and individual user flows	Personalized messages on the website, via email or SMS to specific segments
Data Management Platform (DMP)	Cookie- and first-party data for top of funnel campaigns such as retargeting and lookalike targeting	Understand makeup of website audiences; use for personalization and targeting of web and advertising	Combining first-party cookie data with third-party data to segment and analyze online audiences	Some predictive modeling, specifically likelihood to convert of online audiences	Display advertising centric, some ability to personalize online experiences specially web and email
Email Service Provider (ESP)	Design and send email campaigns	Email automation and email deliverability	Just email behavior, some data cleansing but no fuzzy matching	Some analytics and reporting, but usually limited or no predictive capabilities	Email only; but most ESPs are evolving into full campaign automation solutions
Customer Relationship Management (CRM)	Manage contacts, accounts and opportunities	Funnel management, sales management	Ability to collect, but not to de-duplicate or cleanse customer data	A snapshot of the current funnel, limited historical views and no predictive views	Direct sales, call center campaigns, can power external campaign management
Advanced analytics	Provide data analysis and reporting	Information, visibility	Any data can be collected and mapped	Predictive analytics workbench, build your own models—no turnkey models	None, this is an analysis tool

Figure 15.1 Predictive Marketing Technologies Overview

Web Analytics

Web analytics is a critical component to any marketer's toolkit. There are two fundamentally different types of web analytics: the first provides reports or analysis of web browsing data on an aggregated basis, while the second type performs person-by-person analysis of named (or anonymous) visitors. Enterprise class web analytics tools provide both aggregate and user-level analytics, ad hoc discovery, and data mining now. Web analytics is mostly aimed to help you improve your user interface and site performance. These tools do not aim to deliver omni-channel customer experiences. Some advanced web analytics tools are starting to introduce segment discovery and propensity models, but generally these are highly custom deployments. Web analytics tools do not aim to build customer 360 profiles by linking customer data from sources other than your website, nor execute campaigns across channels.

Data Management Platforms (DMPs)

A data management platform will collect first-party data from a company's owned web properties, layer this data together with third-party, cookie-based data, and provide analysis about the audience segments of the website visitors. This analysis can be used to target specific audiences with display, search, video, and social advertising campaigns. DMPs deal mostly with anonymous, cookie-based information, and the goal is to acquire more new customers through advertising campaigns, rather than to optimize the lifetime value of existing customers. DMP platforms are definitely developing into central data hubs, integrating data from different sources. For the time being, data management platforms and predictive marketing platforms therefore are very complementary, but over time it is likely that these two data platforms will converge, as is outlined in Figure 15.2.

Email Service Providers (ESPs)

Email service providers help you design, schedule, and deliver your email campaigns. Some email service providers also allow you to integrate third-party data sources and use those to segment your email database and to trigger campaigns. For the most part, data integration is cumbersome, doesn't come out of the box, and requires extensive professional services.

Figure 15.2 Convergence of DMP and Predictive Marketing

Most email service providers are evolving to become fully functional campaign management systems, covering more than just email. Several email service providers were recently acquired by larger marketing cloud vendors, and few stand-alone email service providers remain.

Customer Relationship Management (CRM)

Customer relationship management systems were envisioned and designed as sales performance management or funnel management systems. Despite its name, most systems do not yet manage the customer relationship. Rather, these systems provide a central repository of customer data, but most don't include predictive analytics capabilities. CRM systems do not aim to provide omni-channel campaign automation but can integrate with systems that do. Similar to email and marketing automation, CRM systems can integrate bidirectionally with predictive marketing clouds. For example, if you use a CRM system in your call center, then call center interaction data can be imported into your predictive marketing cloud, linked to a customer's profile, and included in predictive analyses.

Advanced Analytics

Business intelligence (BI) solutions provide analytics, though typically this is limited to backward-looking or descriptive analytics. The goal for most BI tools is to give an overview of your business trends overall, not to analyze individual customers. You might be able to see the average order value of your customer base and the sales by region, but not what is the lifetime value of a single customer or whether this customer buys from you in different stores or just one. You can certainly learn a lot about your customers and your business using business intelligence. Most business intelligence tools are general purpose, but some vendors are emerging to focus specifically on marketers with built-in reports and dashboards for this audience. BI tools can integrate, and often clean, data from different data sources. BI tools, however, do not include predictive analyses and do not aim to provide omni-channel campaign automation.

Which Solution Is Right for Me?

Keep your end goal in mind: make your customers happy by delivering valuable, relevant, and meaningful customer experiences in every context. This will build the kind of engagement that leads to profitable relationships with customers. So ask yourself, what capabilities will help me deliver the most valuable experiences and build the most profitable relationships, in the shortest period of time?

The more relevant the predictive models, the more relevant the customer's experience because you will have more ways to anticipate and serve your customer's needs. The more accurate and complete the customer profiles, the more relevant the experiences. If you can link all past customer actions to a single profile, you can better anticipate and serve customer needs. The easier and more accessible the technology is to all marketers, the more likely it will be used in everyday campaigns.

If you are like most marketers, you don't have an infinite budget, so you would like this solution to be up and running as soon as possible and require as little as possible in terms of data integration and ongoing professional services. So in an ideal world, you would have access to a turnkey, out-of-the-box solution, with truly predictive capabilities and advanced data quality that gives you, the marketer, control over your own customer data.

Whatever path you choose, make sure to build these three fundamental capabilities discussed throughout this book:

1. The ability to link customer data from different sources, online and offline, as well as to prepare your data for predictive analysis.
2. The ability to analyze customer data, using turnkey or custom predictive models, to perform advanced analysis and segmentation.
3. The ability to trigger the right action for the right customer at the right time, across your different marketing execution systems.

Then place this system at the center of any marketing infrastructure—forming the central nervous system, operating system, or brain of your customer operations. Make sure the system updates automatically, at least once a day, ideally without manual intervention, to ensure the latest customer data is there.

Whatever You Do—Get Started

If there is only one thing you take away from this book, let it be that you should get started as soon as possible and focus on the very basics and do them well. Choosing the wrong vendor or the wrong campaign is not as bad as waiting. Your competitors are already leveraging predictive marketing today and gaining a significant competitive advantage from their early experiments. Remember that many companies are seeing the lifetime value, retention, and loyalty of their customers increase dramatically using predictive marketing techniques.

Here are three recommendations.

Get Started Small

With a couple of thousand dollars a month and a couple of weeks of integration work, you can begin solving your customer data problem and run your first marketing campaign. The best way to build a case for predictive marketing is to just get started. Given the large returns expected for this investment, you really cannot afford to wait. Ask yourself how you would feel if your competitors deployed this type of technology first. How would your customers feel if they are getting personalized treatment from your competitors first, but not from you? Also ask yourself if there are other projects on your plate that can truly give you a higher return on investment.

Bring Customer Data in House but Outsource the Data Science

We strongly believe that it is not possible to become truly customer-centric without making customer data available to all customer-facing personnel in your organization, starting with you—the marketers. Therefore, we strongly recommend against outsourcing your customer database to a third-party provider such as a marketing service provider. It will be too difficult to access data when and how you want it and the customer insights will reside outside your organization. Bringing customer data in-house does not mean that you need to hire expensive data scientists or technology resources. Easy-to-use, online solutions are available that allow you to own and access your customer data at any time, but use outside vendors to create the advanced statistical models. Data scientists are in high demand, and most marketers do not have the bandwidth and expertise to hire, provide direction, and retain such analytical personnel. The best data scientists that truly make an impact are the ones that have business acumen, which are even harder to find. Data science is a good way to gain insights, but it is hard to make the information available at every customer touch-point without extensive IT projects. Therefore, start with the end in mind and find the most practical solution that gets you to making a difference in the way your customers interact with your brand.

Complement Your Existing Infrastructure with Predictive Marketing

You don't have to rip and replace your existing infrastructure. You can certainly get started by complementing your existing infrastructure with robust data cleansing and predictive capabilities. Start small and expand your deployment over time. This could include embedding predictive capabilities into your different marketing channels, such as email, and perhaps replacing your existing specialized tools with a single campaign management platform to coordinate campaigns across all channels. According to a recent AgilOne survey of 132 retail marketing executives, only 17 percent of marketers use a single solution to coordinate omni-channel campaigns. However, of the remaining 83 percent who do not yet centrally coordinate campaigns, 42 percent plan to develop such centralized capabilities in the next 12 months.

CHAPTER 16

Career Advice for Aspiring Predictive Marketers

If you are fearful of data and machine learning, you are not alone. You may have a job in marketing because you love creating amazing experiences for customers and consider yourself a creative person. Perhaps you were never good at math, and all this talk about data and machine learning makes you feel uncomfortable. You would be surprised how little knowledge you need about predictive analytics to make you an expert! The definition of an expert is somebody who knows more about a subject than 95 percent of the population. Just reading this book will probably place you in that top 5 percent. Plus, while predictive marketing uses predictive analytics under the hood, you don't need to *know* predictive analytics at all to be a predictive marketing expert.

There is a huge career opportunity that comes from being an early adopter of new technologies, like predictive analytics, and new business practices, like predictive marketing. There are very few marketers out there who have direct experience using predictive analytics, or practicing predictive marketing. This means that even a little bit of experience can greatly differentiate you in the job market and place you ahead of more tenured marketers. Plus, the demand for data-driven marketers will only continue to increase.

Here are some career tips for aspiring predictive marketers.

Business Understanding Trumps Math

Hundreds of programs around the world are popping up at universities with degrees in data science or data analysis. Don't sign up just yet! We believe it is a real misunderstanding that in order to be data-driven and practice predictive marketing you need to be able to crunch numbers.

Numbers and stats are useless without people who can draw meaning from the data and turn it into strategies, products, and campaigns. This process requires a unique combination of the creative, analytical, and interpersonal skills so often siloed into different departments and job roles. As big data rises, the need increases for big data marketers who can draw insight and inspiration from the stats and target consumers accordingly.

It turns out that finding people who know the business, target market and customer needs well enough to interpret data is much harder than finding data scientists to crunch the numbers. Plus, new technologies are becoming available that hide the complicated math under the hood and present data in a way that is easy for marketers to understand and use.

Although you don't need to learn to crunch numbers, you still need to feel comfortable using and interpreting them. That means you need to overcome any fear of numbers as quickly as possible. Start by using and learning simple analytics tools such as Google Analytics or even by understanding and reading financial statements of companies you know from your everyday life. Popular books like *Freakonomics*, *NurtureShock*, or *Moneyball* might also help you hone your data-driven way of thinking by applying an analytics approach to economics, education, and baseball, respectively.

Ask the Right Questions

So if predictive marketing is about interpreting and using data, how might a marketer get started with that? The most important thing is to demonstrate curiosity and ask the right questions about your business and customers. Start with a hypothesis. For example, you might hypothesize that you are losing customers because a new competitor is stealing market share or because customers are dissatisfied with your latest product lineup. Once you have a hypothesis it is much easier to go look for the data to support or deny this thesis. Any analytical approach is a tool to solve a problem and not a solution on its own. This is very important to internalize. Many failed projects around analytics are due to this search for the magic bullet that never yields results.

Specifically, ask creative, deep questions about your customers. Increasingly, it is the marketing organization that owns customer data and customer insights. A recent survey of 132 marketing executives found that the marketing department is responsible for customer data in 75 percent of companies. Management is starting to look to marketing to inform major strategic decisions for the company. This type of visibility in the company can be great for your career.

Recently, the director of customer relationship management at a large discount retailer discovered that a larger than average percentage of customers bought from it once but never came back. In other words, a large number of their customers were "one and done," which is a common problem in retail. Increasing repeat buyers became a huge growth opportunity for the company. The board of directors of this publicly traded company discussed these reports. Ultimately the director received a promotion and was asked to lead a worldwide team tasked to increase customer engagement and customer lifetime value.

Do not just look at the data—mix it with real-life customer experiences. Often the best questions come from real interactions with customers. Do not just stay in your cubicle; get out in the field and interact with real customers. There is no substitute for customer face time.

Dominique once worked in Japan for Nippon Telegraph and Telephone (NTT) when it had half a million employees. Every employee in the company was asked to spend a couple of weekends working in the company store to make sure each employee was tuned in to the customer needs. Similarly, Disney asks all new employees—including executives—to work in theme parks in character costume to understand the customer experience up close. If your company doesn't have an initiative like this, you might start one. It will surely differentiate you and make you, and your colleagues, better marketers.

Blend the Art and Science of Marketing

In an episode of the television series *The Crazy Ones* with Robin Williams, a New York advertising agency hires a data analyst against the wishes of Williams's character, Simon. The company has a new client that sells cat food, and the data-driven marketing campaign designed by the young data analyst outperforms the marketing idea of veteran Simon. Initially Simon and the data analyst clash, but eventually they come to a happy place of blending the art and science of marketing. In this case, prime time television is not far off the mark. Successful marketers learn to combine the science of numbers with the art of creativity. Remember: Your job is to differentiate, delight, and disrupt.

Probably the most important thing to realize is that data science will not replace the need for creative thinkers. Dan Pingree, CMO at Moosejaw, described data-driven marketing as a way to inspire and validate the creative process. Using data, you can discover new customer personas and marketing strategies and test that your creative ideas are working.

Netflix and its chief content officer, Ted Sarandos, have been outspoken proponents of data-driven programming, which they say was behind the company's biggest successes in in-house programming, such as *House of Cards* and *Orange Is the New Black*. However, at a Sundance panel called "How I Learned to Stop Worrying and Trust the Algorithm," Sarandos conceded: "It is important to know which data to ignore. In practice, it's probably a 70–30 mix. Seventy is the data, and 30 is judgment—But the 30 needs to be on top."

Learn from Others

There is still a lot you can learn from traditional marketers. Traditional database marketers, who were focused on direct mail campaigns, are the most experienced marketers when it comes to predictive analytics. Because it is expensive to send a postcard or catalog, database marketers have long used likelihood to buy models and clusters to focus their mailers on the highest response segments. Digital marketers and database marketers don't typically spend much time together, but they should! The principles used for many years in database marketing directly apply to modern data-driven marketing. If you have a current or former database marketer on your team, take them out for lunch and learn about advanced segmentation from them. If you don't have a database marketer on your team, perhaps find somebody in your LinkedIn network and make contact.

You are not alone in your desire to learn about data-driven marketing and predictive marketing. There is no need for you to reinvent the wheel. You could look up companies in your industry that you admire and contact peers through LinkedIn. Most will be just as keen as you are to get together to compare notes. Start a formal or informal meet-up group with other people interested in the field and get together on a regular basis to compare notes. You could bring in outside speakers to educate you and your friends. You can even go a step further and make this a larger gathering in the form of a formal meet-up. Leading a meet-up can be a great way to increase your visibility in the industry and to add relevant leadership experience to your resume.

A great source of learning is also technology vendors selling predictive marketing software. These vendors are working with many companies in your industry and can educate you on best practices and benchmarks which otherwise might be hard to get a hold of. Software sales have changed a lot in recent years. Most vendors invest heavily in educational content, training, conferences, and even industry dinners and give you access to all these free resources long before they will ever try to sell you something. You should definitely take advantage of this opportunity and do not feel shy to reach out to relevant technology companies—our company AgilOne included. We would love to talk to you and help you further your career!

CHAPTER 17

Privacy and the Difference Between Delightful and Invasive

This is the time to focus on the customer, and build a valuable brand and personal competitive advantage in the process. However, never forget that you are dealing with customer data, and inevitably there will be privacy concerns that arise. Marketers today are struggling to walk the line between privacy and personalization, not realizing that these goals do not have to be mutually exclusive.

In general, consumers are willing to share preference information in exchange for apparent benefits, such as convenience, from using personalized products and services. A research paper titled "Personalization versus Privacy: An Empirical Examination of the Online Consumer's Dilemma" by the Marshall School of Business found evidence that online consumers' intention to use personalization services (and hence their willingness to share information) is positively correlated with factors that build trust in the vendor offering personalization services. These findings would argue that online vendors that seek to benefit from their personalization strategies should not only be mindful of their consumers' privacy concerns but should also uncover ways through which they can build trust. In fact, the relative reputation of online vendors is one reason why consumers prefer to use personalization from one vendor while ignoring another, even if the services are virtually undifferentiated. Two important factors known to build trust are the consumer's familiarity with the vendor and her past experiences with them.

Here are some more guidelines for dealing with customer data and engendering trust. First, inform online consumers about what information will be collected how and why. Second, give online consumers a choice about how their information will be used and to which parties it will be disclosed. Third, make sure you have adequate mechanisms to protect online consumer information from theft, accidental loss or unauthorized use. You don't want to end up on the front page of the Wall Street Journal after a breach. Adequate protection also requires that there is an effective authority to enforce and impose sanctions for potential violations.

Types of Personal Information

When it comes to personalization, there are different types of customer information that can be used, and consumers may feel different about one type of information over the other.

Anonymous information. It refers to information gathered about page visits without the use of any invasive technologies, typically the standard information sent with any web or Internet request. Such information includes a machine's IP address, domain type, browser version and type, operating system, browser language, and local time.

Personally unidentifiable information. It refers to "information that, taken alone, cannot be used to identify or locate an individual." Information such as age, date of birth, gender, occupation, education, income, zip code with no address, interest, and hobbies fall into this category. The consumer through radio buttons, menus, or check boxes on a web page has to explicitly disclose most of this information. In addition to solicited information, personally unidentifiable information also often involves the use of sophisticated tracking technologies, for example, cookies, clear gifs, and so on. Such technologies, though not identifying a customer individually, enable the information collecting entity to sketch an effective customer profile.

Personally identifiable information. It refers to information that can be used to identify or locate an individual. These include email addresses, name, address, phone number, fax number, credit card number, social security number, and so on. Invariably, such information is almost always gathered explicitly from the customer and is typically collected when consumers register with websites or engage in financial transactions.

There is some evidence that there is an important psychological difference between companies you have chosen to do business with using your personally identifiable data and companies that you have not previously bought from using any data, even if it is anonymous. If you have eaten in a restaurant before, you appreciate it if you get recognized when you return: if the waiter knows your name and remembers that you like your meat medium-rare you will be impressed. However, if a stranger on the street suddenly addresses you by name and asks if you enjoyed the whiskey you drank last night—that is invasive. The same is true on the Internet. If you have bought from Gucci before, you might appreciate it if they recognize you as a high-value shopper and send you a Christmas gift. However, if Gucci competitor Versace is relentlessly targeting you with display ads that follow you around the web, you might find that annoying and creepy.

Get Elastic found that 57 percent of online shoppers are comfortable sharing information as long as it is for their benefit—and being unknowingly followed across the Internet by unknown brands is hardly a benefit. At the same time Consumer Reports found that 71 percent of consumers state that they are very concerned about online companies selling or sharing information about them without their permission, causing more and more marketers to make the transition from traditional third-party cookie retargeting to first-party data.

Avoid Invasive Situations

Use common sense when considering whether a marketing campaign is delightful or creepy. Consider the context of the situation. Some actions that are delightful in some situations might be downright creepy if you change the context. For example, if a sales representative greets me in the store it is fine, but if the same sales representative comes to my house at 10 pm in the evening, it is downright creepy. It seems that customers are more comfortable still with asynchronous communications, such as email, than with real-time personalization such as display advertising. We shared in Chapter 11 that 66 percent of U.S. consumers appreciate an email offer related to something they looked at online previously, but only 24 percent appreciate to receive this same offer in the form of an online advertisement.

Customer perceptions differ greatly from customer to customer and from segment to segment. In general, data from the Columino survey of 3,000 consumers shows that consumers in the United States were much more likely to expect online retailers to personalize experiences than those in the United Kingdom: about half of Americans want to receive a new customer welcome greeting, versus only 34 percent in the United Kingdom. Also, shoppers, aged 18 to 34, part of the "millennial" generation, were more likely to appreciate almost all forms personalization: 52 percent of millennials expect brands to remember their birthday as compared to 21 percent of shoppers aged 65 and over. Because of these differences, it is very important not to generalize: some customers will outright demand personalization, whereas others are categorically turned off by it. What is important is to develop customer profiles for each and every customer, and to track in these profiles what type of personalization a customer appreciates.

Give Customers Control

Consumers will want control over their own data, and companies that give control over their data will win. Large companies like Google and Amazon are already doing this. Giving customers visibility into some of the inputs into the algorithm also makes the whole process of predictive analytics much less scary. There are three effective ways of giving consumers more visibility and control over the ways you are using their data:

1. *Edit data*: Provide customers with the ability to determine which data a company can use for recommendations, so the user can erase specific history (such as a purchase they made for a friend's baby shower) or completely turn off certain data sources.
2. *Explain why*: Explain why a specific recommendation is made, so the user can understand where the relevance comes from. This simple approach usually makes even the mistake seem logical and understandable to the user.
3. *Feedback loop*: Provide user the ability to give feedback, whether the recommendation was good or bad. This is also called *reinforcement learning* that learns not only by observing user behavior (implicit learning), but by receiving input (explicit learning).

Hard Boundaries and Government Legislation

Beyond sound business practice, there are also hard boundaries of privacy. For example, in some cases you cannot collect and sell information without the customer's permission. There are different industry rules and legislations designed to prevent accidental information disclosure or loss. In the European Union, data privacy is governed by the Data Protection Directive. American companies wanting to do business in Europe are required to follow the US-EU Safe Harbor Privacy Principles. Any companies processing credit card information must comply with The Payment Credit Card Industry's Data Security Standard.

The US-EU Safe Harbor Privacy Principles allow for a streamlined process for U.S. companies to comply with the EU Directive 95/46/EC on the protection of personal data. The Safe Harbor Principles are designed to prevent accidental information disclosure or loss. Companies operating in the European Union are not allowed to send personal data to countries outside the European Economic Area unless there is a guarantee that it will receive adequate levels of protection. There are also requirements for ensuring that appropriate employee training and an effective dispute mechanism are in place.

The Payment Credit Card Industry's Data Security Standard, called PCI DSS, was developed by the credit card industry. All merchants that handle credit card information are required to comply with this standard, but in security circles the standard is also widely regarded as a good commonsense benchmark for data protection. Even if you are not subject to PCI DSS, you may look to this framework to get an idea how to best protect customer data. Some of the capabilities that are required with PCI DSS are the requirement to install and maintain a firewall, to encrypt transmission of cardholder data, and to track and monitor all access to network resources and cardholder data. In total, the standard specifies 12 requirements for compliance.

In some countries, like the United Kingdom, Spain, and Portugal, consent of the individual is required to collect and process information, and in the case of sensitive personal information, explicit consent is required. The laws in the United States are somewhat of a patchwork across states, but generally speaking the United States has the least restrictions on data privacy. Consult with a legal expert, especially when doing business in different countries, because local laws and regulations change frequently, and many regions, including the United States and Europe, are considering more stringent data protection laws.

We hope that companies will do what is right so that the government will not step in with legislation that is too invasive. One thing is clear: to bolster consumer trust and confidence, companies should protect and treat customers' data like it is their own. Businesses must think of data privacy not as a back-office activity for compliance, but as a competitive differentiator that improves the customer-experience.

CHAPTER 18

The Future of Predictive Marketing

Upon entering a Rebecca Minkoff store in New York or San Francisco, the very first thing a customer encounters is a wall-length touch screen that offers free drinks. Guests have the opportunity to order a free water, tea, coffee, or espresso. They're asked for a phone number where they will receive a text as soon as their drink is ready.

That perk is not just out of the goodness of Minkoff's heart. That phone number serves as a digital signature, which tracks them throughout the store. That large touch screen also lets them browse the brand's catalog and put together outfits. While shoppers don't know it, the store's employees are plugged into mobile apps, which keep them apprised of who's in the store and what data is being input into that giant video wall. Then, when customers enter the dressing rooms, things get interesting.

All the clothing and accessories in Minkoff's new stores are outfitted with RFID tags—radio signal-emitting tags frequently used in theme park access wristbands and in credit cards. The dressing rooms at Rebecca Minkoff's new stores in New York, Los Angeles, San Francisco, and Tokyo are equipped with RFID shields that allow them to identify which clothing customers bring in to that specific dressing room.

The dressing rooms themselves have mirrors that double as large touch screens. A computer automatically builds an inventory, based on the RFID tags, of the clothing a customer brought in with them.

The touch screen lets the customer switch to a series of mood-lighting setups and, crucially, integrates Minkoff's e-commerce operation into the dressing room.

Different sizes and colors of the items a customer brings in are automatically showcased up on the screen. If something does not fit, they can order a different-size version to be added to their online cart for future checkout. Each piece of clothing they brought in and didn't try on is converted into a lead. The innovation lets retailers like Minkoff see which items individual customers *are not* buying. This lets retailers then send emails to customers urging them to return and take another look at the clothes they didn't end up purchasing.

In this book, we have only scratched the surface of what predictive analytics can do for marketers. We predict that there will be more and more use cases of predictive analytics in marketing. Predictive models will become more easily accessible and available to all marketers, at companies large and small, as time goes on. Also, predictive models will increasingly power real-time, personalized communications with customers both in the digital and physical world. The store of the future will be very different than the store we know today, as we saw in the story about Rebecca Minkoff. Lastly, we believe the widespread accessibility of big data and machine learning will spurn a true culture shift of rebuilding marketing practices around the customer, rather than around products or selling channels.

Advanced Predictive Analytics Models

In this book, we choose to focus on the predictive models that can have the biggest impact on customer value in the shortest period of time and are most widely used by early adopters in predictive marketing. However, there are many other predictive models which advanced marketers could use. Following are just a couple of examples so you get an idea of how widely these techniques can apply.

An engagement propensity model predicts the likelihood of a customer to engage with a brand. Engagement can be defined in various ways, but most of the time it describes events such as opening an email, clicking on an email, or visiting a brand's website. Using an engagement propensity model, marketers can determine the right frequency of emails by throttling the number of emails a person receives based on this engagement propensity. You could also include a directional indicator to the engagement model to show whether a customer is becoming more or less engaged with the brand. Marketers can use this model to target down-trending customers with special messages and offers to prevent them from leaving the brand.

A total size of wallet model can predict the maximum possible spend for each customer. This is often called *size of wallet* or *total addressable market* (we will use the acronym TAM for Total Addressable Market) and is defined as the total yearly spend by a single customer on the products/services sold by a company. A TAM prediction can also be made for a specific product category. Marketers can use these models to identify customers who are likely to spend more with the brand. As with engagement, you can complement a TAM model with a Direction of TAM model. A Direction of TAM model predicts whether the total addressable market for a given customer is growing or shrinking. For example, a hot start-up company may have a low TAM on servers today but its direction of TAM may be very high, indicating it is growing fast and could become an important prospect soon. Marketers can use this model to identify hot prospects.

A pricing optimization model predicts the price that best drives sales, volume, or profitability. The model should be customized based on what you are optimizing for—sales, profits, volume, or any other factor. A marketer can use a pricing optimization model to decide the best price for a given product or service for each customer. A different model can be developed for each product you want to do this for, or a more generic model can be used that predicts price sensitivity of a customer in general. Similarly, an offer optimization model can determine which offer will have the most impact on which customer. This kind of model can be configured to maximize conversion, revenue, or margin. This model helps marketers to send the right offers to the right people.

A keyword-to-contact recommendation model can predict the affinity of a customer to certain content, such as a newsletter or email, based on things like web behavior or past purchases. Similarly, a hot topics detection model would predict what are the hot topics or hot products that customers are interested in based on analysis of a customer's social activity, website logs, sales, and other sources. Marketers could use these predictions to decide on content marketing topics for specific customers.

A predictive clustering model predicts which cluster a customer will fall into in the future. Marketers can use these predictions to start differentiating treatment of customers right after they have been acquired. There is no longer a need to wait for them to express their behavior to understand who they are. Instead, marketers can react before it is too late when customers are moving to lower value customer clusters.

Think Like a Predictive Marketer

Something struck us in our work with successful early adopters of predictive marketing. These people took a different approach. There is a strong win-win here for consumers, companies, and individual marketers alike. Customer satisfaction is up, companies have been transformed around the customer, and individual marketers have gained a higher profile in their companies. One company we worked with was able to double overall revenue by growing its online revenue around a brand that was rooted in stores. Online purchases rose from 20 percent to 80 percent of revenues in the process.

So we finish with some advice, not on what to do, but on how to be. Here are some lessons learned from predictive marketers that will help you make this amazing transition.

First, if there is only one lesson you take away from reading this book it is to focus on the customer and organize your thinking around the customer. Customer-centricity is not a new concept. In fact, marketers have strived to focus on the customer since the dawn of marketing. Just because the concept has been around for a long time doesn't mean it has been implemented successfully. And just because your company might have failed to build a true customer-centric culture so far doesn't mean you shouldn't try again. Big data and predictive analytics truly enable a customer-centric organization in a way that wasn't previously possible.

Second, focus on actions, not analysis. Too many analytics projects fall flat because companies get stuck in the proverbial analysis paralysis phase. Once you get used to numbers, you can get hooked on them. Every revelation about your customers will prompt another question. We only have a low percentage of repeat buyers. Why is that? Are the defectors young or old? Do we have more defections in the store than online? Are there certain products that bring in more repeat customers? Are the defectors returning more products than others? There is no end to the questions you could ask, and answer, using customer data. However, there is a real risk in asking too many questions all at once. The risk is that you *do nothing* with the data. Just having data alone will not change anything. Only ask questions that will lead to an action, otherwise, it's all nice to know. This is what a lot of consultants do, pages of analysis without any action, all interesting facts. You will only improve customer experiences, lifetime revenue, and your company's financial performance if you act on customer data. This means using even just one customer insight to change something, to launch one campaign that might improve things. In this example, perhaps it is to launch or improve a customer welcome campaign with post-purchase recommendations and see if it makes a difference. The sooner you start acting on customer data, the sooner data-driven marketing becomes a way of life. Also, it helps to have some early wins, in the form of improved customer satisfaction and revenues, to give you the mandate inside your company to continue your data explorations.

Third, get started today, keep it simple and iterate. It is true that the technology landscape of vendors supporting predictive marketing is changing rapidly. Newer and better technologies will become available every year. However, that is not a good reason to sit and wait. There is a huge benefit in being an early mover. The companies featured in this book know that. A major challenge we had in writing this book was to get marketers to agree to share the results they have achieved with predictive marketing. Often we heard: "We don't want our competitors to know just yet how big the rewards are from deploying predictive marketing" or: "We view our predictive marketing initiatives as a major competitive advantage and we do not want others to know about it." This tells you something. Take a risk and get started with predictive marketing—even if it is at a small scale. It will take your company a while to get used to the new way to thinking required for predictive marketing, so the sooner you can start this transformation and learning process, the better off you are. Eventually, your customers will demand that you serve them more relevant content, and as your competitors are rolling out predictive marketing, you may start to lose customers to them. If you know you will have to adopt predictive marketing eventually anyway, why not start today and gain a competitive advantage?

Fourth, frequently try new things and measure everything. Don't expect that you will crack the nut on predictive marketing on the first attempt. It will require some trial and error to find the data and the campaigns that work for your company, but the only way to learn this is to get started. However, make sure you formulate a clear hypothesis for every experiment and test your hypothesis by A/B testing or by always including a holdout group that doesn't receive the new treatment. Improve gradually by testing new things. Be patient. It may take a while for your company to catch on. Don't stop after the first failed experiment. Some of our most successful clients run hundreds of campaigns, each contributing a small percentage to the overall experience and lifetime value of their customers. Like football, predictive marketing is a game of inches. Every marketing play helps to move the ball forward down the field, toward the goal of loyal and profitable customers.

Fifth, communicate successes inside and outside your company. As you start to see results with predictive marketing, share these with the world. There is a real advantage in finding a group of like-minded marketers—inside your industry—and comparing notes. Perhaps you can find marketers at companies or brands that you have a lot in common with but don't directly compete. Your learning will accelerate if you don't have to invent the wheel by yourself. Predictive marketing is turning into a powerful movement, and finding like-minded practitioners can be both profitable and fun. We recommend you also tell customers about your experiments, perhaps using your blog or by doing a press release. We would be happy to put you in touch with reporters keen to write about this movement. Customers will like reading about the fact that you are investing in better understanding and serving them, as well as efforts to eliminate irrelevant mass marketing practices. Lastly, blog or tweet about your successes so you can get the credit you deserve as a forward thinking, modern marketer. Why not build your own reputation in the process of adopting predictive marketing?

These are the principles of predictive marketing. We are very lucky to get to witness one of history's most profound technology and cultural revolutions. Aspire to these qualities and you can use the strategies we've laid out to your advantage—or invent your own. You'll be able to build on your successes, both with customers and within the company. And then, as predictive marketing rises and becomes ubiquitous, you will be ready.

Marketing is on the forefront of a much larger revolution. Machine learning will eventually permeate all walks of life and improve the quality of education, philanthropy, and health care, among others. As marketers, we are the pioneers who are exploring how to best use the intelligence of machines to improve our lives—without invading privacy in undesirable ways. What you do truly matters. We wish you the best of luck in your predictive marketing endeavors and encourage you to tell us about your experiences:

Website: www.predictivemarketingbook.com
Predictive Marketing Book LinkedIn group: www.linkedin.com/groups?gid=8292127
Twitter: twitter.com/agilone

Please stay in touch and join the conversation!

APPENDIX

Overview of Customer Data Types

Purchases and Transactions

You can track online purchases by a tag you install on your website or directly from your order management system, which could be your e-commerce platform. You can track in-store purchases from your point of sale (POS) application or an order management system. Often, store purchases are collected by a different system than online or phone purchases. It is extremely important to be able to tie all purchases back to the same person. For example, if you send abandoned cart reminders without reconciling online and phone purchases, people who abandoned a cart online, but completed the purchase over the phone, may receive a discount coupon for checking out their abandoned cart. These customers are going to be upset and complain: "You mean that if I had waited, I could have received a discount for my item?"

Web and Online Behavior

If you are a business marketer, web browsing behavior and email interaction may be even more important than purchases. These two behavioral data points give you a good idea of the future intent of a prospect or customer. Purchases alone would not give you enough information in business, given that there are typically much fewer purchases than in consumer marketing. On the flipside, the decision cycle in business marketing is much longer so there are more of these prepurchase data points. In fact, predicting who will purchase in business marketing is so lucrative, that a cottage industry of specialized "predictive lead scoring" vendors has sprung up to help marketers know which prospects are getting ready to make a purchase. With this information in hand, companies can focus their limited sales resources on the customers that matter most.

You may not be able to recognize all visitors during their first visit; however, using cookies—tags placed on a customers browsing activity—you can start tracking the behavior even for anonymous visitors and tie this back to real people later. You will know who people are when they identify themselves, for example, by making a purchase or by signing up for your newsletter, or by filling in a form before downloading an electronic book or watching a video from your website. You can use progressive profiling to collect customer information without hurting conversion rates. Instead of having to fill out 15 form fields in order to register, a site visitor only visits a couple of fields at a time. For example the first time customers come to the site, they fill just first name, last name, and email and on the second visit are asked for phone number and zip code, and so forth.

Email Behavior

Email opens and clicks can be an important signal of user engagement and likelihood to buy. You can learn much about customers by analyzing which emails they read and how often they open your mail. This information can even be used to make predictions about the likelihood of an individual to unsubscribe from your email list. Unsubscribes are seemingly innocuous, but are actually very expensive. We come back to optimizing email frequency in Chapter 9 of the book.

Household and Account Grouping

Householding was an important data processing step in catalog marketing, where marketers didn't want to send the same catalog twice for two buyers from the same household. Not only does householding help to reduce direct mail costs, it helps you better understand truly valuable customers. By myself, I may not look like a very valuable customer, but if I directly influence the purchases of a number of household members I may very well be a VIP.

The relationship between individuals and the households they belong to is not always easy to see. Using the person's name and address, likely relationships between family members can be established. Software can even be used to automatically assign a head of household, which is the person deemed most influential in that household when it comes to buying from your brand.

In business marketing, the relationship between a contact (a prospect or a customer) and the company he or she works for is often recorded in the company's customer relationship management system. For new leads coming in, you may need to invest in custom code or third-party tools to automatically link contacts to the account they belong to.

Location

After customers make their first purchase, their home address can be derived from the billing or shipping address. It is useful to have software automatically calculate and append the longitude and latitude of the location of a customer's home address. This will allow you to make other calculations later on and to target customers based on attributes like their proximity to a certain store. For example, when you have a new store opening you could send all customers within a 10-mile radius a postcard invitation to come by and check out your new location.

When 100% Pure, a cosmetics retailer that started as an online-only brand, decided it wanted to open up physical stores it turned to the data it collected on existing customers. Based on their shipping and billing addresses collected when they bought products online, the company chose its new physical store locations. You can read more about the 100% Pure experiences with predictive marketing in Chapter 12.

For business marketing, company address is also very important, as salespeople often get assigned based on the location of a customer.

Beyond a customer's home address, it is also useful to collect more temporal location information. In other words, it is useful to know where the customer is right now. Web logs can be used to look up a customer's IP number and marketers can determine a customer location based on this. You might have experienced this technology most vividly when you travel overseas and Google is asking you if you want to switch the default language of your search engine.

Mobile technologies such as iBeacon determine a smartphone location with high accuracy. Supermarkets such as Marsh and Safeway have been early adopters of iBeacon technology. Studies conducted by Coca-Cola and Procter & Gamble among others show an immense difference in effectiveness between offers that are made to consumers right in the store versus at home or elsewhere. The time-of-purchase power is very important. For example, beacons in Marsh stores will be able to trigger alerts such as shopping lists, ads, and other content for customers who use Marsh's mobile app. And because beacons are more accurate than GPS, it can send the alerts when you are in the right aisle.

Call Center Interactions, Meetings, and Social Interactions

Customers may be making phone calls to your company, providing even more important data points. New text analysis software can help you record and analyze the length and frequency of calls, as well as the topics of conversation and customer sentiment. The easiest way to incorporate call center interactions is to classify each call into a category and to append this category to each customer data profile.

Especially for business marketing, the fact that a prospect or a customer agrees to meet with you over the phone or in person is a strong buying signal and you want to record this in your database. As with purchases and call center interactions, there are a large number of data points—direct and derived—that can be recorded about each meeting. Think about the time, location, and length of the meeting as well as the customer sentiment during the meeting.

Social interaction poses the same problems as call center data. These are typically natural text conversations, and in order to append actionable information to a customer profile, you will need to classify or tag the social interaction. Vendors are trying to mine sentiments from social comments, such as whether a customer is making a positive or a negative comment. The problem so far has been that most of these sentiment analysis packages are highly inaccurate and can give marketers more misinformation than helpful data points. Large consumer brands often resort to assigning customer service personnel to monitor social feeds and to manually classify and assign conversations.

Returns, Complaints, and Reviews

Returns and complaints hold very rich information about customers' likely retention and advocacy. Not many customers return or complain and therefore it is sparse data, but it should be highly paid attention to. For example, it turns out that in order to predict customer lifetime value or customer retention, returns or complaints are among the top five most important variables.

Reviews and surveys can provide information that is equally valuable to complaints and returns. The reason we recommend you don't start with analyzing reviews when considering predictive marketing is that often reviews and surveys are left at third-party sites. It is trickier to integrate with these sites and tie back the reviews to a specific customer. Some of this might violate customer privacy, and not all customers are comfortable with it.

Gender

Segmenting your customers by gender is one of the most basic segmentations you can do. It is easy to create a newsletter with a dynamic header that will change based on the gender of the recipient. This has proven to significantly increase click and conversion rates. Also, there really isn't a point to send feminine products promotions to men and shaving promotions to women. Typically the gender of customers isn't collected specifically as part of a purchase but software algorithms can automatically recognize most names and tag many of your customers as men or women.

Beyond targeting men and women with different marketing and offers, men and women also have different shopping behaviors. We recently analyzed 1 million consumers visiting gift and variety sites and found the following differences:

- Men have a 24 percent higher lifetime value than women because they shop more often and have larger transactions.
- Men are twice as likely to buy using rewards points than women.

- Men are slightly more expensive to service, with margins for men being 4 percent lower than women, because they use more rewards and more discounts.
- Men are slightly more likely to buy across multiple product categories, such as socks, pants, and watches rather than buying only pants.
- Men are slightly more likely to buy from Amazon rather than from a brand or specialized retailer's site directly.

If you are a marketer for one of these sites, you may want to offer rewards points to male customers, as they are very receptive to rewards programs. You may also want to focus your retention budget on female customers who are more apt to return and buy frequently.

U.S. Census Data

U.S. census information offers an important source of data enrichment that is often overlooked. U.S. census data is freely available to everybody and can be matched with your customer records based on zip code.

If you know how many people live in a certain area you can compare that to the number of customers you have in that area. So now you can essentially calculate your market penetration for a specific region. Based on this information you may decide to increase your acquisition budget for regions with low penetration. You can learn from U.S. census data what kind of housing is most popular in a specific neighborhood. Especially if you are marketing lawn mowers, it could be very important to know whether this is a neighborhood of apartments or single-family homes. You can approximate household income based on a customer's zip code. Household income has always proven important for understanding customer behavior.

Vertical and Size

In business marketing, the size and industry of a company is probably the most frequently used demographic data for segmentation after location. Third-party databases can help to augment your data with the right company size, vertical, and number of employees. Traditionally companies like Dunn and Bradstreet and Harte Hanks provided this data. Increasingly, the most accurate and up-to-date view of company size, at least the number of employees, is LinkedIn. LinkedIn will not have revenue data, but probably has an up-to-date count of the number of employees. Industry vertical and employee size in business marketing become very important when calculating the total available market or the share of wallet or market share. Business marketers typically don't care about the overall penetration of a market, but about the penetration of a specific market segment—by vertical or company size.

Other Customer Data Points

The amount of data you can collect about customers really has no end. For example, there are many third-party data sources that could be tapped to enrich your customer data. One popular example is to mash up a customer's location with the weather that is predicted for that area. If you could collect both in real time, you might surface umbrellas to the front page of your website just like you would in a physical store during rainy periods. One retailer we work with has experimented with weather-based campaigns, but has not yet found a profitable way to leverage it on its site. First of all, it is not trivial to create campaigns on the fly in response to weather, and second, it has not yet been found that this increases sales materially.

INDEX

NOTE: Page references in *italics* refer to figures.